History, Truth, Holiness

*Studies in Theological Ontology
and Epistemology*

D1593310

Ἀπαρχὴ Χριστός, μεσότης καὶ τελειότης· ἐν πᾶσι γὰρ ὁ ἐν τοῖς πρώτοις, ἔν τε τοῖς μέσοις καὶ τελευταίοις ὡς ἐν τοῖς πρώτοις ἐστίν· τὰ πάντα καὶ ἐν πᾶσι Χριστός.

Christ is the beginning, the middle, and the end. He Who is in the first is in all, and as He is in the first so He is in the middle and the end as well—Christ is all and in all.

St. Symeon the New Theologian (*Chapters* 3.1)

Bishop of the Western American Diocese
Maxim Vasiljevic

to the Keller Library from J Robert Wright

History, Truth, Holiness

Studies in Theological Ontology and Epistemology

Edited by
Daniel Mackay

*To fr Robert
with appreciation
in the Holy Spirit
+ bp Maxim*

SEBASTIAN PRESS
2011

BX
323
.V37
2011

Published by
Sebastian Press
Western American Diocese of the Serbian Orthodox Church
in collaboration with *The Institute for Theological Research in Belgrade*

Edited by
Daniel Mackay

Contemporary Christian Thought Series, number 10
First Edition

Prepress & printing
Ivan Jovanović & Interklima-grafika, Vrnjci, Serbia

Copyright © 2011 by Maxim Vasiljevic and Sebastian Press

Address all correspondence to:
Sebastian Press
1621 West Garvey Avenue
Alhambra, California 91803

Email: info@westsrbdio.org ∵ Website: http://www.westsrbdio.org

Front cover: *Ship* – fresco by Stamatis Skliris

Publishers Cataloging-in-Publication

Vasiljevic, Maxim.
History, truth, holiness : studies in theological ontology and epistemology / Maxim Vasiljevic ; edited by Daniel Mackay. — 1st ed. — Alhambra, Calif. : Sebastian Press, 2011.
p. xxii; 247; cm. 23
(Contemporary Christian thought series; №10)
ISBN: 978-1-936773-01-5
Includes bibliographical references and index.
1. Orthodox Eastern Church—Doctrines. 2. Ontology. 3. Knowledge, Theory of. 4. Religion and science. 5. Philosophy and religion. 6. Christianity and existentialism. 7. Christian art and symbolism. I. Mackay, Daniel, 1974– II. Title. III. Series.

BX323 .V37 2011   2011923963
230/.19—dc22   1102

Contents

For my teachers
Bishop Athanasius Yevtich and
Metropolitan John D. Zizioulas

Crucifixion
(fresco in Studenica Monastery, Serbia, early 13th century)

Foreword

by Aristotle Papanikolaou

One of the most remarkable aspects of contemporary Orthodox theology is its abiding faithfulness to what constitutes the core and central axiom of the Orthodox tradition—divine-human communion. Even though Orthodox theologians disagree about many things—and those differences are becoming more manifest—they share a truly unprecedented consensus on the principle that God has created all of creation for communion with God and that this communion is a real union with God's very life. One would be hard-pressed to find such an explicit consensus on any theological point in either Protestant or Roman Catholic theologies. In affirming that creation is destined for "deification," Orthodox theologians bring the past wisdom of early Christian thinkers into contemporary theological discussion, even if the form of theology looks differently than patristic theology.

The most influential Orthodox theologian in Christian theology since the fall of the Christian Roman empire has unquestionably been John Zizioulas, Metropolitan of Pergamum. Although detractors of his theology are increasing, his influence in contemporary Christian discussions of trinitarian theology, anthropology and ecclesiology is indisputable. In this incredibly insightful and poetic book, His Grace Bishop Maxim—a student of Zizioulas, Athanasius Yevtich, Christos Yannaras (to mention only the most influential)—amplifies and magnifies this relational understanding of *theosis*. He demonstrates with eloquence and persuasiveness that the importance of such an understanding of ontology is not limited to theology, but extends to questions of epistemology and the inter-disciplinary debates on human freedom.

Bishop Maxim also takes his teachers' theology in directions in which Zizioulas, in particular, was hesitant to go. Although Zizioulas was not anti-monastic, there is not much reflection in his writings on monasticism, probably because he was nervous about its tendency toward an individualistic understanding of deification. Given the over-emphasis in contemporary theology in the person of Vladimir Lossky on the singular, ascetical struggle toward union with God, Zizioulas offered a necessary corrective. Bishop Maxim offers a balanced approach in which the monastic understanding of holiness is interpreted as a relational, liturgical event and eschatological event. He offers a way forward beyond the opposition between the ascetical and the liturgical in showing that the ascetical struggle to holiness toward an *ekstatic* freedom is simultaneously an awareness that we are eternally loved by the God who is eternally Other, and as such, eternally unique and irreplaceable. Such holiness manifests itself in relations to others: the holy one now, like God, becomes the unique Other in whose face one is drawn toward personal freedom, toward a relational event of uniqueness and irreducibility.

In this book, the reader will find rich insights through a faithful engagement with the liturgical and patristic traditions, with contemporary thinkers, Orthodox and non-Orthodox, and in conversation with philosophy and science (particularly in the chapters "Truth and History" and "Is There a Biochemistry of Freedom?"). Bishop Maxim offers an invaluable contribution to Orthodoxy's long tradition of thinking on divine-human communion.

Introduction:
History, Truth and Holiness

Theology today is of crucial significance; by being faithful to the Fathers, it serves contemporary man. It is not, nor should it ever be, an exclusive luxury, but rather it is an *ancilla* of existential necessity: an incursion into the heart of humanity wherein compact createdness and unreachable otherworldliness meet. Theology responds to Christ's *ephapax* Incarnation and continual personal engagement in history as the Church, "for us men and for our salvation." In history Christ manifests the constancy of our existence; the Church articulates His everlasting and eternal presence with theology, not as depersonalized ideology but through personal and loving concern for the salvation of all. He meets each person within the communion of the "breaking of the bread", and each person encounters Him within the Church.

The texts collected in this book stem from a debt to contemporary man; aiming to synthesize the existential revelation of the Gospel and the Fathers, they represent man as living a permanent tension between person and nature. And is this not the Christian struggle: to say "yes" to God in an *ekstatic* and personal (rather than natural) action? In so doing do we not say "no" to nature? From out of this struggle within every beating heart emerge history, truth, and holiness. The articles herein inquire about the implications of this personal struggle: What does freedom mean? Why does love expressed through freedom mark the beginning of the advancement for which we were made? How does this *theosis*, an earnest indemnity against corruption and decay wherein God reveals man as God-like, reveal the image of the Triadic hypostases that willingly share their life, being, relation, and communion with us?

There is, however, a difference between theology serving contemporary man and theology unnecessarily burdening itself with the directionless demands of the time. The time, like nature, does not know what it wants. More to the point, unlike the experience of truth revealed in holiness, the time does not know for whom it longs. It is unaware of what stories must be told, and a man is a story of his time. Theology must serve contemporary man, not be served by contemporary man. It attains this lofty and dutiful service through the perspicacity of a person being able to see past human nature, past the fallen nature that burdens time. By articulating that insight in language—a feat only possible if the Church refuses to pay the debt history asks of it—the Church will become a visible icon in which the time is transformed to the Eschaton, wherein nature is redeemed, and wherein the Godly image of each person is fulfilled. The time does not have an a priori need; rather, it is always incomplete, always in making. "In making" means that it is given a chance to recognize itself through the Church.

Sometimes anachronistic problems and questions arise to which the pressing issues and proposed answers of the day are insolvent. In such situations, contemporary man, subject to his time, lacks the sense to recognize them. But as long as there are thirsty spirits, the Church will be the debtor of their thirst, offering the means by which they will be satisfied. The Church cannot change the world, but this is not a deficiency for this is not her purpose. Rather, her responsibility is to reach the other, to pour oil upon the wounds of fellow persons, as modeled for us by the Good Samaritan, an image of Him who is "meek and of a humble heart" (Lk 10:34). Through the Church, Christ "pours oil and wine" over man's tragic dead ends and the perils of the time.

And here we come to the ontological question of the Greek Fathers. Yet, some contemporary scholars do not seem to realize that the Greek Fathers propagated salvation in an existential way—which is *ontological*, of course—that speaks to every context concerned with true being. If "Hellenism" was simply about being "rational and disposed to definitions" or merely "abstract and metaphysical", then why would it matter at all? This is the crucial question. By placing the dogma of Resurrection at the center of their concerns, these Fathers— unlike the Syriac, Arabic, Coptic, Ethiopian or Armenian Fathers—responded not to psychological, moral or other "contextual" questions (as did the abovementioned Fathers of non-Greek traditions, because ontology was not in their "blood"), but to the problem of existence. (By the way, the non-Greek Fathers were not concerned with the dogmatic aspects of the heresies of Arius, Nestorius, etc.) Even the Jews in Jesus' time had not developed the idea of resurrection sufficiently. This work was done from as early as the 2nd century, when we encounter a developed theology of resurrection by those Fathers who were in charge of "translating" the Gospel for the Greek-Roman world. And this happened, as Florovsky explained, because salvation—having come "from the Jews" — "has been propagated to the world in Greek idiom." And here the relevance of the Greek Fathers comes to the surface. Their epistemological tool was faith in the Resurrection from the dead, i.e., response to the existential problem of *to be* or *not to be*, because "natural" immortality was excluded. Christ himself asks his disciples an ontological question: τίνα με λέγουσιν οἱ ἄνθρωποι εἶναι, (lit. "whom me say men to be"), who do people say that I am? The preaching of the Resurrection is the nucleus for the genesis of dogma. "If Christ has not risen, your faith is a vain thing" (1 Cor. 15:16). "Christ has risen" is the message to all people, but the Greek answers: "Truly He is risen"!

Since the ontological question, i.e., the issue of true being (τὸ ὄντως ὄν) has been at the foundation of Western philosophy until our own time, the problem of death remains its main preoccupation. This is what the Greeks called the "ontological" question. When our Western philosophy stops using the word "to be" in its vocabulary (even giving a negative answer to ontology, as Nietzsche did) it will cease to be "Greek;" but not until then. Hence Florovsky's assertion: "the Christian message has been forever formulated in Greek categories". Even Post-modern thought does not pose new questions, it rather answers ontological, Greek, questions. It is no use having the right answers if you are not asking the right questions.

Orthodox theology must articulate the meaning of salvation so as to prevent it from being falsified by accommodation to the demands of culture. Inquiries into the meaning of life haunt contemporary man. This demands from the Church an existential interpretation of dogmatics and a new theological language in the face of a pluralistic culture. The question of the meaning of life resonates within us only to the extent that there is a vacancy within us for it to occupy. As Christ fills us up, it evaporates, replaced instead with a joyful need to express our union with Him to our time, addressing our anchorless culture with fundamental theological questions that challenge its stale presumptions. These inquests and their answers have immediate consequences for man's general attitude toward the world and life. Ideally, the question provokes a reorientation from time to history, from contemporaneity to Christ in the effort to posit an answer...

Terms of relationship such as love, otherness, freedom, and communion have neither stable nor static meaning because they always refer to a desired fullness, to a parousia of the Spirit. This expectation forms our theological engagement so that we look to our biblical faith and, even more, to the Christian Church as the experience of God as the par excellence personal and Holy Being. These presuppositions about God lead to anthropological implications for man who is created "in the image of the holy God", they also lead to questions: Is there more than a mere formal correlation between "be holy, because I am holy" and person and otherness? Does one entering into communion with God become unique and special, seeing that God is really the One Who is fully and radically special as "completely other" (*ganz andere*)? As far as both theology and the experience of the Church are concerned, each man may be considered distinct and unrepeatable, but this is only applicable to him who reaches out from the anonymity of individuality towards the uniqueness of personhood. This transformation occurs through inter-personal communion, through *communio sanctorum*. Church tradition acknowledges the specialness and distinction of each Saint because of his special and unrepeatable relationship established with the Special and Unrepeatable Holy One within the liturgical experience of the Church. The notion of holiness itself contains both a personal and ethical meaning, both of which are emphasized in biblical tradition, although the former carries more weight than the latter in this volume because of the transformative possibilities implicit in the transition from ontology that is naturally conditioned to one that is hypostatically oriented.

Different meanings (or no meaning) have been attributed to "holiness". In this book, we use it to refer to God's personal sanctifying presence and its different manifestations in both anthropology and also in the experience of the Church. It is not perchance that the Orthodox Church denotes both the faith of the saints and the space of sanctification. It is a faith that produces holy persons, "enriches the world with saints" and insists on an ethos of holiness. It is well known that in contrast to the major natural religions, holiness in the Church is considered a free gift of God and a free accomplishment by the human person (unlike the naturalistic *mysterium fascinandum et tremendum*) and is, furthermore, experienced as a catholic and communal act. This does not mean that holiness refers to an "objective" appraisal of a person's degree of intellectual consciousness of the teachings of the Church (θεωρία) achieved by means of "purification" (κάθαρσις) of the body from the passions and of the soul from prejudice or ignorance. On the contrary, hagiography, especially in the early centuries, is predominantly concerned with overcoming the tragedy of existence, that is, of mortality. This is no mere coincidence, for the very existence of the Church cannot be understood outside the parameters of death and corruption. Holiness is a gift bestowed upon those who are open to the experience of communion whereby death and corruption are overcome.

The Truth is that death has been trampled down, overcome, defeated. The relevance of truth cannot be objectively understood, but it can be encountered as a Person; furthermore, that Person can be encountered through persons. The Fathers proceed from the assumption that the Truth, encountered in time, sets one free (John 8:32). They realize that our procession is one from corruption to death; however, this is the case only when truth is hypostatically, and not naturally, united to creation. Truth dwells in communion of man and God, where He is ever imparting an uncreated mode of existence to His creation. The Incarnate Truth, Christ, illumines and justifies history, affirming the human body as the center of human existence. No historical institution can monopolize truth because the faith and life of the Church and her position are *epicletic*, that is, dependent on God. As a consequence of this dependency, an individual does not "possess" a given truth; rather, truth is bestowed according to the measure of one's participation in the divine life offered in the Body of Christ through the grace of the Holy Spirit. The validation of these theological claims does not occur through observational methods because they are not susceptible to "objective" assessment since epistemology cannot "control" theological facts. In theology, God, the subject, confers knowledge of the truth out of freedom and love. The recognition that our consciousness is mainly a natural-biological product does not deny that God "touches" those existential chords in human beings that surpass all neurobiological processes.

Recent developments in the field of natural sciences shed a light on a theological-medical approach to the human being. Recognizing that neuro-molecular biology-based medicine can say a lot about "spiritual" processes, we undertake to verify theological implications about man's freedom through observations based on the premises of modern medicine in "Is There a Biochemistry of Freedom?" We can temper the unpleasant enslavement and conditioning suggested by the chemical and biological basis for the individuality of human "nature" by readjusting our premise to that of the ascetics, who labor in their feats of self-denial so that they might receive a personal inheritance, promised to all, and grow with ever increasing sanctity into the likeness of God. St. Maximus the Confessor and the contemporary elder Porphyrios Kapsokalibite are examples of theologians operating from such an ascetic premise. Of all human characteristics, freedom— experienced as transcendent impetus and gift—is the least submissible to objective testing precisely because it is initiated by God in love, emerges in successive moments of Truth-recognition, and is realized for salvific ends, spiritually saving those yoked to the world and subject to death and decay. Spirituality gives birth to an ethos that, in turn, produces habits and conducts that influence biological life. The personal characteristic of freedom, then, determines the very biochemical substance that some would place above both freedom and spirit. The eschaton—the true state of existence—enlightens our understanding of man's biochemical substratum decisively. The person, experienced eschatologically, is not subject to "laws of nature" that cannot be changed. Rather, the human body as biochemical mechanism is so subject, but the eschatological person is subject to thorough epigenetic changes to the "tropos of existence."

This multidisciplinary approach to the biochemistry of freedom has pedagogical, missiological, pastoral, bioethical and other implications. In the double jubilee of 2009, commemorating the 200th anniversary of Darwin's birth and the 150th anniversary of the publication of *On the Origin of Species*, we reject a biochemistry of freedom and conclude that evolutionary laws do not exclude the transcendent cause, i. e. the Personal God and His intimate relationship with both the world and history. The Church offers the possibility of overcoming our fallen biochemistry through the two Holy Mysteries of Baptism and Eucharist. Baptism is humanity's participation in the death of Christ—i. e. the dying of the old man and his "methods of knowing" and natural passions—and the new man's entrance, through immersion, into the resurrection of the

God-man Christ. The Eucharist, on the other hand, bestows not only a foretaste, but also an earnest and advance experience of eschatological health and healing. Theologically, it could be admitted that there is a biochemistry of the natural will but not a biochemistry of freedom, for God's salvific activity and His transcendent dwelling within and among men ensure that our freedom escapes the determinations of biochemistry in a mystical, but no less experientially and realistic, way. In that sense, hopeless determinism seeking to reduce freedom to mere instinct is naught but a chimera. Orthodox theology must develop a corresponding ethos of freedom and love in order to establish a bioethical culture ruled by freedom, acknowledging that there is no real freedom without transcendence nor is there complete healing without Christ.

In order to develop the future of Orthodoxy at the beginning of the third millennium after Christ, we need to examine postmodern pluralism, since such is the cultural framework within which Orthodoxy is called to act and to which it must adapt, although, importantly, not align itself. Certain key concepts in the Orthodox theological tradition—among them Christology, Patricity, Neopatricity, and culture—can bridge the gulf between Orthodoxy and Western postmodernity. Despite all the answers, solutions, and propositions that have emerged from the inculturation of the Gospel into various historical conditions, most notably the age of the Fathers in the fourth century, the task remains difficult, although not without precedent. The solutions of the past, however, do not automatically transfer to the present, and, therefore, theological criteria are first and foremost required, as well as steadfastness in the face of severe spiritual struggle (podvig). Although every age has lived and experienced Christ in a way as unique as those persons encountering Him, and although every age has articulated this experience through its own means (theoretically, intellectually, politically and so forth), there have always been challenges to developing the cultural expression of this experience. The relationship between Christ and any given culture is always both dialectical and critical ("now is the judgment [κρῖσις] of this world", John 12:31). One could go even further and claim that every age has a legitimate need—even a right—to receive (in the same sense that the Apostle Paul uses the word) Christ—Who is the same forever—in its own way. But we must proceed cautiously for therein lurks the temptations of secularization, utopianism, romanticism, sentimentalism, and aestheticism. Once appropriate criteria are established, we can discern those elements received by the Church from among cultural achievements, recuperating those Christological elements that help us to discriminate the ontological from the epistemological.

The Church, as the icon of God, is the only place where the freedom of being "other" represents sanctity in itself, for through her structure and salvific mission she expresses the freedom of otherness (*alteritas*). Holding true as it does within both Triadology and Christology, the freedom of otherness must also hold true for ecclesiology, where the same ontological principles apply. This is the reason we speak, primarily from a theological standpoint, of the synodality of both the Orthodox and Catholic Church. Orthodox and Roman Catholic concepts of conciliarity differ from each other even though they stem from the same synodal tradition. Our creative and more profound encounter is, nonetheless, beneficial and even necessary if we endeavor to fulfill sincerely the petition of the Lord's Prayer at Gethsemane. Although the differences that exist in both general and historical interpretations of the one and same conciliar tradition are not insurmountable, overcoming them will be daunting unless expressly pursued through theological dialogue, from whence ecclesiology derives. Primacy (or *primus*) represents the *conditio sine qua non* of synodality, but the converse is true as well. Despite its relevance today (in view of preparation for the Great and Holy Synod of the Orthodox Church), our study on conciliarity is not focused on the evolution of conciliarity in the life of the Church. A close study of the Church's historical development already reveals the message or idea essential to any genuine theology of synodality. Our primary interest is the ecclesiological elements forming this institution. Such an approach makes it easier to grasp the manner by which the fundamental ecclesiology of the synod has remained unchanged despite the adoption of new expressions of Church unity. In the light of these theological, historical and ecclesiological considerations, we must be clear about which guidelines, related to the institution of the synod, should inform the Canons of the Orthodox Church in order to ensure that fundamental concepts such as community, otherness and freedom remain essential pillars of life in the Church.

Among the most essential of Church pillars is reception of the Eucharist, the nature of which is fundamentally eschatological. In the Liturgy, we see the Truth of the Kingdom of God. The Church provides us with windows into this future kingdom in our liturgical use of icons. From the very beginning of Christianity, icons have been fundamental to theology, especially Christology. Although the means of expression derive from fallen nature, iconography refers to inexpressible Truth by encouraging personal relations with the Truth; a proper icon creates true personal relationships. That is why an icon is indivisibly linked with Love: we cannot speak about Truth without Love, and we cannot speak about iconography that does not lead us to Love, which for Orthodox Christians means the Church, wherein we meet the other in his or her true state. As St. Justin (Popovich) used to say, "in the Church we are taught to see (iconically) in every man our future brother/sister [as he or she is in] Paradise". There, in the Eucharistic synaxis, we will see and meet God through our communion with others. So, the icon gathers (in a synaxis) the community we call the Church. The icon, then, is not only an object that we kiss and venerate, but also an eternal synaxis that exists in moments, movements, and actions during the Divine Liturgy. Outside the Church, there is not the Kingdom of God; inside the Church, all is iconic.

The identification of the selfsameness of Christ with His image leads to the assertion that Orthodoxy is the Church and not an ideology. It is a gathering of the people and, particularly, a Eucharistic gathering of living icons. This is what we must emphasize today: not an Internet—on-line—virtual illusion of communication, but the icon as the visible and true communication of the Kingdom; such must be the future of Orthodoxy because such is the future Christ promises His Church. In the Eucharist, we are taught not only to venerate and greet icons, but also the other members of the synaxis, not passing the living icons—people—by, but greeting and embracing them. So, the icon is indeed the right method of looking at the world. Only this iconic approach will save Orthodoxy from becoming a secular organization conforming to the image of the world.

The thoughts and insights in the following pages are the fruit of the author's dialogue with the patristic "mind" of modern fathers and teachers of the Church, especially George Florovsky, Metropolitan John Zizioulas, Bishop Athanasius Yevtich and Christos Yannaras. Thanks to them, an important trajectory of thinking within contemporary Orthodox theology, we hope, may continue.

I dedicate this book to Bishop Athanasius and Metropolitan John, my teachers in theology who have maintained this trajectory. From them, I was able to learn the criteria with which patristic Christology freely and creatively incarnates in space and time, transforming it, i.e. changing the mode—the *tropos*—of existence and not the reason, or logos, of nature. Our journey is one beyond romanticism, nationalism, and utopianism to history, truth, and holiness. I am especially grateful to Aristotle Papanikolaou for his forward and Deacon Daniel Mackay for his diligent work in editing this book.

**I am the Vine,
you are the branches** (John 15:5)

Holiness and Otherness

From Holiness as an Ethical Concept to Holiness as a Hypostatic Concept

The idea of personal holiness is deeply rooted in biblical faith, especially in the Christian Church. God is called and experienced as the personal and Holy Being par excellence.[1] Because the biblical God is the only foundation of true holiness, it follows that only He can state: "Be holy, because I am holy" (Lev. 11:44, 45; 1 Peter 1:16). Bearing in mind that man was created "in the image" of the *holy* God, it is not surprising that the Church has a well-developed sensitivity for the holiness of the *human* person. The idea of holiness, sanctified because of its connection to Christ and the Church, is profusely rich in both its content and inferences. For this reason, the Church understands any sin committed against the sanctity of the human person to be a sin against God Himself (regardless of intention or justification).

When we examine the idea of *holiness* within "be holy, because I am holy" before subsequent meanings are attached to it, we note an implied personal understanding of holiness apart from the more explicit ethical meaning emphasized in biblical tradition. This personal meaning, in turn, changes our understanding of anthropology and ecclesiology.

I. The biblical concept of otherness

1. The semitic word *qdš*/קָדֹשׁ= kadosh or godesh / which the Seventy translated from the Old Testament into ἄγιος[2] (*holy*) is related to the

---

[1] In 1 Sam. 6:20 *God* is identified as *Holy* within the same context. Refer to footnote 7 for further comments.

[2] Cf. *Ecclesia: A Theological Encyclopedia of the Church*, ed. Christopher O'Donnell, O. Carm, Minnesota, 1996, pp. 198–202. Also: *The Oxford Companion to Christian Thought*, ed. Hastings, Mason and Pyper, Oxford, 2000.

1

Assyric word *kudduchu*. It means "to cut," "to separate (to exempt)," "to radically differentiate," "to clean."[3] It follows that: a) holy is he who is separate from the rest (definitely applicable to God), b) a holy person is someone who is different and exempt from other people, and c) holy are those things that are separate from the rest, especially those that are reserved for the service of God and are consecrated to God.[4] This is the etymological concept of holy. Etymology without theology, however, does not provide a complete explanation. Therefore, let us see what theology can offer us with regard to this subject.

2. The biblical approach goes beyond the etymological meaning of holiness (holy = *separate, different, independent*); it also, however, exceeds the psychological meaning of holiness emphasized by the ancient Greeks, i.e. dread, fear, being in awe of a higher power or its carrier.[5] Simply speaking, through offering an ontological encounter with love, the Bible surpasses the concepts of holiness as a) an expression of ethical individualism, or as b) *mysterium fascinandum et tremendum* (a mystery that arouses fascination and trembling),[6] and leads us to theology precisely when the

[3] The relationship between purity and innocence is derived here. The subject of purity and purification is the dominant theme in Leviticus 17–26, especially with regard to the "code of holiness." Compare the study of Mary Douglas, *Purity and Danger—An Analysis of Concepts of Pollution and Taboo* (1966) written from an anthropological perspective, which demonstrates the different ways in which the idea of holiness serves the purpose of preserving the categorical system of separation and distinction in society. Cf. Mircea Eliade: "Holiness is always expressed as the reality of a different order compared to the 'natural' realities" (*The Sacred & The Profane* [1957], Belgrade, 1988, p.12).

[4] Wisdom 6:10: "For those who keep the holy precepts hallowed shall be found holy." God is *Holy*, therefore, according to the Bible, our holiness consists only in what is *consecrated* and *surrendered* to such a God. Hence, holy are, for example, the *bread* offered to Him, the *child* dedicated to Him, an *oath* given to Him; as is written in the Holy Scriptures: that is "*holy to God.*" There are also the ἱερὰ γράμματα, βιβλία, ἁγίασμα (holy water), τὰ ἱερὰ καὶ τὰ ὅσια." The philological difference between ἱερὸς (Latin: *sacrum*) and ἅγιος (Latin: *sanctus*) has been preserved in the Slavic "sveto(st)" (holy, saint) and "svešteno(st)" or "osveštano" (sacred, sacré). See "*The Encyclopedia of Religion*," ed. Mircea Eliade, vol. 6, 1987, p. 435. According to M. Kardamakis ("Ἁγιότητα καὶ ἐσχατολογία," in: Ἁγιότητα, ἕνα λησμονημένο ὅραμα, Athens, 2000, p. 176) their difference consists in the more personal (intimate) character of holiness (ἁγιότης) compared to the less personal and inaccessible domain of the ethical and metaphysical character of the sacred (ἱερότης). See the work of E. Levinas with the characteristic title: *Du sacré au saint*, Paris, ed. De Minuit, 1977.

[5] See G. Kittel, *The Theological Dictionary of the New Testament*, vol. 1, p. 88–89.

[6] The expression originates from Rudolf Otto (*The Idea of the Holy*, Oxford University Press, 1923).

concept of holiness is connected with (God's) absolute otherness through the absolute Other. It is not difficult to conclude how the Bible identified the Holy One with God, Who is not an isolated Entity but the Trinity. In His absolute transcendence in relation to the cosmos, Yahweh[7] alone is the Holy One, in His Trinitarian, perfect and unique fashion ("there is no one holy like the Lord," 1 Sam. 2:2); holiness is not abstract.

3. The prophet Isaiah, who is characterized as the "prophet of the Holiness of God" emphasises the uniqueness and particularity of God's Holiness in the Old Testament through the triple repetition: "Holy, Holy, Holy is the Lord Almighty" (Isaiah 6:3). In its Hebrew form, the threefold repetition[8] signifies perfect, infinitely Holy and All Holy (πανάγιος). The Church has valued this moment *liturgically* in her Eucharistic prayer (both in the East and in the Western *Sanctus*) and *canonically* (the Eucharistic reconciliation with others was the objective of the Council), which we will discuss later. The Church Fathers interpreted Isaiah's threefold *Holy* as triadological for hypostatic-existential reasons rather than according to a narrow "dogmatic" interpretation. In view of this, holiness should not be understood as one of the qualities of the *nature* of God but as the fundamental characteristic of the Triune *Persons*, unique, unrepeatable and personal Hypostases. When God, the only Holy One and the only Truth, invites[9] us to holiness according to a *life in Truth*, this invitation extends to a manner of existence that is appropriate only to Him: "Be holy, because I am holy" (Lev. 11: 44–45). This is the most perfect invitation, which nothing can surpass either in this or in the next world because it enables the acquisition of a true hypostatic existence for every participant. Christ even ends His

---

[7] It is interesting that biblical science has not noticed and examined the crucial connection between the name Yahweh (He Who Is) and the name *Kadosh* (the Absolute Other). The identification of *Yahweh with the Holy One*, which we encounter in 1 Sam. 6: 20 and the entire context of the Old Testament provide a solid foundation for biblical personalism. More detailed studies are found in the works of John Zizioulas, "Deification of the Saints as the Icon of the Kingdom" (in Greek: "Η θέωση τῶν Ἁγίων ὡς εἰκονισμὸς τῆς Βασιλείας," in: Ἁγιότητα, ἕνα λησμονημένο ὅραμα, Αθήνα: Ακρίτας, 2001, 23–41, and Athanasius Yevtich, *Jesus Christ Is the Same Yesterday, Today, and Unto the Ages* (Sebastian Press, Los Angeles, 2010).

[8] According to Jewish tradition the threefold repetition of a number is an indication of its infinity. See J. Zizioulas, "Deification of the Saints...," in: Ἁγιότητα, ἕνα λησμονημένο ὅραμα, *ibid.* p. 28.

[9] The meaning of this "call" is worthy of more thorough research, which we cannot conduct here due to a lack of space.

Sermon on the Mount (Matt. 5:48) with words in the same vein: "Be perfect, therefore, as your heavenly Father is perfect" (let us remember here that the threefold repetition of *qadosh* [holy] means *perfection*).

4. So, this correct, *theological, ontological* understanding of holiness is indeed biblical; that is, it pertains to the Old and New Testament. "Be holy, because I am holy" is an invitation extended to the community as well, not only to the individual.[10] This is most significant, for the aim of creation is the arrival of God the Logos in history; indeed, there is no other aim than to recapitulate not only man but also all of creation in the Person of God the Son, and to thereby unite them with the only Holy One. Both man and all of creation seek none other than this Holy God, Who, as it was said to Israel, is "The Holy One, Whom you are awaiting."[11] Otherwise, it would mean that God created the world without the aim of uniting *hypostatically* with Him. The Holiness of the Father that Christ as High Priest invokes in His prayer (John 17:11) is the foundation of His request for all the faithful to remain in communion with Him.[12] No one has ever reached perfection without a personal relationship with the *Holy One*, that is, with the Absolute Other. Hence, man's first *fall* can be explained within this context.[13] Adam's rejection of God meant a rejection of holiness, which properly understood is, of course, constitutive of existence—otherness, and not merely some quality. In his aspiration to become a god on his own, that is, without the other, Adam rejected the Other as the constituent of his existence and proclaimed himself as the final explanation and ultimate end of his own existence. In his "fallen"

---

[10] Cf. the study of H. Wheeler Robinson, "Corporate Personality in Ancient Israel," Philadelphia, 1964.

[11] Prophet Malachi 3:1, St. Clement of Rome, *1 Cor.* 22:3.

[12] Cf. W. Pannenberg, *Systematic Theology*, vol. 1, Edinburgh, 1991, p. 399.

[13] Within the context of modern scientific discussion about the first-created man, it suffices for our topic to accept Adam as the first being in creation that God personally invited to become a god in communion with Him, and to thus transcend death and corruption inherent in the nature of the world. His subsequent rejection of this invitation represents the "Fall." See the brilliant analysis of St. Maximus the Confessor: "For this reason the anthropos was introduced last (ἔσχατος) among beings, as a kind of natural bond (σύνδεσμός τις φυσικός), mediating between the extremities of the universe through its proper parts, and leading into one in itself the many (εἰς ἕν ἄγων ἐν ἑαυτῷ τὰ πολλῷ) that are set apart from one another, according to nature, by an interval, in order to bring about the union of everything with God as its cause, beginning first of all with its own division, [and] then, proceeding successively through the intermediate steps by order and rank to God, it receives the end of the lofty ascent through everything occurring by union..." (*Ambigua* 41, PG 91, 1305).

state, holiness, otherness and union cannot coincide with each other at all, as they do in the case of the Divine Triune existence.

5. Meanwhile, the central question is as follows: "Who can stand in the presence of the Lord, this holy God?" (1 Sam. 6:20), since Adam, the first man, did not succeed in this? In other words, how can the hiatus between the uncreated, holy God and the created world be overcome? Since the biblical God is completely extraordinary, beyond the Other and Otherness, how can the ontological abyss (ἄβυσσος) between God and the world be overcome? St. Maximus the Confessor (7th century) answers these questions through the hypostatic union, that is, through the Hypostasis of the Son. God does not overcome the abyss through nature or through some of His energies, but through the adaptation of His *tropos*, through His way of existence. Herein lies the mystery of Christ.[14] In this way God's relationship with the world is not foundationally ethical, psychological, or religious but *ontological*. Man achieves complete realization only through hypostatic communion with God in Christ. Holiness stems only from Him and through a relationship with Him. Thus, he who enters into communion with God can become exceptional and unique because God is the One Who is completely and radically unique, i.e., "completely other" (*ganz andere*).

Now we arrive at the central question of our discussion. Does being exceptional, which *qadosh* implies, entail separation and partition? Indeed, some scholars have gone so far as to translate "Be holy, because I am holy" (Lev. 11:41) as "Be separate, because I am separate."[15] Let us examine this idea, which at first glance implies a transcendental dimension and in the final analysis identifies holiness with uniqueness. The Bible insists on the holiness of God precisely because He is special, *separate*, and therefore *completely different* from everything else. Bishop Athanasius Yevtich[16] perceives a radical gap between the classical Greco-Roman notion of holiness, shared with eastern and other traditions, and the Hebrew-Biblical

---

[14] *Ambigua* 5, PG 91, 1056 and 41, PG 91,1308c and 1313. According to St. Maximus λόγος φύσεως does not change nor is there any need to replace it in contrast to its τρόπος ὑπάρξεως (*Ambigua* 42, PG 91, 1340 BC 1341 C). This is precisely what occurs in the Incarnation of Christ. The tragedy of the Fall lies in the "mode of existence" which is contrary to the "logos of nature."

[15] Mary Douglas, *ibid.*

[16] "O svetosti i odgovornosti," *Živo predanje u Crkvi* ["On Holiness and Responsibility," *Living Tradition in the Church*], Trebinje–V. Banja, 1998, pp. 378–80.

tradition. He asserts that Plato's idea of God as the supreme Good is the highest and best link in the chain of beings; however, it only remains a link because it is not the biblical God. Evidently, the biblical *Kadosh* (Holy) means something entirely different also with regard to cosmology. With this in mind, we can claim that this world is *sacred* (ἄγιον in the sense of being different) even to God. This is true because God the Father recognizes the world as an extension of "His Own Will" (ἴδια θελήματα), returning us to Maximus the Confessor's notion of God's hypostatic union with humanity.[17]

6. Holiness as *mysterium fascinandum et tremendum* (Rudolf Otto) inadequately expresses the encounter between holy God and man because *separation* is fundamental to this relationship as defined by the *mysterium* experience. The biblical God, by contrast, paradoxically moves toward creation through eros and love—ekstasy—respecting the holiness of the world,[18] i.e. its otherness, distinction, dissimilarity. Although Otto's approach is profound and complex, it still remains typically essentialist, a Western approach wherein holiness is recognized by its attributes (*fascinans* and *tremens*), implying a substantial need and irrationality that arouses fascination and trembling.[19] The biblical approach points to God as *Holy* because he freely reveals Himself as a loving Being and invites us to encounter Him, to experience a relationship with Him ("We love Him because He first loved us"; 1 John 4:19). His appearance to Elijah on the mountain was not manifested in lightning and thunder (which indeed would have caused fascination and trembling) but in the "tiny whispering sound" (1 Kings 20:12). The energies of God, which reflect the infinite dynamism of His Being, do not emanate "ἄνευ προαιρέσεως" according to Plotinus' concept. Rather, they are always within the realm of the Divine

---

[17] *Ambigua*, PG 91, 1260c.

[18] "God moves in such a way that He instills an inner relationship (σχέσιν ἐνδιάθε-τον) of eros and love in those who are able to receive it (τοῖς δεκτικοῖς). He moves naturally, attracting the desire of those to Him who are turned toward Him." *Ambigua*, PG 91, 1260c.

[19] Already Mircea Eliade noticed this inadequacy in Otto's approach. Cf. *The Sacred & The Profane* (1957), (in Serbian) Belgrade, 1988, p. 12. Levinas' approach to this problem should also be emphasized: "The presence of the face coming from beyond the world...does not overwhelm me as a numinous essence arousing fear and trembling. The Other does not only appear in his face...infinitely distant from the very relation he enters" (*Totality and Infinity: An Essay on Exteriority*, Pittsburgh, 1996, p. 215).

Persons so that the personal and loving God is always revealed in His sanctifying energies. This encounter with the holy God that the Orthodox liturgical experience values has almost nothing in common with the "natural" idea of a God Who arouses fascination and trembling.[20] This is further confirmed in Patristics, in liturgical, and in ascetic literature. The relation with the only Holy One—Christ, is a loving relation; completely and infinitely intimate, a wholesome personal—holistic encounter, precisely because Christ is a personal and a relational Being par excellence.[21] Therefore, the dimension of holiness, which natural religions lack, can be termed *hypostatic*. This dimension complements that part of holiness characterized as "ekstatic," which is man's experience when stepping forward in order to encounter the Holy One.

So in the Church, each saint differs from others in his absolute otherness, an otherness that is unique, non-repeatable and irreplaceable. Any phenomenon that violates or undermines the absolute uniqueness of a person, which emerges through relations, changes it into a thing, into a means toward an end. There is nothing holier than the unique person experienced as absolute otherness. Let us illustrate this through a number of historical examples.

II. The emergence of holiness in historical figures

1. According to the Old Testament (or Covenant), holiness is not attainable other than through separation. Yet, within both theology and the Church, a holy man is not only he who is distinct and unique, but he whose uniqueness is achieved *free from the anonymity of "individuality."* Because a person does not exist for himself alone—and here is the quintessence of hagiology—realization of one's authentic self occurs through the communion of persons, that is, through *communio sanctorum*. This is the reason why Church Tradition teaches that each saint is unique and distinct: his personal distinction is a result of a unique and irreplaceable relationship attained with the Unique and Irreplaceable Holy One. Importantly, this relationship takes place within the liturgical (common) experience of the Church. This Holy God bestows holiness, uniqueness

---

[20] St. Augustine conveys a similar experience, in *Confessions* 9, 9.

[21] As in the *Little Prince*, wherein Exupéry writes: "When a mystery makes such a strong impression a man does not dare disobey." However this is the result of an astonishing and inspirational event, caused by the personal encounter of two persons.

and irreplaceability upon him. Here, it is important to emphasize how the call "Be holy..." (Lev. 19:1) requires one to love one's neighbor as one-self ("love your neighbor as yourself; I am the Lord"; Lev. 19:18). Holiness requires a special kind of separateness that is inexplicably, but inevitably, connected to an experience with others.

2. Therefore, in view of the ethical and personal dimension of holiness, we can assert that the objective of every human being is not moral perfection *through* holiness but *uniqueness*, that is, an otherness, manifested through communion with others. Here, one should point out that otherness and distinction—that is being different—are not the same. Distinctiveness can be expressed in terms of qualities that all share, but it does not apply to otherness because personal otherness and uniqueness exclude it.[22] After all, in the Divine Liturgy the Church commemorates[23] *particular* saints and not saints as a general category. They are commemorated by their respective calendar dates: every individual ascetic and martyr. Only through their uniqueness and irreplaceability can they serve as inexhaustible sources of inspiration to Christians. Consider, for example: Abba Sisoe's attitude toward death, Abba Anthony's sober vigilance of the mystery of God's judgments, holy Martyr Polycarp and other martyrs in their ekstatic passion during martyrdom for Christ, or the challenges of St. Simeon the Fool for Christ. They are all permanent and eternal examples of a sacrificial love "stronger than death." At the same time, they pose an existential challenge to man. Perhaps a maximalistic anthropology stems from their hagiography, which at first glance seems unattainable for modern man and difficult for those who are used to a leisurely lifestyle. However, this kind of anthropology causes an awakening from a "dogmatic," as well as from a likely ethical, "slumber." After all, the higher one aims, the deeper one repents. The lives of the saints show

[22] This is the reason why certain theologians are in favor of the introduction of the so-called "ethical apophatism" in the realm of culture. For more detailed information, see John Zizioulas, "On Being a Person: Towards an Ontology of Personhood," in: *Persons, Divine and Human*, eds. Christoph Schwoebel and Colin Gunton, pp. 33–46 (T & T Clark, 1991).

[23] One should keep in mind that the most accurate meaning of holiness is by way of liturgical remembrance. Namely, ontologically a saint is remembered only *liturgically*, in a union that reveals permanence (eternity, intransience) here and now, and not psychologically through the function of memory but by the remembrance of God the Father through His Son in the Holy Spirit.

that the search for holiness *here* and *now* turns man into a being who is unafraid of death and who leads all of creation into communion with the Holy God. The martyrs who offered themselves wholly to God serve as an example. Their being was united with God to such an extent that one can no longer speak of any *separation* between them, although *distinction* (i.e. otherness) certainly continues to exist and remains forever. The saints of the Church are those persons (the Theotokos, the Apostles, the martyrs and ascetics) who in one way or another, have overcome the anonymity of nature (λόγος φύσεως) in their own and irreplaceable manner, and have united themselves with Christ, the "only Holy One" in a personal and unique way.

3. With a concept of holiness, we paradoxically arrive at the understanding of *eschatology*, and *vice versa* as well. Namely, every saint is regarded as a future resident of Heaven, although in his lifetime he continues to bear both the marks of history, including the fall, and also man's infirmities. Christ, however, retains the *ultimate word*. Were it not for the vision of the *Eschaton*, that is, were we not given a foretaste of the Kingdom in the Liturgy, of that ultimate *communion with the saints*, we would never know what is meant by either "holiness" or "holy man." In other words, it is only the vision and the liturgical experience of the *true*, end state of the world that provides us with the possibility of knowing something about the true world, man and God. This dimension of theology and of the Church is of paramount importance and should be of greater significance in contemporary theological thought.

4. As we resume the previous thought, we can assert that the eschatological dimension of the presence and action of the Holy Spirit[24] has a profound influence on our perception of the "saints," i.e. on the other members of the Church and on their identity. Christian recognition or acceptance of a person does not depend on one's past, but rather on the foundation of one's future image (icon) in holiness. The memory of our experience, positive or negative, is stored in the mental perception of our mind, and determines our attitude toward the other person.[25] Therefore,

[24] Of the two hundred and thirty times the term "ἅγιος" (holy) is used in the New Testament, ninety refer to the Holy Spirit.

[25] "The field of facial recognition is located at the lower region of the temporal lobe, in the area of the *gyrus occipitotemporalis lateralis*. An isolated lesion on both sides of this cortical area of the cerebrum causes an impairment in the recognition of familiar faces" (Aleksandar Ilić et al., *Anatomija centralnog nervnog sistema*, Belgrade, 2004, p.

it is only in the Church that man can remember someone as holy, independent of his past or, to be more exact, *in spite* of his past. This is in accordance with the position of eschatological ontology, which imparts to us that nothing exists or has *truly* existed if it does not exist in the Eschaton. Since the future is entirely in God's hands, our approach to other people should not be weighed down by criticism (judgment) of the other person. Every "other" person (the evangelical *neighbor*) is a *potential saint* in the Holy Spirit, even if he is and continues to be a sinner. It appears that the ancient Christians were more aware of this when they spoke: "You have seen your brother—you have seen your Lord!" Thus, the icon reveals an existential position. Just as we venerate the *eschatological image* of a saint and not merely a photograph, so too should we also perceive primarily the future, the re-established and the resurrected image of each of our neighbors, free from passions; we should overlook his current weaknesses and faults.[26] The iconographic tradition of the Orthodox Church teaches this, where particular emphasis is placed on the role of *light in the depiction of the saint's image.*

5. This leads to reflection on the significance of the *body* in the ontology of holiness. A saint's body is not used for some alternate purpose, nor is it rejected once the intended objective is reached. The body is ontologically fundamental to the reality of sanctity. In paraphrasing George Florovsky, we may state that in the anthropology of *holiness, incorporeality is a phantom*, and *corporeality without holiness is a cadaver.* The eschatological character of iconography *depicting saints in a glorified body* points to the following truth: although the body is par excellence the place of conflict in man's existence, it also embodies his end solution (see Orthodox icons). Death of the body (as sanctuary) is sanctity's greatest enemy because its aim is to destroy the corporeal dimension of our salvation, and to erase and abolish the "otherness," the communion and the love that follow from it. This corporeal dimension of holiness has a special place in ecclesiology; namely, the Church is the space wherein we learn to love one other, including those whose *physical characteristics leave something to be desired.* The Church explicitly teaches that every man is

---

148). Cf. also Eric R. Kandel, *In Search of Memory: The Emergence of a New Science of Mind*, Norton, 2006.

[26] Cf. Stamatis Skliris, "Eshatološki karakter pravoslavnog slikarstva," *Vidoslov* 15/1998, p. 47.

unique and irreplaceable, which is why he is sacred. A number of observations should be made here. In her eucharistic and philocalistic teachings, the Church emphasizes the value of human beauty. However, it is also true that in respecting "otherness" (i.e. differences) as sacred, the Church receives all in her embrace, independent of physical characteristics. Therefore, the Church affirms the human body. However, the *physical* (natural) attributes are not absolute, instead they are seen through the prism of *relativism*;[27] it is not the human attributes that are holy but man's otherness. The person, and not nature, takes priority over man's existential issues.

III. The Church as the space for holiness and otherness

How is the theology of holiness illustrated thus far realized within the Church? Certainly, the respect for personal "otherness" is essential to Orthodoxy. The Church prizes the theology of holiness through her Holy Tradition, which cherishes the Eucharistic encounter with persons where each is accepted, as both other and different, irrespective of all other qualifications or disqualifications, such as sinfulness, morality, sex, or age. Contrary to Sartre's axiom: : "the others are hell," the saint, according to Patristic thought, always needs both the *Other* and the *other*. It is this type of logic that makes Orthodoxy so valuable to all those who lately are in favor of otherness and differences. Let us first have a look at how otherness is experienced in the Orthodox Church.

1. In Patristics, which emphasizes relational, rather than "objective" holiness,[28] the "other" is a *conditio sine qua non* of holiness, rather than a "given fact." The other is the one who represents holiness within the context of Church communion. The Desert Fathers, who lived apart

---

[27] This is the ethos of saints that has been cherished by the Orthodox Tradition throughout the centuries. This explains the reason for individual female saints (Katherine, Anastasia, Pelagia, Eufimia, Irene, Thecla and others) concealing their natural beauty. We can then understand also why Abba Agathon was ready to give his healthy body in exchange for the infirm body of a leper as a gift to him. It is not his physical being that he was giving but his healthy body that he was "transplanting" onto someone else. Unfortunately, the recent culture of art and science is leading us in the opposite direction through the predominance of physical traits. Man is not free when he is reduced to a being of nature, when he is not irreplaceable.

[28] The idea of venerating icons in *relational* terms (σχετικὴ προσκύνησις) which was developed by theologians (St. John Damascene, St. Theodore the Studite, and others) is closely connected to the idea of "relational sainthood."

from the "world," were nevertheless equally dependent on the other[29] as their brother. There is no other principle than the one expressed by St. John the Theologian: "Whoever loves God must also love his brother" (1 John 4:21), and "We know we have passed from death to life, because we love our brothers. Anyone who does not love remains in death" (1 John 3:14). Sanctity cannot exist outside of the "other" (ἐπέκεινα τοῦ ἄλλου) because the other serves as the "terminal" or "reference" of holiness. The "other," at the same time, is also the "cause" of my holiness. If existence is understood dynamically as movement, it follows that holiness should be understood as the eternal movement from one saint to the next (compare the expressions of Maximus "the state of eternal movement" and of Gregory of Nyssa "from glory to glory"), each of whom are affirmed through their mutual relationship and communion with one another. The ultimate destination of this movement of holiness is the only Holy One (Ἅγιος) par excellence, Who affirms each individual "saint" and in Whom every individual saint finds his ontological foundation (which Maximus termed "rest"[30]). However, we must not understand this relation like Buber does, since the fullness of the I-Thou relationship requires *communion* and not just *relationship*. Let us examine this closer.

2. The basic problem of any union consists in how the *individual* is treated. The individual should not be represented as part of a holy entity so that he can offer himself as a sacrifice to any societal Moloch. In ancient philosophy, the unity and totality of the human being—of which the individual was only a part—represented the highest value. Plato is clear about this when he states, "the sum total was not created because of you but rather you were created because of it: You forget that creation is

---

[29] The collection of the lives and the sayings of the Desert Fathers, the *Gerontikon*, abounds in examples that show how each saint is a point of reference to another saint. Their freedom lies not within themselves but in the other, which surpasses Buber's concept of a relation wherein "I" does not exist because of "You" but only in the relationship with "You." Even Levinas could not find a solution to the problem of a reconciliation of otherness with communion because he rejects the idea of the latter and considers it as a threat to otherness. Levinas does not regard holiness as otherness.

[30] This is Maximus' key idea in his interpretation of the 14th Oration of Gregory the Theologian. "The state of eternal movement" is the continual and uninterrupted *enjoyment in the Desired One*" which further means "participating in the *supranatural* Divine realities" (μέθεξις δέ τῶν ὑπέρ φύσιν θείων) Maximus, *Ad Thalassium* 60; PG 90, 608d.

not for your benefit: *you* exist for the sake of the universe."[31] The Apostle Paul, however, stresses that a union (here he refers to the Eucharistic communion) must affirm and sanctify not only the totality and entirety but also the *otherness* of its members.[32] This is the reason why Paul calls all Christians *holy* (see Corinthians, Galatians, Thessalonians, etc.), and *qadosh* (holy), we have already clarified, refers to uniqueness or exceptionality. It is precisely in the Church that this uniqueness or otherness (διαφορά, difference) ceases to be a division (διαίρεσις), or something negative, but becomes positive, good, and at the same time indispensable, that is, a prerequisite. The personal charisms of holiness in the Church are so varied that no member can say to another one: "I don't need you" (1 Cor. 12:21). According to Maximus the Confessor, this is so because in the Church the διαφορά of a saint does not lead to διαίρεσις but to unity and communion.[33] The diversity of the saints and their otherness are affirmed in the Eucharist. In Christianity this means that *when we respect someone's holiness, we actually respect his otherness and vice versa.* Whenever this principle is not applied, the meaning of holiness is violated; it becomes void of any value, even if all other conditions for its fullness are satisfactory or have been met. So, "holiness" that in any way excludes those placed in a second category, whether by race, sex, age or profession, depersonalizes relationships and, in fact, is *opposed* to holiness. Any spirituality that prefers monastic ascetics, children, black or white saints over others also defies holiness. The Church must include the communion of all saints in her Eucharist because only through the coming together of the various personal charisms of the entire Body will the impersonal differences of nature and society be overcome.[34] The Church that does not celebrate the saints in the Eucharist, but merely attaches importance to sentimental *pseudo-holiness*, is in danger of losing her catholicity.

[31] Plato, *Laws*, X, 903 c–d.

[32] Within the context of the modern philosophical and sociological problems regarding otherness, Christian Tradition cherishes all the basic values of the human person of which the value of respect toward otherness or distinctiveness takes first place.

[33] *Division* (διαίρεσις) is one thing and *difference* (διαφορά) another; difference is desirable whereas division is not. This is one of Maximus' key ideas in his brilliant analysis of existence, accurately presented in the second chapter of Thunberg's study, "*Microcosm and Mediator*," Lund, 1965, pp. 51–67. Cf. John Zizioulas, *Communion and Otherness*, New York: T&T Clark, 2006, pp. 22–24.

[34] Cf. John Zizioulas, *Communion and Otherness*, p. 8.

3. We have already mentioned that the Church has valued the moment of holiness both *liturgically* (in the East and in the West: "Ἅγιος" or "Sanctus") and *canonically*. The point here is that the purpose of Church councils is found in the Eucharistic *communion* (κοινωνία) as well as in reconciliation with the Other (the only Holy One) and with the others (the "neighbors" of the Gospels). The most frequent topic of the canons with regard to receiving those who are excluded (τῶν ἀκοινωνήτων) from participation stems from this (see, for example, the fifth canon of the First Ecumenical Council). Great consideration ("...may it be examined...") is given to the subject of correct relations and of a salvific functioning within the assembly of the Church, which is the obvious reason for summoning regular councils ("it has been found beneficial for councils to take place in every region twice a year," from the same canon). Whereas "to be separate" or "to put aside" implies *judgment*, in the Church, judgment does not pertain to an individual but to the community. As a result, according to the canonical tradition of the Church (the apostolic, ecumenical and local councils of the Holy Fathers) questions related to participation or non-participation, that is, receiving or excluding someone from communion, are most frequently answered by the canons. The Eucharistic reconciliation with *others*, i.e. individuals or church communities, has been the objective of the Councils. The canon laws were instituted in order to a) safeguard the canonical unity of the communal spirit and communication in the Eucharistic Communion of Christ with the Grace of the Holy Spirit, or b) rectify and reestablish the *unity* and *communion* that has been violated while safeguarding and respecting the otherness. Therefore, the objective is to reestablish the *other* (our neighbor who has gone astray, been deceived, or has gone away from the Church) in the communion of holiness[35] (the 102nd can-

---

[35] The sixth canon of the Third Ecumenical Council, for example, prohibits the consecration of a bishop without the designation of the place of his diocese. This is indicative of the fact that in the Church personal otherness does not exist without other persons, with whom the respective bishop is connected and from whom he extracts his identity. In contemporary practice, the Serbian local Church included, the consecration of vicar bishops, and furthermore the transfer of a bishop from one diocese to another reflects the neglect of the original understanding of the link between the bishop's otherness (and person) and the otherness of his diocese as his Bride. Here, it appears that the Orthodox Church has been affected by yet another influence of universalistic ecclesiology. This is not a judicial but rather a theological issue. A local

on of the fifth and sixth Ecumenical Council was instituted in this spirit). It is therefore the canons that pronounce judgments (or exclude where necessary), and thereby serve either one's salvation or, if one has independently set himself apart (excommunication) from the Church, one's judgment or condemnation.[36]

4. We have already successfully indicated the way in which church ministries (τὰ χαρίσματα) are also a part of the cited image of holiness. The Apostle Paul explains the Church charismas in terms of love, understood as *relational* and not sentimental or moral. Since a relation makes the personal existence dependent on others, it follows that every saint is confirmed only within the context of relations. Therefore, *each saint is different from every other saint.* For the value of a saint consists only in his relation with "others" in *communio sanctorum*, that is, in a structured, grace-filled community with a bishop at the head, like those about whom ancient ecclesiology testifies. The community is consecrated through the bishop as the head of the Eucharistic assembly.[37] The presiding bishop is not merely an "administrative power," as some erroneously understood him. He confers the grace and the sanctification of the Divine Eucharist, all the charismas included, onto all the branches of Church life.

Church (diocese) together with her members is the bishop's only bride representing the icon of the Bride of Christ with her eschatological sign.

[36] The idea of judgment leads us to the following observation: "sanctification" does not have, or did not initially have, a moral meaning only, but meant rather "to put aside" (someone or something), and even to "withdraw from the world." The canonization of a saint was also a kind of "judgment." The Church "separates" him from the community of the faithful so that he can serve others as a paradigm and as a standard of ascetic struggle. Likewise, the Church as the community of saints is "not of this world" so that it is precisely She who will *judge the world.* It is only within this context that we can understand the statement of the Apostle Paul, namely that "the saints will judge the world" (1 Cor. 6:2). John Zizioulas observes that this judgment or separation is the essential element of eschatology because at the dawning of the end times the judgment with which to judge the world will be established (Matt. 25:31). "The world will be judged according to the relationship of its communion with 'the least' (Matt. 25:40–45), which is synonymous with the Body of the Son of Man ('whatever you did for one of the least of these brothers of mine, you did for me', Matt. 25:40), a multitude, nations of saints, the Church" (J. Zizioulas, "L'Eucharistie: quelques aspects bibliques," in: *L'Eucharistie*, Paris, 1970, pp. 58–59).

[37] This is the ancient perception of the Church testified to by the early Christian Fathers. See sources in J. D. Zizioulas, *Eucharist, Bishop, Church: The Unity of the Church in the Divine Eucharist and the Bishop during the First Three Centuries*, transl. Elizabeth Theokritoff, Brookline MA, Holy Cross Orthodox Press, 2001.

5. A historical explanation is called for here. Specifically, the term "holy," referred to this way in New Testament theology, and which became a *terminus technicus* for the early Christians, particularly for the members of the community in Jerusalem, was replaced by the expression "Christian" already during the apostolic epoch in Antioch (Acts 11:26). Initially the term "hagios" (holy) was mainly used for martyrs (whom the Christians held in very high esteem) and later, following the persecutions it was applied also to other persons who led venerable lives in asceticism.[38] Therefore, we can state with some certainty that historically, but in a period (4th–5th century) and manner unknown to us, the Church decided to place special emphasis on individual saints. She *separated* them from the "*community of the saints*" as an example and as the "proof" for the attainment of that particular, personal, and unique relationship with Christ which the *holy martyrs* had attained before them, and which all others are invited to acquire. This notion of holiness has *essentially* prevailed up to now; from time to time, greater emphasis is placed on the anthropological (individualistic) perception and less on the ecclesiological one.

Here it is necessary to make a few remarks:

a) There is no *elitism* among saints, nor is there any "pyramidal" structures, aristocracies, or exclusive "models" of holiness. There exists only one "ecclesial" aristocracy, which is affiliated with the Church of God and is completely independent of social status. With regard to the objection that there is an over-emphasis in favor of saints from specific categories, as in the example of "monastic" orders, or that there is a prevalence from within the ranks of the "clergy," we say that it is true that the "writer" who records the tradition, i.e. who is responsible for the commemorative documents of his time, writes them in keeping with his world view, interests, etc. Frankly speaking, we admit to certain "inclinations" toward specific types of saints in hagiographic literature, known by the name of "*The Lives of the Saints*."[39] Here it becomes evident that the authors within the monastic order discover holiness for the greater part in monasticism. The hesychast finds holiness in contemplation and

---

[38] So the epithet of *holy* gradually became imparted at the end of one's life, in contrast to the original practice recorded by the Apostle Paul.

[39] There is a difference in the ideal of holiness between, for example, *The Spiritual Meadow* by John Moschos and Simeon Metaphrastes' *Menologion*. See our study "La conception de la sainteté dans l'oeuvre hagiographique de Syméon le Métaphraste," *Revue des études byzantines* 66 (2008) pp. 191–207.

hesychasm. The outwardly active person finds it in activities, such as missionary work, and educated people find holiness in the teachers of the Church. However, this kind of "partiality" should not lead us to the wrong conclusion that holiness is defined according to their respective evaluation or model. On the contrary, holiness is accessible to every member of the Church for, according to the trustworthy words of the Gospel, it is given "without limit" (John 3:34) to all: to priests, peasants, soldiers and farmers,[40] to all. The unreserved desire to attain holiness is sufficient.

b) It is precisely in the Church where man learns (acquires the habit) to love and to be loved, freely and without exclusion. This is a community in which, according to Maximus the Confessor, "perfect love does not divide the nature of man...but always embracing it, loves all men equally...For our God and Lord Jesus Christ showed His Love to us by suffering for all of humanity..."[41] For this reason the ascetic ideal (the sign of perfection), inspired by the above words of St. Maximus does not divide people according to their sex. As an example, there was a traveling monk who, on his way, met some nuns who were desert-dwellers. In order to avoid them he crossed to the other side of the road. Then the one who was the abbess called out to him and said: "Had you been a perfect monk you would not have noticed that we were women" (*Gerontikon*). With regard to modern feminism, it is important to emphasize in this context of holiness the following obvious fact: there is absolute equality between man and woman in the entire ecclesiology of the Orthodox Church. This is crystal clear particularly regarding the topic of holiness: equal honor is given to women and men alike who have devoted themselves to a venerable life or martyrdom.

c) During the course of history there have been some tendencies to limit the members of the Church to the "saints" who most frequently belonged to one "category." However, the Church resolutely rejected the views of the Novatianists, Pelagians, Donatists, Luciferians, Eustathians, Messalians, and others,[42] in their defense of what is known as the *Ecclesia*

---

[40] Cf. St. Justin Popovich's *Preface* in *The Lives of the Saints* for January.

[41] Maximus the Confessor, *On Love* I, 71; PG 90, 976bc. Also see Ἐπιστ. 2: Περὶ ἀγάπης.

[42] For more information, see John Meyendorff, "Authority and Structure in the Church," *The Byzantine Legacy in the Orthodox Church*, Crestwood, NY: St. Vladimir's Seminary Press, 2001, pp. 197–255.

permixta (Augustine), which includes all the faithful. According to St. Augustine, the authentic Church consists of sinners and saints alike.[43]

d) Insofar as sanctification is consistent with becoming an authentic and unique person, there is a legitimate and an inalienable right to become holy (to realize the authentic Self). We have seen in what manner this is realized within the Judeo-Christian tradition. Christians have accomplished this "right" regardless of prevailing conditions, as has been documented in the early Christian text of the *Epistle to Diognetus*. In contrast to other human rights, this right can be achieved under every government and in any society, regardless of "external" conditions, precisely because it is independent of government and society.[44]

e) It is interesting to note that the saints from the iconoclastic period were not primarily ascetic figures but were theologians and hymnographers, and above all, guardians of the icons. Thus, the aspiration of the ascetic ideal shifts toward the struggle of protecting the teachings of the Church, the veneration of icons in this instance (Andrew of Crete, Germanus of Constantinople, John Damascene, Cosmas of Maiuma, Theophanes the Branded, Theodore the Studite, etc.). During the time of iconoclasm, the saint's path to holiness went in the "opposite direction" so to speak, especially when compared to the ascetic model of early Byzantium: "...not only are they not forsaking this world for the sake of stillness in the desert, but they remain in the capital and conduct their struggle using their pens and by means of their daily actions. In their hands, theology is becoming more than the contemplation of God with their intellect; it is becoming a weapon against the heresies..."[45]

---

[43] Cf. *Ecclesia: A Theological Encyclopedia of the Church*, pp. 198– 202.

[44] V. Perišić has provided an exceptional example of the connection between otherness and holiness: "The true realization of I is possible (I am not asserting that it is necessary or desirable) even in situations in which the person is deprived of his so-called human rights. I will give one example: martyrs were martyrs precisely because they were deprived of all human rights—even the right to life. (One can also describe it this way: the deprivation of human rights provided them with the opportunity of martyrdom). A world without human rights is truly awful however, even in such a world man can still be a true man. Moreover, *prima facie* paradoxically, a world deprived of human rights often provided man with the chances to prove to be an authentic man in his daily life with his fellowmen"(Vladan Perishich, "Ličnost i priroda" [Person and Nature], *Raskršća*, Belgrade 1995, pp.109–110).

[45] N. Tsironi, "Ἅγιοι τῆς εἰκονομαχίας" ["The Saints in the Period of Iconoclasm] *Ἁγιότητα, ἕνα λησμονημένο ὅραμα*, p. 162. Later, after the end of iconoclasm, we observe

6. What connection is there between the holiness of the Church and the holiness of an individual? Our experience of the Church reveals a mystery. Her holiness reveals our shortcomings and leads, thereby, to repentance. The higher the awareness of the sanctity of the Church as the icon of the Kingdom of God, the deeper our repentance. Orthodox ecclesiology, in emphasizing the holiness of the Church, does not and should not lead to triumphalism, but rather to a profound capacity for compassion and *repentance*. The experience of holiness is the experience of the Cross. Holiness divested from the Holiness of God and the Church as its point of reference would be "demonic," a paradoxical yet so true *contradictio in adiecto*. Authentic saints are aware that their sanctity is an icon of the Kingdom to come, and they experience the gift of holiness as a gift of God's love toward them of which they are wholly unworthy.

IV. Concluding remarks

So far, we have seen from this analysis how holiness as an ethical concept arrives at holiness as a hypostatic (personalistic) concept. We wish to emphasize the following in our review of what we have here attempted:

1. If we understand holiness exclusively as a category of *nature* (an attribute of God's nature, as in dogmatic textbooks), instead of becoming recognized as a *hypostatic* otherness it will appear as *mysterium fascinandum et tremendum*, a mystery that remains forever *separate* and *out of reach* for us, precisely because it does not have an ontology of love that "drives out fear" (1 John 4:18). If, however, we understand holiness as part of a *hypostasis* (like the Church Fathers who did not perceive the relation between the nature and the Person of God as in conflict), we will not experience this separation, i.e. this distance, but rather we experience a loving union of the two Hypostases, detached *by nature*—God and man—wherein "perfect love drives out fear": the fear implied by *natural* holiness. In this union, man's holiness is manifested as a unique and personal otherness, as a gift from the Only Holy One (the Other) and not as a trait of nature. The inquiry into holiness merely as a Divine attribute does not lead to the ontology of the person.

that holiness is "evaluated" also in the field of social, political and economic struggle in the life of the empire.

2. Even with the inclusion of all the former meanings of holiness, it is clear that the concept of the *holiness* of a person remains deeply rooted in biblical faith. Because God is called and is experienced as a personal and holy Being par excellence and because man is made in the image (according to the icon) of the Holy God, it is obvious that any sin against the holiness of a person (irrelevant of its aim) simultaneously represents a sin against God Himself.

3. *Relational holiness.* Every individual manifestation of holiness of the Christian person within the life of the Church points to the only Holy One, Jesus Christ. The iconographic principle of *relational reverence* (σχετ-ική προσκύνησις = relational, conditional reverence, dependent on the prototype) applies to the reality of holiness. Thus, any holiness without a reference to the holiness of God and the Church is oxymoronic, i.e. a "demonic" holiness and a *contradictio in adiecto*. The "fall" is an attempt to attain one's own holiness, with the individual's self as the point of reference, which is why it leads to death. Therefore, every saint out of humility consciously and deliberately "transfers" and directs holiness to the Prototype of holiness—Christ,[46] that is, he lets it "ascend to the prototype."[47] In short, in the experience of the Church, *holiness* represents the immediate grace-filled reality of an existential and mystagogical nature, experienced here and now only partially, as an "icon," but which will be fully and perfectly experienced in the future timeless Kingdom of God.

---

[46] The example of the holy Prophet Elijah is quite indicative. Endowed with the power and grace of God, he "removes the lightning from the heavens" and hurls it onto the prophets of Baal. He halts the three-year drought, and so forth. Then a woman, Jezebel, banishes him, humiliated and powerless (compare this iconographic moment), and he is forced to hide himself from her for forty days! This is the "mystery of weakness," a so-to-speak "ontological" weakness, a crisis that is not simply psychological although profoundly human, through which the greatest saints must go through. They pass through this in full awareness and in all humility so that they may demonstrate by their own example the truth of salvation, which does not come from oneself (from man) but from the only Holy One. Similar examples of the "endurance of saints" are recorded in the Book of Revelation (14:12).

[47] Ἡ γὰρ τῆς εἰκόνος τιμὴ ἐπὶ τὸ πρωτότυπον διαβαίνει (St. Basil the Great, *On the Holy Spirit* 18,45, PG 32, 149c.)

Truth and History
Implications in Theology and Science

"The Word became flesh and made his dwelling among us"
(John 1:14)
"If there is no resurrection of the dead, then not even Christ has been raised"
(1 Cor. 15:13)

In this presentation, we intend to succinctly examine—in light of the problem of truth—the following three basic questions concerning the ontology of the Christian faith and the resulting implications with regard to theology and science:

a) What is truth for created beings, among whose number we belong?

b) How can we reach an understanding of the historical Jesus Christ, the Incarnate Word of God, Who embodies the *truth* of the created world?

c) How do uncreated and final Truth and created and immanent human existence relate in space and time, i.e. in history? Furthermore, what is the outcome of this relationship?

This problem has been studied in the past. However, in view of the *existential (metaphysical) suppositions* of modern man and his contemporary world, it appears that a contemporary answer to this ancient[1] question, crucial to Christian thinking, has gained in significance. It is a difficult task to argue for a satisfactory case in the age of *pluralism*, where the most diverse and, more often than not, conflicting explanations and interpretations of universal realities, are respectively claimed as the truth by

---

[1] We use the term "ancient" because it denotes and condenses the problem, which from time immemorial has captivated men's thought, namely, the triumph over all that is *transient* in the way of that which *truly is*. This, for instance, was the main preoccupation of ancient Greek thought, and is still today; more about this later.

21

dismantling history and tradition.[2] The vision of Church theology that we portray contrasts with the psychological and ideological approaches of modern man who has a genuine desire to re-examine everything that has become known to him by means of tradition. We emphasize the faith of the ancient Church in the Truth—Christ was not a matter of psychological and ideological conviction but was instead a revelation, an ontologically new historical *experience of the truth*, that is, the experience of God as Truth. Within this Christian perspective, every question about the truth is manifestly connected to *theology*, i.e. to the discussion about God, Who is the Truth par excellence, and is particularly discussed in Christology.[3] The theology we have inherited from Church Tradition deals with the *true* life, the *whole* life in all its dimensions of catholicity,[4] and argues that it is precisely *this* life and its foretaste that affects contemporary man and the world to which he belongs. In the text that follows, we shall attempt to examine the question about *true life* from every angle, with each one corresponding to the fundamental aspects of the Christian faith. We shall consider whether theological principles support empirical evidence. Furthermore, we shall see how the authentic life links one to God, particularly to the Persons of Christ and the Holy Spirit, by taking into consideration how patristic Christology and ecclesiology are inspired by and established through Pneumatology as the eschatological reality. Importantly, it is this reality that illumines the problem of truth in history.

I. Truth and history

According to biblical faith, it is possible to speak about Truth from the historic Incarnation of the Son of God. From this moment, and especially from Christ's Resurrection, Hebrew tradition becomes inter-

---

[2] The worldview of a man is inevitably associated with and conditioned by his intimate preferences and surroundings. Therefore, every world view is "a description of the treasures that man loves, that he has perceived, transformed and 'appropriated'" (G. Florovsky, "The Metaphysical Premises of Utopianism," *Collected Works* 12, p. 76). Generally speaking, everything we observe has already been selected and organized by the very act of observance. See more in IV, 5–6.

[3] In the Incarnate Christ "all the fullness of the Deity lives in a bodily form" (Col 2:9) and on account of this: "Christology is the sole starting point for a Christian understanding of truth" (J. Zizioulas, "Truth and Communion," *Being as Communion: Studies in Personhood and the Church* (London: Darton, Longman & Todd, 1985), p. 67).

[4] This entails the triumph over confessionalism and all forms of exclusiveness.

ested in *truth in history*, as well as in the deliberate Incarnation of the Truth.[5] At the same time, however, Christian tradition also maintains that the truth is a reality of the *future* and not of this age.[6] Hence, the first question is on the nature of the established relation between Truth and History from the moment of the Incarnation of Christ-Yahweh. The next immediate question that follows is the manner in which the relation between Truth (in this instance understood as hypostatic) and man's existence unfolds in space and time, i.e. in history. In order to understand the extent of the implications that this relation has in both the ontology of history and also in the life of mankind—his creativity in history as well—we commence with this inquiry.

1. In order for truth to be concerned with the fate of creation, it must be in a relation of love. Namely, in order for truth to be freely accepted by history, it must be capable of creating a relation of love with something outside itself, respecting the other's otherness, i.e. the other's *truth*. Freedom, be it the reality of the uncreated God or the created world, does not tolerate a relation by necessity. In the Old Testament, it is not by chance that the relation between God, Yahweh, and the world is understood, experienced, and described as a *covenant*, a *pledge*, and even as a *marriage*. The idea of a *pledge* (*berit*, a concept taken from daily life) pervades the entire history of the people of Israel, although it is often erroneously misconstrued by the Israelites themselves as a type of legal "contract." We learn from the Bible that Yahweh entered into *marriage*, into a union and into a relation of love with something completely "other" and different from Himself. Even if the fate of this relation remains uncertain until the end,[7] there is nothing to suggest a desire for a "divorce" from His part, that is, a breach of this covenant. A relation with the world is a novelty for God (eternal, absolute, unchangeable) as well; it is a delight, for to Him the world signifies a joy of love.[8] So, according to the Bible, God, a

[5] Cf. John 3:21: ὁ ποιῶν τὴν ἀλήθειαν and 1 John 1:6. See A. Yevtich, "A Prolegomenon to the Gnosiology of Hesychasm," *Emmanuel*, Los Angeles 2008, p. 143.

[6] "...and what we will be has not yet been made known" (1 John 3:2), "Now we see but a poor reflection as in a mirror; then we shall see face to face" (1 Cor. 13:12), etc. Cf. the Gospels, the epistles of John and Paul, and so forth, where the basic idea is expressed about us. Namely, that we are able to truly perceive and know the Truth only at the Eschaton. More on this topic in II, 2.8.

[7] We emphasize the word *end* and will turn to this topic in III, 1–2.

[8] "I have loved thee with an everlasting love: therefore with loving-kindness have I

loving God, in His man-loving Providence, in the Person of His Son Jesus Christ, Who is the Alpha and Omega of all and everything (see Revelation, Maximus the Confessor, etc.), wondrously sets history in motion and invites all creation to emerge from division and fragmentation—the result of which is that all is subject to decay—to enter into a *true existence*, which He Himself embodies: the *true life* (John 3:15–16; 14:6; 17:3) and the true communion of *love.*[9]

2. All the problems in the relation of God with the world, accurately illustrated in the Bible, establish the background for the way in which mankind experiences in every way ignorance of a life without death and corruption. "True life" cannot be experienced as a lasting *inner worldly reality*, inherent to the nature of creation, nor can it be experienced as an integral part of an empirical reality. As a result, a natural union of truth and history is not possible because it is not permissible for truth to act upon history and creation in a *natural* way, for the pivotal distinction of truth is its constancy and uniqueness. Namely, these two characteristics make truth unalterable toward either change or decay, to which both history and creation are subject.[10] Those who are well acquainted with this theme remind us that ancient Greek thought, in all its forms, was mainly concerned with the question of overcoming the *transience* of individual beings using terms of what truly is. For, according to the Bible, all created beings are mortal and continue to be "creatures of death" (which we are reminded of by the existentialists and by Heidegger in more recent times), that is, they are corrupt, untrue, dependent, as long as they find themselves outside the relation with Someone who is the synonym of Life and Truth (John 14:16). They have a feeling of *homelessness* of which they

drawn thee" (Jer. 31:3). Through this the purpose of life is understood as the recognition of Christ's Image in God—the Bridegroom and the Lover of man; man, who although sinful and mortal, is wounded by His Love = "τετρωμένοι τῆς ἀγάπης Αὐτοῦ" (Cf. The Song of Songs 5:8). This idea imbues all of the Old Testament Books and culminates in "*The Song of Songs*" and in "*The Proverbs of Solomon.*" Israel, God's faithful people, is the betrothed, the fiancée, and the bride while the Lord Himself is the spouse, the bridegroom. Israel is the wife; Yahweh is the husband. Israel's faith and love signifies matrimonial fidelity; their idolatry is adultery (Archimandrite Irinej Bulović, "The Testament of Kosovo in Light of the New Testament," *Bogoslovlje* 1–2/1989, p. 5).

[9] Compare St. Maximus the Confessor's idea of the logos, which says that Christ, the Logos, embraces all the basic logoi; therefore, the final and "pleromatic" designations of all things are found in Him. *Ambigua*, PG 91, 1068–1105.

[10] Cf. John Zizioulas, in "Truth and Communion," p. 70.

cannot divest themselves; they lack a foundation and are therefore bereft of any *reference* (anaphoricity) to an other that is *outside* of themselves.[11] This feeling is a result of the experience of death.[12]

3. Because of the fleetingness of mortal life, those with a biblical perspective conclude that the truth of creation is a *conditional-created* truth, which depends on its *participation* (μετοχή) in or *communion* with the Truth of God. The Truth of God is the uncreated Truth of κοινωνία and has no need to participate in something other in order to become the Truth. Adam, the first man, was invited to do precisely this, that is, to lead creation into fellowship with God. This is the basic idea of the Holy Fathers and endless examples can be given thereof.[13] Meanwhile, true union depends on the manner in which this fellowship is realized: through nature or something else?

a) If participation were to imply that reality is attained by transferring individuality to a common denominator (a stable nature that guarantees survival[14]) whereby it could participate in God, then biblical ontology would become little more than naturalism: a closed ontology unable to manifest *personal* truth.

b) If, on the other hand, participation implies a *hypostatic* unity (as affirmed by the Chalcedonian definition), we can then talk about free-

---

[11] We maintain that the very reference of existence together with the feeling of "homelessness" are sufficient to suggest that man is still not a *complete* man, and that he has to yet become an *authentic* man. More about this in another place.

[12] As the contemporary biologist Clark observes: "Human beings, uniquely among all living creatures on this earth, know that one day they will die. It is a painful knowledge. We have spent most of our history as a knowing species devising belief systems that help us either accept or deny that single fact. No human culture ignores it. It colors our experience as individuals, and often influences our collective actions. Death is a subject that simultaneously terrifies us and fascinates us. Understanding that terror and fascination is an important part of human psychology" (W. R. Clark, *Sex and the Origins of Death*, Oxford University Press, 1996, IX).

[13] Cf. St. Athanasius the Great, St. Gregory the Theologian, St. Maximus, and other parts of our study: *Man in Communion in Christ — "Participation in God" in the Theological Anthropology of St. Gregory the Theologian and of St. Maximus the Confessor* (in Greek), Athens, 1999, pp.16–21. The basic idea of these Fathers is to present and describe the concept of μετοχή (participation) as a dynamic anthropological expression of the more general concept of κοινωνία (communion). These concepts are used as synonyms, or almost as synonyms, in the Holy Scriptures and very frequently by the Holy Fathers; however, based on the theological statements of the Holy Fathers, a distinction should be made.

[14] Indeed, from the viewpoint of the ontology of nature, is there anything more lasting than *nature* (φύσις) itself, in which individual beings appear and disappear?

25

dom, otherness, and the bond between truth and history. Adam failed to achieve this union while, as we shall see further on, Christ succeeded.[15]

c) This participation concerns one's very being (ontology) and not just one's well-being (ethics). Namely, in this instance the act of participation is more important ("it is important to participate") than the measure and quality of the participation itself. Some show greater participation than others; however, all are gathered around the table of the Kingdom as its "citizens" (see IV, 4).

4. It is, therefore, evident that existence is permanently threatened by *death* (nothingness[16]) and is constantly limited by it. Biology assures us (and in this case it coincides with patristic thought) that according to nature every being is born as "dying," meaning that one begins to die biologically from the moment of conception and birth.[17] The whole created world is dying while it exists and exists while it is dying; the life of the world, as well as our own lives, does not embody "true life."[18] Each individual created being, and thus *homo sapiens* too, is tragic by nature; his existence is determined by a paradox which reconciles two absolute and

[15] God gave Adam a personal *invitation* to become a god in communion with Him, and, as a result to transcend death and corruption, inherent in the nature of the world. His refusal to accept this invitation represents the "fall." Cf. the brilliant analysis of St. Maximus the Confessor: "For this reason the anthropos was introduced last (ἔσχατος) among beings, as a kind of natural bond (σύνδεσμός τις φυσικός), mediating between the extremities of the universe through its proper parts, and leading into one in itself the many (εἰς ἕν ἄγων ἐν ἑαυτῷ τὰ πολλῷ) that are set apart from one another, according to nature, by an interval, in order to bring about the union of everything with God as its cause, beginning first of all with its own division, [and] then, proceeding successively through the intermediate steps by order and rank to God, it receives the end of the lofty ascent through everything occurring by union..." (*Ambigua*, 41, PG 91,1305).

[16] Therefore, "nothingness"—non-existence—from which the world has been brought forth, is ontologically absolute, that is, it has no connection with existence and is void of any ontological content.

[17] This could be the reason why certain Fathers have placed nature, sin, and sexual reproduction in the same category. For example, compare Maximus the Confessor *Ad Thalassium* 21 (PG 90, 312). "The form of *programmed death* seems to have arisen at about the same time that cells began experimenting with sex in connection with reproduction" (W. R. Clark, *Sex and the Origin of Death*, Oxford University Press, 1996, XI).

[18] It is interesting to note that Guyton & Hall (*Textbook of Medical Physiology*, 2006, p. 6) consider even reproduction as a homeostatic function: "It does maintain homeostasis by generating new beings to take place of those that are dying." On a more poetic note, compare the words of T.S. Eliot (*Choruses from 'The Rock'*): "Where is the Life we have lost in living? Where is the wisdom we have lost in knowledge? Where is the knowledge we have lost in information?" Popular wisdom: "Joy is as sensitive as a drop of dew; while it is still laughing it already dies."

mutually exclusive elements: life and death, existence and nothingness. Life is in fact a "process of being" that inevitably ends in death, which is genetically transmitted. The aphoristic *death is inherited through birth* points us toward the realization that the death of every being begins with the initial death of just a few cells.[19]

II. Truth and the Incarnation

So, we arrive at the following question: how does the relation between Truth (which is Christ for the Christians) and human existence unfold in space and time, i.e. in history? As we read the Holy Gospel according to John (1:14; 16), we encounter the following words, which help us answer this question:

> The Word became flesh (σὰρξ ἐγένετο) and dwelt (ἐσκήνωσεν) among us, and we beheld (ἐθεασάμεθα) his glory, the glory as of the only begotten of the Father (μονογενοῦς παρὰ Πατρός), full of grace and truth... And of his fullness we have all received (ἐκ τοῦ πληρώματος αὐτοῦ ἡμεῖς πάντες ἐλάβομεν), and grace for grace (χάριν ἀντὶ χάριτος).

From the biblical point of view, as well as from the perspective of the Holy Fathers, this Gospel passage points to the following conclusions, linked to the ontology of *truth* and to the ontology of *history*:

1. First of all, in the prologue of the fourth Gospel, the Logos of God is the Son of the Father, "One of the Holy Trinity" ("we beheld his glory... as the only begotten of the Father"). This *meta-history* (ἐκτὸς τοῦ κόσμου) of the Logos is paradoxically the basic pre-condition of Christ, the Logos, as the Life and Truth of the world. He is the second Hypostasis of the perfect Being and Communion of the Holy Trinity.[20] Had Christ, the

---

[19] Cf. the aforementioned study of W. R. Clark, *Sex and the Origins of Death*.

[20] Life and existence in the Holy Trinity is regarded as identical to the Communion of the Triune Persons (see Basil the Great: "οὕτως ἐπὶ τῆς θείας καὶ ἀσυνθέτου φύσεως ἐν τῇ κοινωνίᾳ τῆς θεότητός ἐστιν ἡ ἕνωσις," *On the Holy Spirit* 18, PG 32, 194c) that reveals the perfection of Existence. The Truth, that is, the true being in his authentic metaphysical condition, is thus regarded as *identical* with communion and is revealed as an ontological, and not an epistemological (gnosiological), category. "The way in which God exists involves simultaneously the 'One' and the 'Many'" (J. Zizioulas, *Communion and Otherness*, New York: T&T Clark, 2006, p. 164). On the other hand when the Church speaks about the unity of God, of the *one* and at the same time *triune* God, She does not ascribe the *oneness* to the ontological primacy of the Essence but to the ontological principle or cause of the personal-triune life of God, which is the Person of God the Father (cf. Ch. Yannaras, *Philosophie sans rupture*, Labor et Fides 1986, p. 175).

Messiah, been anybody from the created world (for instance an angel,[21] a righteous figure of the Old Testament, or any man) then true salvation could not have been wrought, as demonstrated by St. Athanasius the Great (see further below in II, 5). Therefore, the *identity* of the Logos, the Savior, ("Who") must be *divine* in the absolute sense of the word.[22] None other than He, the eternal and uncreated Son, the Word of God, "by Whom were all things made," can *hypostatically (personally)* unite the two worlds, which are incompatible by nature. A distinction in the spirit of the Cappadocians should be made here. Namely, *true life* in God cannot be ascribed to His uncreated nature but rather to His *personal mode of existence*, which hypostasizes nature. Since the immortality of the divine Hypostasis is not an essential given natural occurrence, it follows that *true* life does not represent a *natural* predetermination, contrary to free will. The personal freedom of each respective Hypostasis hypostasizes nature by transcending itself in an act of love. This is why true life is found in the personal mode of existence and not in "nature." The *Hypostasis*, that is, the Person of God the Father is the ontological principle and *cause* (αἴτιον) of existence. The nature of the Persons of the Holy Trinity is authentic because of the free communion of the three Persons in love. After all, according to the Bible, Christ is the *Hypostatic* Truth, the pure Truth ("full of grace and *truth*"). Such an assumption is necessary in order to arrive at the next significant position, a position that the holy Evangelist John emphasizes.

2. "*And the Word* (Christ) *was made flesh and dwelt among us.*" By means of the Incarnation, the truth of all beings and creation became immanent in man and the world, and dwells (ἐσκήνωσεν) in the very heart of history, in the mortal foundations and corruption of creation. How is this possible, and what can be obtained by this? This is possible because the Christian God is *ekstatic*, and, this means that Love (John 4:16), that only a loving God (ὁ ἀγαπῶν Θεός), is able to create a relationship of love outside of Himself—He does not impart but comes out of Himself—and to personally become united with something *other* (τὸ ἑτερούσιον) that is not Himself, that is beyond Himself. It is precisely at this point that the

[21] Living in the Church, the Christian does not simply imitate the angels, but draws his existence and ethos from the Incarnate God-Man Christ.
[22] The struggle against Nestorianism and Monothelitism and similar heresies confirms the significance of this identity.

Christian Fathers surpass ancient Greek ontology[23] through their statement that "the Existing one comes into being" in the event of the Incarnation (ὁ Ὢν γίνεται[24]); furthermore, they abolish Greek ontology through the theology of the Resurrection. The dwelling or the *parousia* of God—the Truth in history—is of a twofold nature and is realized in both *receiving* and *giving*. a) Christ "descended" *vertically* and, as the New Adam (a corporate person), he *horizontally* received the *history* of the Israelite people to whom he belonged; b) Christ becomes incarnate and implants a divine and *personal* mode of existence (τρόπος ὑπάρξεως) in our human nature (λόγος φύσεως), thereby radically transforming the anthropology and ontology of the world.[25] Notwithstanding this, His body[26] should be understood in an *ecclesiological* sense and not merely Christologically; that is, Christ should be understood as the *Church*. Christ, the Incarnate Truth, is salvific not simply because He is God by nature but because human nature, united with the Divine One, is freed and healed in His Hypostasis from the corruption and death inherent within it through a hereditary inheritance. If the body is par excellence the *focus* and *locus* of human existence, it follows that the Incarnation is the *sine non qua* of salvation. And

---

[23] Gregory the Theologian states verbatim: "He Who Is becomes"; the Incorporeal becomes flesh, and the Son of God becomes the Son of Man (*Oration* 38, 13, SCh 358, 134, PG 36, 525b). The point here is that God, Who is beyond all measure and is immeasurable, becomes the *present* in time and in the world.

[24] This has to do with an open provocation. "Likewise, in affirming that Christ, i.e., a historical being, is the truth, the New Testament hurls a challenge to Greek thought, since it is in the flow of history and through it, through its changes and ambiguities, that man is called to discover the meaning of existence" (J. Zizioulas, "Truth and Communion," p. 71).

[25] From the anthropological viewpoint, Christ sets human nature free from its submission to death, by a true manner of life and so achieves what Adam had missed. This is why He is the "other, the new Adam." He is born of the Virgin, which means that He hypostasizes nature, for He is not subject to its *mode* of existence, that is, its birth instinct that eternalizes death, as we have already concluded in I, 4. From the ontological viewpoint, the mode of existence of the Truth—the Holy Trinity—becomes the mode of existence of man and of creation. The essential role of the Holy Trinity in this metamorphosis is of immense significance; however, more about that later on.

[26] By this we wish to emphasize something which is often overlooked by theologians, namely, the words: "The Logos became (ἐγένετο) flesh," and not simply "took flesh." These words among other things, point to the fact that man *is* a body and not simply *has* a body. In this case, moving the emphasis from "have" to "be" is of paramount importance. Here, we are merely pointing to the implications, which are usually not taken into consideration.

so at any given moment of His life, Christ's own individual body "is not subject to corruption because it lives in the bosom of Life, in the Hypostasis of the Logos Who is Life."[27] This perception of human nature reveals the wondrous mystery of the Lord's love toward His creation, the mystery of the *kenosis*, which is paradoxical, yet not illogical.[28]

3. Had Christ passed through an historic phase (let us say, during the rule of Tiberius in Palestine) merely as a man, as a guest,[29] He, the Truth and Life, would be of no significance *to us*, who are His successive generations. Yet, we read: "And of his fullness have we *all* received, and grace for grace." These words prove to be just as important as the previous ones. Let us remember that in the Old Testament, God directs history by means of certain events and persons toward His great purposes. However, with His entrance into both space and time of the world, Christ as the Eschatological Reality (namely, as the Alpha and Omega of history) establishes the last days, that is, the *ultimate* truth of the world in history[30] and thus *frees*[31] and *heals* it. Here it is important to note how the Jewish linear concept of time has been complemented: if Christ is the Alpha and Omega of history, it follows that, in a certain way, the end of history in Christ through the Holy Spirit becomes present already *here* and *now*.[32] The argument consists in the following: if the end were not present *now*

---

[27] G. Florovsky, "Redemption," *Collected Works*, 1976, p. 139.

[28] Christ "emptied" Himself of His divine glory by denying every claim to life and existence separate from the (human) nature He had embraced. "His complete renunciation of any claim to a life-in-itself and existence-in-itself liberates nature from mortal life and transposes it into the mode of immortality" (Ch. Yannaras, *Variations on the Song of Songs*, Holy Cross Orthodox Press, 2005, p. 123).

[29] The idea of Christ as a stranger/guest (ξένος) and as a passerby (πάροικος) in this world, found in Luke's Gospel, is rather interesting (Luke 2:4; 2:39; 8:1; 13:22; 17:11; 4:29–30; 9:53; 9:58; 24:18); however, this does not exclude His hypostatic relation with the world. Regarding this important Christological aspect, see A. Denaux, "A Stranger in the City. A Contribution to the Study of the Narrative Christology in Luke's Gospel," *Louvain Studies* 30, 2005, pp. 255–272.

[30] "...Grace and truth came (ἐγένετο) through Jesus Christ," John 1:17. Truth appears as historical reality with Christ, and is present and accessible to man. According to the words of Bishop Athanasius ("A Prolegomenon to the Gnosiology of Hesychasm," *Emmanuel*, Los Angeles 2008, p. 145), Truth "became" or "appeared" not through His "ousia" (essence), but through His real *parousia* (personal presence) in the world and in history.

[31] "Then you will know the truth, and the truth will set you free" (John 8:32), and, "So if the Son sets you free, you will be free indeed" (John 8:36).

[32] Cf. J. Zizioulas, "Truth and Communion," p. 71.

(with and in Christ) it would then *never* be present (which we will clarify later). This, of course, occurs pneumatologically: the Holy Spirit is the
eschatological force that—following Christ's Resurrection—brings into
the world and history the last days (Acts 2:17). This is of extreme importance to anthropology, which is otherwise limited by a *choro-chronic*
structure (space and time) and that we may, therefore, call "tragic." God's
condescension towards *history* represents one of the main features of the
Judeo-Christian tradition that is contrary to the anti-historicity of the
classical and more recent religions and of certain erroneous forms of
Christianity (like Monophysitism and Nestorianism). These conceptual
philosophical, religious, and pseudo-Christian approaches overlook basic truths, such as the fact that Christ" belonged to a definite historical
period, a definite generation, and did not speak except *in* and *through*
that which was historically given to Him within His own context."[33] In
this way, Christ, the God-Man, is not a global, totalitarian truth—*auctoritas*—that everyone must unconditionally accept[34] and Who imposes
conditions upon us that are projections of His eternal being. No, indeed;
rather, He comes as a *Person* extending and conferring the option to freely believe in Him, to freely adopt Him *in a communion* of love, and to
freely recognize Him as our own truth within our *historical* circumstances[35] (this is why Dostoevsky chooses this truth, a personal truth). It is in

[33] J. Zizioulas, "The Theological Problem of Reception," *The One and the Many*, p.
118. After all, Christ Himself explains to us "His eternal, God-Man mysteries that are
beyond understanding and are inexpressible in a concrete and human language like ours.
Furthermore, the biblical language is not something abstract, a new language of God
that is outside time and beyond history, but it is the word of the body, the speech of the
Incarnate Logos, marked by time and history, and moreover, to a certain extent, marked
by a respective culture and its manner of expression," (Hieromonk Irinej Bulović, *Novi
prevod Svetoga Pisma Novoga Zaveta*[*The New Translation of the Scriptures of the New
Testament*], Belgrade 1985, p. 9).
[34] As J. Sikoutris cleverly observes ("Platonski eros i hriscanska ljubav" [The Platonic Eros and Christian Love], Srbinje–Belgrade–Valjevo, 1988, p. 67): had Christ
remained on earth after His Resurrection as the true God, then people would not have
had any alternative other than to acknowledge Him as such. Also, according to His own
words, He was able to summon a whole legion of angels to His aid. However, how would
their human freedom have found its expression? Faith entails freedom.
[35] Christ did not elevate His truth to the level of an absolute legal decree, which
would have been independent of time and of the diversity of human persons. Therefore,
this diachronicity of a pentecostal freedom reconciles the "singularity" of the individual experience with the "diversity" of influences which are found in scriptural texts. This

this sense that ontology gives birth to gnosiology and not vice versa.[36] Furthermore, one should know that in Christ-the Truth, creation does not survive by force. This would be the case if immortality were *natural* (therefore, necessary) to creation or to the soul in particular (as is the case in, for instance, ancient religions). Christ offers and extends His truth and life to human freedom and love. He does not impose it upon an external subject as some objective reality (*auctoritas*), as a *principle* of "value," or as an impersonal and moral imperative. With this in view, historically speaking, His truth is "powerless" to impose itself. However, paradoxically, herein is the "invincible power of truth unarmed" (Pasternak) or the "divine weakness" (θεαρχικὴ ἀσθένεια),[37] about which Eastern Christendom speaks. Such expressions are not self-contradictory but *apophatic*, meaning that they express the freedom of communion in Christ (e.g. Church hymnography apophatically defines truth).

4. Understanding the *reception* or acceptance and adoption of Christ–Truth in space and time is particularly significant in our postmodern times[38] and can be of some importance to culture and philosophy. The faith and position of early and later generations of Christians,

remains a challenge to every new generation of Christians. It is not by chance that the Church translated the dogmatic truths through hymnography, so that both the "icon" and the "text" converge into one and the same concept. The comprehension of scriptural texts through the icon, that is, in an "iconic" manner, is a sensitive way of finding a wise solution. The multi-layered canvas of truth and its meaning are akin to a multi-layered picture, and is revealed only gradually, and thus "speaks" to people in many ways.

[36] The term *gnosiology* refers to the experiential way of acquiring spiritual knowledge, and is used by Fathers like St. Isaac the Syrian and contemporaries like St. Justin (Popovich) of Chelie (see *Orthodox Faith and Life in Christ*); it can be contrasted with epistemology, which refers to the study of more conventional, intellectual, and often scientific means of attaining knowledge. Gnosiology tends to emphasize ecclesial asceticism (and the acquisition of the virtues) and is, therefore, more communal in character.

[37] The Areopagite and the hymnography of the Church talk about this. Although Levinas deals with this problem ethically, his insight deserves attention: "The idea of a truth whose manifestation is not glorious or bursting with light, the idea of a truth that manifests itself in its humility, like the still small voice in the biblical expression—the idea of a persecuted truth—is that not henceforth the only possible modality of transcendence?" (*Entre nous: Thinking of the Other*, Columbia University Press: 1998, p. 55). Contrary to the desire of the world: the more knowledge and power there is, the greater the totalitarianism and injustice, in which truth has too great of a significance so as not to be defended by lies and by force.

[38] See our consideration of postmodernity below, in "Neopatristic Christology in Postmodern Culture," pp. 155-188.

who asserted that Christ is the Truth and the Life of the world, originated precisely from existential circumstances, that is, from the authentic experiences of personal communion with Truth ("which we have heard... we have seen...our hands have handled"[39]) and with Life par excellence in the experience of the free communion of the Church, which the Holy Spirit builds (1 Cor. 13:13). This communion in the form of the Eucharist is not merely "passed on" (παράδοσις = tradition) as an historical inheritance and memory—"For I received from the Lord what I also passed on to you" (1 Cor. 11:23)—but as an eschatological event. For the Eucharistic remembrance (ἀνάμνησις) is not a higher mental operation on a historical (or sociological) level, but is rather an existential realization since it is, literally, a grace-filled incursion of the End into this impenetrable world; it is the *Eschaton*, which is never identified with history (we shall consider the reason for this later). As a result, the existential consequences for contemporary culture are enormous. Currently, the Orthodox nations appear to have difficulties in relating creatively to their own Tradition, while they take a negative and polemic approach toward modernism, so that their art is generally limited to repeating and copying the achievements of previous Christian generations. This is most clearly evident in art (highly indicative in iconography[40] and architecture). However, it is important that we understand Tradition not as something received from the *past*, but (in addition) something dynamically adopted from the *eschatological* (that is, future) charismata of that Spirit Who equipped and inspired past Christian generations, from the Apostolic times up to the present, with holy gifts; for ours is "the faith that was once for all entrusted to the saints" (Jude 1:3). Then, we exhibit the freedom and the right to express Tradition in *our* way,[41] through our particular

[39] "That which was from the beginning, which we have heard, which we have seen with our eyes, which we have looked at and our hands have touched—this we proclaim concerning the Word of life," (1 John 1:1).

[40] See the attempts of contemporary iconographers such as, for example, Stamatis Skliris, whom we consider to be inspired by this kind of experience of Tradition. See his book: *In the Mirror*, Sebastian Press, Los Angeles, 2005.

[41] One of the contributions of philosophical hermeneutics lies in its statement of the impossibility of the imposition of rules on others, which they would have to comprehend and make use of in a certain text. In an ecclesiastical context, such a problem cannot occur thanks to Pneumatology: the Holy Spirit acts in such a way that the past is brought into an existential (not simply an abstract or a ritualistic) relation with the present, leaving the present open to the future. Following the Res-

time and culture. Christ's mystery has been *given* once and for all but is constantly *renewed* in the world through the Holy Spirit for the salvation of all humanity and creation. Hence, the Christian expectation of the resurrection of the dead is not a passive expectation but is instead an active collaboration in Christ's historical work.

5. The dynamic tension between *true* life (given in Christ) and "false" life (the logos of this world without God that does not accept Christ—John 1:10–11) in John's Gospel (and in Luke's[42] also) is aimed at clarifying another key question. From what is Christ saving creation? St. Athanasius the Great maintains explicitly that He saves creation from *nonexistence*, from "non-being,"[43] which constantly threatens creation. This is possible because Christ embodies a Truth "not of this world" but of the Future. Christ plans to bring all created beings into communion with His very Life through His Incarnation—namely, that which He Himself shares with the Father and Spirit in the Trinitarian union of freedom, love and existence—so that these two need to come to know Him and themselves in the act of communion, and thus be preserved from nonexistence. Initially, Baptism was understood as the new birth where human existence is hypostasized anew in a manner true to Jesus Christ's being (Gal. 3:27). New Testament texts abound with examples of the withdrawal of death, revealed as a lie,[44] in encounters with Christ—the

urrection, the Holy Spirit enables the Church to "embody" Christ in any new context (culture) of time and space.

[42] "Luke interprets the Lord's travels as His visit to the city of Jerusalem through His prophet Jesus, which end tragically, considering that the City refuses to accept God's messenger...However, the City does not recognize in Jesus, the moment of God's 'visitation,' 'because you did not recognize the time of God's coming (ἐπισκοπή) to you' (Luke 19:44)," (A. Denaux, op. cit., p. 270).

[43] Cf. the reasons in favor of the Incarnation, which St. Athanasius the Great cites. In this instance they have a crucial, an existential meaning. If the world (creation) possessed a *given* immortality of itself, the Incarnation of the Logos would have been unnecessary. What purpose would the Incarnation serve? For the forgiveness of sins? Was repentance not sufficient? Creation was threatened by annihilation, and only the Incarnate God was able to prevent this. "He saw the rational race, wasting out of existence, and death reigning over all in corruption...He took to Himself a body..." (*On the Incarnation*, 8).

[44] Compare the miracles of Christ, for example, the resurrection of the son of the widow of Nain, and the many healings. The God of the Judeo-Christian Revelation is merciful to His creatures. He created all beings for eternity but sees that they are tormented by death and pain. For pain is the sting of death. He came to participate in the suffering

Life and Truth. On the other hand, creation retains the freedom to *reject* communion with Christ. It is as if the spirit (the logos) of this world does not accept but rather rejects Christ, the Logos of God, which is in accordance with the words: "He was in the world ... the world did not recognize him. He came to that which was *his own*, but his own did not receive him" (John 1:10–11; cf. the opposition between the Church and the world in John 15:18–20; 16; 33; 1 Cor. 3:19; Gal. 6:14). However, this opposition is not based on nature but on one's freedom to choose and the aim directing that choice. It is a biblical fact that Christ, the Truth, is revealed and offered as an act of communion in Whom man participates as a *person* (cf. Luke 24:30–32), and so truth is identified as free co-participation in communion.[45] Truth can never be the property of an individual rational being who handles it as he pleases. Once again, ontology and gnosiology coincide, pervading each other.

6. Based on what has been said so far, the mystery of the Incarnation of the Logos, according to St. Maximus the Confessor, is "the key to all the riddles and images (types) in the Holy Scriptures, offering the knowledge of all intelligent and created phenomena."[46] According to this Holy Father, it is obvious that man and the world do not possess true life outside of the communion and *relation* with God. This also shows something else, namely, that Christ embodies the only true *meaning* and that He is the *archetype* of all created beings. From the beginning, everything was created in view of Christ (the Logos or the Son Who would become incarnated) and this is why His Incarnation is the objective of the world even without man's fall.[47] For what sense would

of man, not to stand aside and observe man from a distance like the god of Islam; neither is He the god presented by the eastern religions, a god that watches man's pain with disinterest. On the other hand, God did not come to merely participate in man's suffering but to abolish death, to destroy it (cf. the church service of the Resurrection). The goal of the Incarnation is the abolishment of death and the eternal life of creation. There is no death where He reigns, and so there is no compromise between God and death.

[45] Cf. the exceptional analysis of this in the text by Stamatis Skliris: "From Portrait to Icon," in his book *In the Mirror*, pp. 88–96.

[46] *Chapters on Theology and Economy* I, 66, PG 90, 1108b.

[47] St. Maximus, *Ad Thalassium* 94, 60, PG 90, 621; G Florovsky, "Eschatology in the Patristic Age: An Introduction," *Studia Patristica*, II, 1957, pp. 235–50. Considering that perfection is not a feature of the original condition of creation—such a notion was, therefore, not adopted by Patristics—it is permissible to assert that not only the *fall* of man, but the very creation of creation demands a Person, Who, like Christ, would unite the created with the uncreated.

it have if man knew that the Truth existed as a reality void of death, corruption and bitterness, but that despite this fact he did *not have and feel it* as the foundation of his own being and life? It is precisely because of this that Christ, *Emmanuel* ("God [is] with us"), is "the newest of all that is new, the only new thing under the sun" (cf. John Damascene), because He introduced into history the absolute reality of truth and life—incarnate through His Incarnation—by becoming man, and so it is possible to see "His glory" here and now and to commence a "true life" (John 3:15–16; 14:6; 17:3).[48]

III. Truth and Resurrection

In the previous pages we emphasized that Truth possesses an eschatological character. If God reveals Himself as the Truth only at the end, in the Eschaton, then the question arises: why is He not the obvious truth *always*, that is, at all times, and therefore at the beginning, too? This is an important question and the answer must be searched for in the theology of the Resurrection.

1. Christ—the Incarnate Truth—by means of His Resurrection is Victor over death, the principal enemy of creation. Therefore, the hypostatic revelation of the Truth culminates in the Lord's Resurrection, which represents essentially one eschatological event. The Apostle Paul is very clear here when he brilliantly inverts the logic, which prescribes a cause-and-effect relation in history, in a passage of his Epistle to the Corinthians. "If there is no resurrection of the dead," writes the Apostle, "then not even Christ has been raised" (1 Cor. 15:13). If this paradoxical statement is taken literally, it could then be worded this way: "*If the resurrection of all people does not take place at the end of history—then neither has the resurrection of Christ taken place!*" If the Eschaton (the last day or the end of history) will occur without the event of the general resurrection, then no resurrection (not even Christ's) has ever taken place. "For if the dead are not raised, then Christ has not been raised either" (1 Cor. 15:16). So, the cause and *truthfulness* of the Resurrection can be found only in the Future which is *already and not yet* present. Therefore, according to the Bible, the Kingdom will begin with the Parousia and Judgment, revealing

---

[48] By using the term "true life," the Holy Fathers do not mean a "higher," "more spiritual," (etc.) life in contrast to a "material" life, but rather a life *devoid of death*, a life not subject to that deceit that presents itself as the only measure.

history through the judgment of what is deserving of eternity (one necessary aspect of Eschatology will be the unveiling of evil in history, which is often camouflaged as good).

Considering the diverse viewpoints encompassing the Revelation of Yahweh, the Apostles begin from the *Event*, and that event is above all Christ's Resurrection. It should not be overlooked that the Apostles recognize the Saviour only after his practical response to the problem of death at Pascha, and not at the time of his teaching. The event of the Risen Christ serves as the foundation of Revelation and not vice versa. It is from here that the witness of the Apostles derives its superb dogmatic "formulation" and, from an anthropological perspective, an epistemological "verification" of the truth of God, and that is the truth that there exists a God strong enough to conquer death and to judge the world, thus saving it (John 5:26–27; Acts 17:31). For the Apostles, who were people of a Hebrew mentality, Christ's Resurrection was proof that He was the eschatological Messiah, and not just the One who truly exists. Accordingly, they do not base their Christological witness of Yahweh on some "principle" thet would therefore need to be understood (i.e. reinterpreted by means of yet another principle), but base it on a *resurrectional* experience of Christ, which the Church experiences within the Eucharist.[49]

2. Therefore, it is empirically impossible to claim that God is Truth simply because we think that this results from the fact that He is *God*. God is the superb Truth for us because, based on the Resurrection, we anticipate (not in the psychological sense of the word, but in the true meaning of the word *anticipare*, which means "to accept in advance," "to have a foretaste") that He is the *final* Truth Who conquers and abolishes the "last enemy"—death. Only the End will reveal "Truth is the state of the future,"[50] and that only that which is real at the end is actually *real*. Were it not for this eschatological foretaste, all knowledge of God would be impossible. Only when God reveals Himself as Love, also *at the End*, will we recognize the meaning of Paul's "love never fails" (1 Cor. 13:8); this means that if God loved us in history but does not love us also at the end, it is as if He had never loved us and had never

[49] For a similar exploration of this subject, though one different from our own approach, see J. Behr, *The Mystery of Christ: Life in Death* (SVSP 2006).

[50] Let us remember here the words of St. Maximus the Confessor (*Scholia Ecclesiastica hierarchia* 3, 2; PG 4, 137d). This is not a unique instance in his thinking, which is completely marked by Eschatology.

existed. The significance of Eschatology[51] in theology is so great that Maximus the Confessor writes about it the following way: "For after the fall (of man) the end is not revealed at the beginning but the beginning at the end; neither does one look for the logoi (=causes, principles) of the beginning but searches for those (logoi) which toward the end lead to those in motion (τοὺς κινουμένους = beings in motion)."[52] If love is not ontological and eschatological, then it is as if it does not exist, that is, it is insignificant for eternal survival. Therefore, precisely because of the ontology of His love, Christ will lead with Himself others into communion with God even if these may be "unworthy," be it in an ethical or some other sense. We can assert that already now their existence is *true*, only under the condition that they will exist at the end (which will actually be the beginning: "in seeking his end (τὸ τέλος), man, thus, encounters his beginning, which exists essentially in his end", says St. Maximus in his *Ad Thalassium* 59). It is as if Christ says to God the Father, Who loves Him and Who declares: "You are My truth and my picture/icon"[53]: You have given me the Kingdom but I want those who are mine to be with me (this is the basic meaning of Christ's prayer as the HighPriest, John 17:1–26). This way, through the ontology of love, He leads all of humanity into communion with God the Father.

[51] "Thus, in his exploration of his end (τὸ τέλος), man arrived at the beginning, which is naturally found at the end, which after having forsaken his search (for the beginning), he engaged in exploring the end (=the goal) since the end is natural (i.e. the end of the beginning). For it was not possible for man to avoid his (initial) limitation because it encircled him from all sides and restricted his movement. For that reason it was not possible to look for the beginning, since as I have said, he remained in the back, and so he explored the end (=the goal), which is ahead, in order to find the unbequeathed beginning because he had not recognized the end from the beginning." (*Ad Thalassium* 59; PG 90, 613d). In his commentary, Bishop Athanasius says the following regarding this (note by the translator in *Vidoslov*, 36/2005, p. 15): "Further on Maximus will say the following: 'after the transgression (man's), the end does not reveal itself at the beginning, but rather the beginning reveals itself at the end'. That is, the beginning can be found and understood only at the end. This is not tautology, or philosophical verbalism or a dialectic, but is a profoundly biblical understanding of the creation/beginning of the world and man, that finds and reaches his end=goal=fullness only in Christ, Who is the Beginning—Ἀρχὴν and the End=Goal—Τέλος of everyone and everything; the Fulfillment of the purpose of creation= the realization of God's original Plan—the Dispensation."

[52] *Ad Thalassium* 59; PG 90, 616a.

[53] Athanasius the Great, John Damascene, and Romans 8:29: "For those God foreknew he also predestined to be conformed to the likeness of his Son, that he might be the firstborn among many brothers"; the same in 2 Cor. 4:4.

3. This ontology of love leading to communion justifies the centrality of the Resurrection in the economy of salvation. This centrality induces St. Maximus to emphasize the Resurrection as the meaning of existence: "He who is sanctified with the ineffable power of the Resurrection has come to the knowledge of the *aim for the sake of which God had formerly created everything.*"[54] It is the Resurrection (and not the Incarnation or the Cross) that has the power to remove the sting of destruction.[55] We mentioned above (in III.3) that history is tragic because, following the fall of man, space and time acquired "negative" dimensions, through which they appear to be responsible for separation instead of unity. To this aspect of the fall we can apply Kant's very accurate insight into space and time: he concludes that the limits of the senses establish boundaries to all sensible reasoning about the world.[56] Here we touch upon the key anthropological aporia on the *identity* of man. The problem of man in *history* consists of the tragedy of man's inescapable condition, which sets the conditions for man's relation with God, with himself and with the world, and—this is the paradox—man does not have the option of transcending this tragic condition within the *framework of history.*[57] M. Frayn argues that all attributes of external realities have been

---

[54] See Maximus the Confessor, *Chapters on Theology and Economy* I, 66; PG 90, 1108ab. Here, we quote the following section: "The mystery of the Incarnation of the Logos contains all the enigmas and prefigurations in the (Holy) Scriptures and the knowledge of (all) visible creation. And whosoever has come to the knowledge of the mystery of the Cross and the burial (of Christ) has come to the knowledge of the logoi of the aforementioned (things). And whomsoever the ineffable purpose of the resurrection has been revealed to, has come to the knowledge of the purpose for the sake of which God has created everything beforehand."

[55] However, here the Incarnation and the Resurrection are not understood as opposites, as it appears to be at first glance.

[56] E. Cassirer (1874–1945), a German-Jewish philosopher whose main work *Philosophy of Symbolic Forms* (4 volumes, 1923–29) is considered central to the philosophy of culture. In it he claims that man is a "symbolic animal" (in his popular *Essay on Man* of 1944). While animal perception of the world is based on instincts, man has created his own universe of symbolic meaning with which he gives his perception of reality a structure and form. Regarding this, Cassirer is greatly indebted to Goethe's morphology and Kant's transcendental idealism, which states that the world cannot be known *on its own*, but that man's view of reality is formed by the mode of perception of the same. But then how can we know what is true in such a world? We maintain that Christians "know" what is true in such a world only because they anticipate (not just "feel") in Christ the final truth of creation through faith.

[57] Cf. Dr. Justin Popovich, *Dostojevski o Evropi i Slovenstvu* [Dostoevsky on Europe and Slavism], Belgrade 1940, p. 37.

imprinted in our mind based on the information received by the senses in a two-way communication with the world.[58] He developed this idea via two concepts from quantum mechanics—the non-predetermination of sub-atomic particles and the role of the observer of experimental results—and applies this construct of solipsism, quantum mechanics, and Zeno's paradoxes to the fascinating diversity of human experiences.

4. This leads us to the discussion of the significance of the body to the truth of history. Man does not make use of his body for any other goal; neither does he discard it once he has reached his specific goal. The body is ontologically the ultimate hypostasis of reality. By paraphrasing G. Florovsky, we can say that in anthropology *the truth without corporeality is a phantom and corporeality without the truth is a cadaver.* The eschatological character of iconography, which depicts saints with a glorified body, demonstrates the following truth: although the body is the site of conflict in human existence, it is also the site and means of the ultimate solution to the problem of death. Death is man's chief enemy precisely because it seeks to destroy the corporeal dimension, to erase and abolish otherness, communion and the love that it embraces. This corporeal dimension occupies a special place in ecclesiology. Namely, the Church is the place where we learn to equally love those who are and are not physically endowed with features corresponding to *our* desire. The Church explicitly teaches that every man is unique, unrepeatable and irreplaceable, and is therefore sacred. A few remarks should be made here. With her Eucharistic and philocalic tradition, the Church emphasizes the value of human beauty that is connected with the incarnate Christ, and not with the mere idea of beauty. Meanwhile, it is also true that the Church, in respecting otherness (and, therefore, variety) as sacred, embraces everyone independent of physical attributes. It follows that the Church affirms the human body, however, not through an absolutism of physical attributes but mainly through their *relativism*[59] (human characteristics are not sacred, rather man's otherness is sacred). The person, not nature, represents the principal issue of man's existence.

5. However, if this is true, why do we speak of a metamorphosis of history? In his thoughts about the Kingdom of God in the realm of salvation of human beings as well as in the realm of survival and well-being

---

[58] M. Frayn, *The Human Touch: Our Part in the Creation of a Universe*, Picador: 2008.

[59] Indicative of the Prophet Isaiah (chapter 53) is his portrayal of Christ as ordinary in appearance, inconspicuous, even aesthetically unacceptable.

of all creation, Methodius of Olympus (early 4th century) wrote his treatise as a refutation of the erroneous concept of certain contemporary Origenists, presenting his conviction that God created the material world not in order for it to cease to exist, but for it to exist forever.[60] Space and time taken within the perspective of the Resurrection and the Eschaton are—thanks to the Parousia/Presence of God—freed from these negative dimensions and become the basis of unity. The natural order of existence (psycho-physiological self-preservation) in the Kingdom of God will be replaced by *grace*; then, the hypostatic energies of God will flow through all beings.[61] Christ, the Truth, will endow the *law of nature* with freedom from division and individualization in its new *mode of existence*. This is the reason why He is experienced as the *Land of the Living*, "the firstborn among many brothers" (Romans 8:29), as the "topos" and "horos" (choro–chronos) of God's encounter with His creation; the "head" of all and everything (Ephes. 1:10) in the eschatological Kingdom. The Resurrection of Christ abolishes all *forms of hierarchies* of beings, which ancient Greek ontology and even Hebrew ontology insisted upon: "Who is this King of glory" (Psalm 24:8) the angels ask, amazed without end at the fact that *Man* ascends to sit at the right hand of God the Father as *equals in divinity* according to the measure of participation (ὁμόθεος κατὰ μετοχήν). Human nature (not the angelic nature) and not merely its external shell, is the most authentic participant (μέτοχος) in the God-Man Person.

6. That is from whence the Church derives its eschatological identity, not from this world. Christ's words (John 17:16) to his disciples can be paraphrased the following way: "You are in the world, therefore, the structure of the choro–chronos applies to you (with all its consequences); however, you are not of the world (you are not reduced to this structure) for you have been born unto a *new life*." History is a battlefield of truth, but it will not be abolished. The Apostle Paul finds the meaning of the historical "sighing" of the Christians when he declares: "For while we are in this tent, we groan and are burdened because we do not wish to be unclothed but

[60] In view of this, the belief that the Kingdom of God is a place where only human souls will exist represents a dangerous reduction.

[61] Herein lies the meaning of the hesychastic teachings of the energies. God's energies are His personal emission, emanation, and flow of divine life, that is, the entire wealth of glory, life, love, beauty, light and goodness, which are given through one's personal meeting in the free union of love in Christ, through the adoption as a son by the Father, by the grace of the Holy Spirit.

to be clothed with our heavenly dwelling, *so that what is mortal may be swallowed up by life*" (2 Cor. 5:4). For the sake of our discussion, an emphasis should be placed on "unclothed," which does not refer to the material structure (i.e. the body) but to *corruption*. St. John Chrysostom brilliantly expresses: "I will, therefore, take off this foreign substance that is not suitable for me, this foreign substance being not my body but corruption and death. The future life destroys and eliminates that which adheres to the body and not the body itself."[62] This thesis continues to be very significant to the relation between theology and science regardless of the many shadows certain neoplatonic elements of ascetic theology (from the 4th century onward) have cast on this fundamental truth, which influenced the creation of specific stereotypes still relevant to this day.

7. Once again, we repeat that history—symbolic of the Cross—is in a crucified state between the true and false life, the latter signifying failure. This is a great mystery of the life of the world prior to the Resurrection. Evil continues to impose itself upon history as a reality, as the truth (cf. the Book of Revelation); however, every engagement with it unfolds "kenotically." God Himself suffered death in order to abolish it ("abolished death by death"). The God-Man emptied the cup of all human pain and suffering on the Cross (Matt. 26:39). All of the saints of the Church without exception have and will pass through death,[63] while the Apostle Paul declares: "I die every day..." (1 Cor. 15:31). The martyrs, the venerable saints, all of them inevitably pass through the Cross and death, for suffering is immanent in created and fallen nature. The saints did not avoid the Cross, for it is impossible to avoid; St. Maximus explained that everything that falls into the realm of creation seeks the Cross.[64] Hence,

---

[62] *On the resurrection*, 6, PG 50, 428. "Ἵνα καταποθῇ τὸ θνητὸν ὑπὸ τῆς ζωῆς, τουτέστιν, ἵνα ἀφανισθῇ, ἵνα ἀπόληται· ὥστε ἀπώλειαν οὐχὶ τοῦ σώματος λέγει, ἀλλὰ θανάτου καὶ φθορᾶς. Ἐπερχομένη γὰρ ἡ ζωὴ οὐχὶ τὸ σῶμα ἀφανίζει καὶ δαπανᾷ, ἀλλὰ τὴν ἐπιγινομένην αὐτῷ φθορὰν καὶ τὸν θάνατον."

[63] Even those who are still alive at the Second Coming will die. Both Elijah and Enoch, even though they are an exception, will have to pass through death at the end (cf. Col. 4:15 ἡμεῖς οἱ ζῶντες οἱ περιλειπόμενοι εἰς τὴν παρουσίαν τοῦ κυρίου οὐ μὴ φθάσωμεν τοὺς κοιμηθέντας).

[64] "τὰ φαινόμενα πάντα δεῖται σταυροῦ", Maximus the Confessor, *Chapters on Theology and Economy* I, 67, PG 90, 1108b. This emphasis on the characteristics of the Cross and Resurrection of human existence (as well as the organic interdependence of the Cross and Resurrection) is, unfortunately, often absent from contemporary Orthodox theology. This, however, makes up the foundation of the Holy Fathers' approach to the problem of history.

the Church's invitation to the ascetic struggle does not signify "submission" of the world and nature to man, but signifies a "kenotic" experience of the struggle with demonic forces and their enslavement. The community of the "least" permanently rests on the Lord and on His Spirit, emphasizing not so much "freedom from nature" as much as "freedom *for* nature." The realization that the mortification of our self-love and egocentricity, the sources of biological death, leads to the birth—once again through Baptism and repentance—unto life in the Kingdom has implications beyond our humanity, that it represents a cosmic deliverance for nature itself, is sobering.

8. Summarizing history itself from the perspective of the future Kingdom, St. Maximus the Confessor places all of Revelation in the foreground of the development of history, which finds its justification in the Eschaton. Christ's Incarnation in history, the most significant of all historical events,[65] affirms history. At the same time, the eschatological reality of Christ's Resurrection frees us from the shackles of history. This is the reason why Maximus declares in the above section that it is the Resurrection that *gives meaning to creation* (protology), *to the Incarnation as well, and therefore to History*. The Resurrection so bestows meaning to History because Christ's Rising on the Third Day envelops the unification of the created with the Uncreated, a process that began with the Incarnation. The Resurrection represents the presence of the Eschaton in history, and the overcoming of the antinomy of history since it is the victory over the "last enemy"—death. Maximus does not declare faith in the Resurrection as faith in the eternal life of the "soul and body" because, in the language of the Gospels, that would not have much meaning. He speaks about the recapitulation (ἀνακεφαλαίωσις) of all and everything in Christ (Ephes. 1:10), which to him means eternal life for all in the entirety of history through the Grace of the Holy Spirit, which transforms everything through the Eschaton. In view of this, a summary of Dostoevsky's words can lead to the following conclusion: if truth is a created and mortal reality, or an epistemological principle that simply explains the universe,[66] a "principle" or a "value" that is not iden-

---

[65] See Maximus the Confessor, *Chapters on Theology and Economy* I, 66; PG 90, 1108a.

[66] "There is the *experience of Truth* and there is a visionary and empty *experience of falsehood*. The transition from delusion to truth is not only a transition from 'subjectiv-

tical to a *personal existence* (but just an *adaequatio rei et intellectu*); if truth is not Christ, the uncreated, absolute and *personal* reality without death ("I am the truth," John 14:6), the *life of the world* in Whom all beings find their purpose and incorrupt existence, then I gladly choose Christ, "in accordance with the truth that is in Jesus" (Ephes. 4:21). This position, a stumbling block for rationalistic thought, means that if the truth of creation is not the Person of Christ then such a truth is so much the worse, and so is all of creation. Here, too, St. Maximus provides profound insight:

> Even if (man) reached the highest (possible) level of (virtuous) works and contemplation during his lifetime, however, as long as he is here, he will have knowledge, the gift of prophecy and a pledge of the Holy Spirit in part only, but not fully. Should he reach beyond the limits of this age unto his perfect measure where he will stand before the praiseworthy *Truth and shall see face to face* (1 Cor. 13:12), he will no longer have (just) a part of the fullness but thanks to his having communed, he will be endowed with the fullness.[67]

IV. Concluding remarks

We now arrive at our initial question about the *relation* between absolute Truth and human existence, about the *application* of truth in anthropology. Taking into account the right and the freedom of each generation to find its *own* way of receiving the truth as the Tradition within the framework of its *respective* context, we must also question the nature of the reception or the adoption of Truth.

1. As we have already stated, the faith of Christians regarding Christ as the Truth and Life of the world does not stem from ideological or psychological convictions, but represents an existential fact, the living experience of communion[68] with this Truth and Life par excellence, in the

---

ity' to 'objectivity' but is above all a transition from a bad subject to a good subject, and therefore, a transition from bad subjectivity to good subjectivity...The transition from the former to the latter occurs only through ascetic struggles, through a new birth 'with water and the Spirit', in a fiery baptism, in a metaphysical, noumenal transfiguration of the person" (G. Florovsky, "The Metaphysical Premises of Utopianism," *Collected Works* 12, p. 77).

[67] *Chapters on Theology and Economy* II, 87, PG 90, 1165c (our italics).

[68] "That which was from the beginning, which we have heard, which we have seen with our eyes, which we have looked at and our hands have touched—this we proclaim concerning the Word of life," (1 John 1:1).

experience of the Church "when the whole Church comes together" (to be more precise: "into one place," 1 Cor. 14:23), i.e. in the Holy Eucharist as a place of truth, as the synaxis, communion and community.[69] The Eucharist is a *koinonia*, the "body," and not the sum of individuals. Since we are corporeal, Christ did not leave us any possibility of an encounter with the Truth other than by communing His Eucharistic *Body*.[70] The Eucharist is the mystery or the practice of the union of all of the faithful and of all creation, centered on the Person of Christ, and is the guarantee of their immortality (cf. φάρμακον ἀθανασίας of Ignatius of Antioch). Therefore, "for us the truth is not in words but in realizations;"[71] it is not a matter of epistemology only but of participation in Eucharistic communion.[72]

2. Here, we encounter a paradox. On the one hand, Truth is not given to us as the fruit of our individual achievements and is not our possession since it is not of this world, but it is "grace"—a gift of revelation, "an extraordinary, and a non–predetermined division in the solid immanent reality."[73] The Truth of the Incarnation or Resurrection represents the interruption of the coherent universe, or the compactness of that which the ancient Greeks considered as "nature."[74]

---

[69] Hence, the indissoluble unity and link between *lex orandi* and *lex credendi* in the faith of the Church.

[70] "God revealed Himself as Truth, Love, Wisdom and Life, so that man could actually participate in, partake of, take an active part in all of these. The best proof and guarantee of the fact that man is truly capable of partaking of all that is divine is that God in Christ became a real, historical man, giving witness that human nature is Godlike and truly capable of containing within itself the entire Godhead" (A. Yevtich, "A Prolegomenon to the Gnosiology of Hesychasm," *Emmanuel*, Los Angeles 2008, p. 159).

[71] "Οὐ γὰρ ἐν ῥήμασιν ἡμῖν, ἀλλ' ἐν πράγμασιν ἡ ἀλήθεια" (Gregory the Theologian, Maximus the Confessor, Gregory Palamas).

[72] At the same time the truth is a *synaxis* of the people with a specific structure that portrays the Eschatological Communion of the Kingdom, in which the Bishop is *the servitor of the Truth, the servitor of communion*.

[73] Peter's confession, "You are the Christ, the Son of the living God" (Matt. 16:16), is not his own individual achievement or possession, as Christ makes clear to us. According to the words of Yannaras, Peter's confession "represents an extraordinary and a non-predetermined break with the solid immanent reality; hence 'grace'—a gift of revelation is not linked with a virtue or with Peter's actual talent" Ch. Yannaras, "Who Do Men Say that I Am?," *Vidoslov*, 20 (2000) p. 30.

[74] See B. Šijaković, *Mythos, physis, psyche. Ogledanje u presokratovskoj "ontologiji" i "psihologiji"* [*Mythos, physis, psyche. Reflections in Pre-socratic "Ontology" and "psychology"*], Beograd–Nikšić, 2002, pp. 30–34.

True life is not dependent on any immanent feature of creation (on *entelechy* or even virtues of people). On the other hand, the ascetic effort to which Christ and the Church invite us is necessary because the attainment of true knowledge is obtained only by living truthfully (and vice versa or simultaneously: the subject seeking to know must himself become "authentic" and exist as "true" in order to see and contemplate the Truth[75]). Thus, the true condition of human existence, which in biblical terms and in the language of the Holy Fathers is called immortality, sanctity, deification, salvation and similarly, is not a consequence of nature, but of one's personal relation with the One Who realizes and embodies that condition within Himself. A saint of the Church (the Theotokos, the Apostles, the martyrs and ascetics) indicates a person (a human-biological individual) of our faith who transcends nature in one way or another and who unites himself personally with Christ, "the only Holy One."

3. If the relation between God and the world is so understood, theology does not appear in opposition to the truth of science. Namely, if science researches the nature of this world (its *modus existendi*; science is understood as physics[76]), while theology recognizes the obvious scientific facts in its attempts to find its own *modus* of transcendence, then their joint cooperation on the same planet on which the Incarnation of Christ took place becomes inevitable. In this case, within the context of discovery and validation, the theologian possesses basic existential terminology and his instruments (the dogmas): freedom, love, person, and otherness; values and doctrines that he translates into existential practice. The distinction lies within the theologian's expression of his faith in the possibility that this world *can* exist in a different way, that is, in an uncreated way—although he simultaneously recognizes all of science's insight

[75] Cf. G. Florovsky, "The Metaphysical Premises of Utopianism," *Collected Works* 12, p. 77.
[76] Biology will be for the 21st century, what physics was for the 20th century, and DNA will make up its most important contribution. In the 20th century, physics offered a more subtle advantage by revealing the insignificant place that man occupies within a universe structured according to subtle laws. According to William Blake, physics enabled men to hold mankind in the palm of their hands and eternity in the span of one hour. However, biology can do much more besides describing man's position in the universe. It describes the very nature of existence. The relevance of DNA may be a very significant part of this description. The biological web of life points to the idea of interdependence.

into the structure of the world.[77] This means that the world can be independent of the deterministic laws of nature, which denotes the discontinuity of structure by means of transcendence. For the Church, the final truth of this world is found *outside* the substance of created beings, outside the temporal–spatial structure and is, furthermore, independent of it. If the continuum of cause and consequence of nature (or of substance) signifies the truth of the world—evidently it cannot guarantee the continuity of individual beings—then the final ontological outcome of creation would be disastrous. In any case, the truth is concerned with the mode of existence (the person) and not merely with the status of existence (nature). Rather than an *a priori* given substance (even if it were divine), the eternal existence of historical beings requires their *communion* with something outside this substance, with a Person Who exists *outside* created space and time and Who can *freely* take things as they are, that is, Who can accept the immanent reality.[78] Therefore, events and facts that are formed by personal discovery are not abolished with death.

4. This demonstrates that the path of ethics, i.e. the attempt at the improvement of the disposition of nature (not by chance has ethics been called *natural* theology in the past) does not necessarily lead to the truth. Concerned with true *being* (τὸ εἶναι) but not with well-being (ethics), theology surpasses moral utilitarianism and occupies itself with the truth of being, with the very existence, as it will appear in eternity ("an eternal state of grace," Maximus the Confessor). After all, the *positive sciences* (physics, chemistry, and astronomy) maintain the position that historical beings can exist eternally only if they are in a different mode of existence. In theological terms, this means that they are grafted like vine branches onto the

[77] For instance, let us say that theology values the discoveries of geology, paleontology, microbiology, nuclear physics, and so forth. Its concern is to reach the common *logos* that brings within a single perspective all these insights (Cf. the similar approach in philosophical undertaking of B. Lonergan, *Insight: A Study of Human Understanding*, 1958). Theology considers the given world as the foundation (worthy of investigation by the positive sciences) and points to ways of transcending the created, ways given through the Revelation in Christ. Epistemology, which does not take the end into account, the *omega* of existence, cannot even provide meaning concerning the beginning, i.e. the alpha, and even less concerning history. "The truth lies outside the authority of human beings" (Popper); however, it is precisely because of this that our search for knowledge, a careful search for the unknown, exists, through the critical appraisal of our presuppositions.

[78] Consequently, outside the nature of creation there is not just the *purpose* (as formulated by Wittgenstein) but there is also the rational *personal cause* of being.

47

grapevine—Christ in the Church—and exist in a mode consisting of the *relation* and *connection* of all that exists, in communion with some other Being Who is *outside* the world. Finally, this fundamental *existential* fact leads to the position maintaining that every autonomous observation of the creature and the world as "nature," devoid of ontological assumptions of a personal *communion* with someone *outside* the world and being, is incorrect. If beings exist authentically, thanks to the ontology of *personal communion*, it follows that their current phenomenology is unstable and their epistemology unreliable. They reveal that their *being* is permeated by *non-being*, not only on account of their inconsistent physical structure, but also primarily because of the possibility of an absolute and ontological nothingness, which is a disruption of the relation of the person. Contrary to natural determinism, personal communion leads to freedom.

5. At the anthropological level, the question of freedom and love remains decisive. All other questions, such as, for example, "to what extent is man determined by his genetic code?" (*the law of nature*) cannot cancel the ontology of personal choice and basis (*the mode of existence*). Whether man's freedom is a result of impersonal biochemical processes as suggested by modern biology (neurobiology) is immaterial if the initiator of salvation is someone Other than man himself. Whether our functionality is dependent on the "practice" and "training" of learned suggestions,[79] be it a theistic or an atheistic approach, is irrelevant because the Son of God became the God-Man. The recognition that the greater part of our consciousness is a natural–biological product cannot deny the truth that God "touches" the existential cords within us, inherent in our neurobiological processes.[80] This applies even in the case of understanding the core of man

---

[79] This "type of interpretation in light of a theory" applies to the field of natural sciences as well as pseudo-sciences. According to Popper (*Conjectures and Refutations: The Growth of Scientific Knowledge*, 1963): once your gaze has been directed in a certain way, you detect everywhere examples which confirm your theory. The world is full of verifications of that theory; no matter what happened the theory was always confirmed. The truth of it always seemed as something obvious. Those who did not believe were evidently people who did not want to see the truth as disclosed. Popper even famously asserted, "Darwinism is not a testable scientific theory, but a metaphysical research program." (*Unended Quest: An Intellectual Autobiography*, Glasgow: Fontana/Collins, 1976, p. 151).

[80] "God moves in such a way that He instills an inner relationship (σχέσιν ἐνδιάθετον) of eros and love in those who are able to receive it (τοῖς δεκτικοῖς). He moves naturally, attracting the desire of those who are turned toward Him" (Maximus the Confessor, *Ambigua*, PG 91, 1260c).

as an immaterial soul–entity, separated from the body, or in the case of identifying him in certain physical characteristics and processes (the condition of the brain, memory, etc.). Since, as we shall see further on, the purpose of salvation is already articulated by the revelation of the personal God, it cannot be validated by epistemology. This, however, on the other hand, does not imply that theology is exclusively apophatic, supporting the relativism of knowledge due to a pessimistic epistemology.

6. According to the observations of neurobiology (neuroscience) and in the spirit of the Popperian theory of science, we can concur that every man has a *selective* view of the world. For instance, more often than not a "religious" person demands and searches for his already selected object, his defined goal, interest, viewpoint, and problem. So, we observe that a hungry animal selects edible and non-edible material so that "the object changes according to the need of the animal," and by the same token, the religious person is selective of the world in terms of that which is sacred and that which is profane, accepting the former as good and rejecting the latter as bad. Indeed, the viewpoint of every man, whether religious or not, is determined by his theoretical interests, his investigation of specific problems, his assumptions and anticipations, his background theories, his frame of reference, and the horizon of his expectations.[81] Hence, objections raised by science maintain that theological principles are irrelevant for science, that they are pseudo–empirical like astrology. Yet, can the criterion of refutation be applied to theology? What validates a scientific theory and what validates theology?

7. Neurobiology itself overthrows man's empiricism, the shortcomings of which are evident whenever man exceeds natural religion and freely accepts transcendence. Observation alone will not validate this observation. First, because this experience is not subject to an "objective" examination, since epistemology cannot "control" a theological fact. Second: a) in theology, God as the subject stipulates the knowledge of truth, and b) this act is the fruit of freedom and love. Since He loves us, we can truly exist and are capable of knowing Him.[82] Without this supposition

---

[81] Cf. the remark of 2c at the beginning of this study. There is not an observation that does not use descriptive language in its description, i.e. predicates. Every view of the world (κοσμοθεωρία) presupposes similarities and classifications, which in turn presuppose interests, viewpoints and problems.

[82] In his most recent book on communion and otherness, John Zizioulas makes corrections of the paraphrases of some contemporary theologians "*I love, therefore I am,*"

of love and freedom, there can be no Christian epistemology. As V. Perishich observes: "God is not *an objective subject of an objective science* but is always and only the subject, the initiator and the instigator of interaction with man (and consequently the instigator of man's process of knowledge). He is *not the object of knowledge* and its 'mastery' does not depend on our skills toward the acquisition of knowledge (whichever they may be). All our efforts toward the acquisition of knowledge (both empirical and rational) would be sterile if He, toward Whom all these efforts are aimed, would not *appear*. Namely, God grants (or allows) to become known *exclusively* when He wants this, and only to the one He selects, and to the measure and manner in which He desires."[83] In contrast to natural religious experiences, the God of the Judeo-Christian tradition is not subject to investigation because He freely reveals Himself only to those who love Him (Eph. 3:1–19). "We cannot know Him against His 'Will' and (equipped with all our cognitive abilities) we cannot gaze into His intimacy without asking Him. The knowledge of God is, therefore, not a subject-object relation, but is instead exclusively a subject-subject relation, and as such is independent of natural religiousness. The Personal God, in communicating with man as a person, is the Alpha and Omega of the Orthodox knowledge of God! Everything outside of that bears the seal of insecurity and arbitrariness."[84] Christ is synonymous with Truth because He reveals the purpose and meaning of all choro-chronos beings in history through the Holy Spirit, and grants freedom from death (Resurrection) as a personal experience here and now, generating eros and love in man with which true knowledge is realized through relationship with Him.

Our study purports that Truth is only significant to man (not morally but existentially) when it is a Person. Only then does Truth set one free from the restraints of history, that is, from corruption and death (because of the "hypostatic"—and not the natural—unity). Furthermore, to

which like Descartes' *cogito* is not free of subjectivity nor arbitrariness, so that Zizioulas goes one step further by formulating "*I am loved, therefore I am*," which expresses more fully the ontological character of love in the ontology of otherness (*Communion and Otherness*, p. 89).

[83] "Nad Ljubostinjskim stoslovom," [On the Hundred Chapters of Ljubostinja] in *Holy Bishop Nikolaj of Ohrid and Žiča* , Žiča–Kraljevo, 2003, pp. 401–404.

[84] Ibid.

be authentic (ἀληθεύειν) means to be in a communion (κοινωνεῖν) that imparts an uncreated mode of existence to creation. The Incarnate Truth illumines and provides history with meaning, also affirming the human body as the center of human existence by which immanent reality is validated. No historical institution can monopolize truth. On the contrary, as we have shown, the faith and life of the Church are *epicletic*, which means that She is dependent on God *at every moment*. There is no given truth that someone "possesses"; rather, truth is given according to the measure of one's participation in the divine life, offered in the Body of Christ through the grace of the Holy Spirit. The truth is bound up with the arrival and with the granting of the Holy Spirit (that is the "Spirit of truth": John 14:17; 15:26; 4:23), Whom the Resurrected Christ[85] bestows upon disciples, i.e. the Church and the world.

---

[85] "But when He, the Spirit of Truth, comes, He will guide you into all truth" (John 16:13); "Receive the Holy Spirit" (John 20:22).

Lord Jesus Christ *The Land of the Living*
(mosaic in Chora Monastery, Constantinople, 13th century)

The Ethos of Holiness:
Between Ontology and Gnosiology

Different meanings have been attributed to the word holiness, and for some people, the word has no meaning at all. In the following text we will review this word as God's *personal sanctifying presence* and its different manifestations in anthropology and in the experience of the Church. It is not perchance that the Orthodox Church is regarded as the faith of the saints and the space of sanctification. It is a faith that produces holy persons, "enriches the world with saints"[1] and insists on an *ethos* of holiness. Let us take a brief look at the phenomenon within Orthodoxy of which holiness consists.

It is well known that in contrast to the major natural religions, holiness in the Church is considered a free gift of God and a free accomplishment by the human person (unlike the naturalistic *mysterium fascinandum et tremendum*) and is furthermore experienced as a *catholic* act, a communal act. Holiness should not be understood as the reflection of a particular "objective" state of an individual who has attained intellectual consciousness of the teachings of the Church (θεωρία) by means of "purification" (κάθαρσις) of the body from the passions and of the soul from prejudice (ignorance).[2] On the contrary, hagiography (especially in the early centuries) is not predominantly concerned with this but rather with

[1] Holy Bishop Nikolaj of Žiča summarizes the problem of this topic with a schematic but correct assertion, which should, however, not be interpreted ideologically: "While the West [meaning the contemporary West] is increasing the world's wealth with books, Orthodoxy is enriching the world with Saints."

[2] This method of fallacy elimination is represented in Socrates' maieutics, Descartes' method of doubt, Bacon's inductive methodology etc. See more in K. Popper, "On the Sources of Knowledge and of Ignorance," in *Conjectures and Refutations: The Growth of Scientific Knowledge*, Routledge: 2000, pp. 3–32).

overcoming the tragedy of existence, that is, of *mortality*. This preoccupation is not trivial, for even the very existence of the Church cannot be understood outside the parameters of death. Holiness is a gift bestowed upon those who are open to the experience of communion.

With this in mind, let us inquire into the connection between knowledge and holiness. Does "having knowledge" stand in contrast to "being holy"? From the philosophical perspective, how do ontology and gnosiology relate to a saint's experience? We shall briefly attempt to analyze this issue by means of specific texts. Let us take a look at the so-called hagiographic literature, the ancient *Lives of the Saints* in particular: their sayings, the ascetic lessons, and the works of the early Desert Fathers.[3] Later, we shall attempt to identify how this relates to the ecclesial ethos.

I. Dogmatic knowledge in the ascetic ethos of the Church

What we initially observe in this type of text that deals with a saint's relation to God is a diminished use of metaphysical categories in reference to God and an emphasis on the expressions of communion, relation, and love. In this case, there is a kind of "dogmatic" restraint[4] and an "apophasis," at least with regard to a rational articulation and formulation of faith. In the eyes of a saint, God is not simply "absolute," "the Supreme Being," "the immobile driving force," "the initial cause," but is a Father[5] first and foremost; He is the Savior, the Desired One, and the

---

[3] The sayings of the Desert Fathers and the hagiography of the Judean Desert and of the desert of ancient Egypt have a particular significance. Distinct from the dry and matter-of-fact monastic instructions and the stereotypes of hagiography, this corpus exposes the psychological tensions, moods, frustrations, and elations in the daily existence of the monks, revealing them as creatures of flesh and blood (Cf. B. Bitton-Aschkelony and Aryeh Kofsky, *The Monastic School of Gaza*, Brill, 2006, p.1).

[4] Keep in mind the prohibition of public interpretations (not readings) of biblical texts in the Gerontikon. This was not an attempt to put a stop to the acquisition of knowledge and dogmatic information. The intention was rather to emphasize the predominance of *relation* over *opinion*, since the latter can prove deceitful and "weaken" holiness. Compare Paul's claim that words of human wisdom could "empty" Christ's cross of its power (1 Cor. 1:17). Abba Ammoun of Rhaithou asked Abba Sisoes, "When I read the Scriptures, my mind is wholly concentrated on the words so that I may have something to say if I am asked." The old man said to him, "That is not necessary; it is better to enrich yourself through purity of spirit and to be without anxiety and then to speak"(Abba Sisoes, *The Sayings of the Desert Fathers*, 17).

[5] Cf. J. Zizioulas's study of "The Father as the Cause" in his book *Communion and Otherness*, New York: T&T Clark: 2006, pp. 113–154.

Merciful One. The relationship with God is not one of "apathy," an "ideological perception" (*theoria*), a "catharsis," or some other similar psychological or emotional movement. It is, rather, the adoption as a son, deification, and a communion[6] in love. In the first instance, God is the object of knowledge, which relies on our cognitive and sensory abilities, whereas in the second instance, He *appears* and freely reveals Himself to those who love Him.[7] The dogmatic-biblical experience is applied to the community of *baptized* members of the Church in an ascetic and ethical manner, and the relation to God is tested by none other than the relation with one's neighbor (1 John 4:20) whose "guarantee" is Christ Himself. "Our life and our death depend on our neighbor. If we gain our brother, we have gained God, but if we scandalize our brother, we have sinned against Christ."[8] Metropolitan John Zizioulas makes the following observation in a recent book about communion and otherness: "The idea of God as Father did not arise as a speculative reflection about God, but emerged from ecclesial experience. Only in and through incorporation into the ecclesial community can there be recognition of God as Father. This is what the baptismal origin of the idea of divine Fatherhood implies."[9]

The dogmatic formulations of the ancient Church were "doxological" statements of the liturgical community, as "the hope entrusted to the saints" (Jude 1:3), something that is constantly received anew from the

[6] For example, even when St. Maximus takes advantage of complex philosophical terminology, he formulates the experience of God using expressions of love and freedom. Cf. for example "the divine itself is subject to movement since it produces an inward state"—(σχέσιν ἐνδιάθετον)—"of intense longing (erotic force) and love in those receptive to them; and it moves others since by nature it attracts the desire of those who are drawn towards it" (St. Maximus the Confessor, *Philokalia: Fifth Century*, 84).

[7] "All our efforts in gaining knowledge (empirical and rational) would be futile if He toward Whom those efforts are directed would not have appeared Himself. God, namely grants (or allows) a measure of knowledge of Himself solely when He wants and only to whom He wants to and in a manner which He chooses. *We cannot know Him against His "will" and we cannot (with the aid of all our cognitive abilities) peek into His intimacy without asking Him* (V. Perišić, "Nad Ljubostinjskim stoslovom," *Sveti Vladika Nikolaj Ohridski i Žički* ["On the Hundred Chapters of Ljubostinja," *Holy Bishop Nikolaj of Ohrid and Žiča*], Žiča–Kraljevo 2003, pp. 401–404; our italics).

[8] The Sayings of the Desert Fathers: Abba Anthony, 9.

[9] J. Zizioulas, *Communion and Otherness*, p. 113.

consciousness of the "community of the saints" in new forms.[10] Therefore, dogmatics was not an unapproachable and inaccessible field of
knowledge as some "conservative" theologians claim (otherwise the dogmas of the Church would have turned into fossilized remnants of the
past). On the contrary, dogmatics is "experienced" as an existential *ethos*,
a "doxological" chant of the community,[11] which seeks an ongoing regen-
eration and is always open to the future. A saint accepts the dogmatic
teachings as the experiential legacy of the Fathers[12] (or Councils) and not
as a collection of mechanically repetitive formulas. *Knowledge* is tanta-
mount to *being in communion* with the saints. Hence, sanctity is the *existential* reality of life in the community whereas the reality of *knowledge*
comes in second place. *Being* prevails over *thinking* or *knowing*.[13] For this
reason equal honor is given to the learned and the unlearned saints in the
Church. Their "equality" and equal honor are indisputable even if their
respective *church services* differ.[14] In fact, we differ very little from each
other with regard to the quantity of our knowledge of the Divine (i.e. the
amount of information about God) since we are all more or less equal in
our infinite ignorance. It is precisely this reality, and not some other *human reality in history*, with which the lives of the saints confront us.
Hence, it is more appropriate to talk about the *quality* of one's knowledge
of God, since God "gives the Spirit *without limit*" (John 3:34). The differences here are enormous depending on whether our knowledge of
God is *personal* or not.

Let us first examine how we associate sanctity with apophatism. We
have previously stated that the latter entails a certain theological "restraint" in appraisals, opinions and statements regarding both the quality

---

[10] These forms are presented in iconography, hymnography, hagiography, etc. We
maintain that Orthodox painting is the "most perfect dogmatic language expressed in
colors" (S. Skliris).

[11] Cf. the Creed as a liturgical confession, or as the Synodic of Orthodoxy (743).

[12] "But," Amoun replied, "When I am obliged to speak to my neighbor, do you
prefer me to speak of the Scriptures or of the sayings of the Fathers?" The old man answered him, "If you can't be silent, you had better talk about the sayings of the Fathers
than about the Scriptures; it is not so dangerous" (The Sayings of the Desert Fathers,
Abba Amoun of Nitria, 2).

[13] Bishop Athanasius Yevtich's study "A Prolegomenon to the Gnosiology of Hesychasm," *Emmanuel*, Los Angeles 2008, pp. 121–186, demonstrates the most comprehensive patristic validation of a gnosiological-ontological approach to knowledge.

[14] See further down, i.e. footnote 18.

of God and man. Apophatism in the East has never been "negative theology." On the contrary, the ascetic Fathers hardly ever commented on the Bible[15] for they were cautious of creation-based epistemology (epistemology without revelation); they stated the paradoxical truth: "It is not knowledge that is light, but light is knowledge."[16] This means that he who acquires light, the illumination from God, is the one who has come to the knowledge of God whereas there is no guarantee of the opposite case. Indeed, saints as depicted in the Church's iconographic tradition are deified under specific conditions, which more often than not are independent of creation-based gnosiology.[17] This "undetermined" parameter of sanctity is reflected in the following ways: a) since God glorifies the saints, they all participate in His Glory–Light, and are glorified by Him, symbolized by the iconographic *halo*; b) this glory shines and is *often* manifested in signs and miracles (supernatural powers of saints, healings, etc.); however, this glory can also appear as *foolishness* in the eyes of the world as in the case of the appearance of Fools for Christ; c) there are saints who are completely unknown to us,[18] in a twofold sense: first, they are as yet unrevealed and second, some of them live among us disguised by their ordinary lives so that their sanctity does not stand out; d) there are also some saints who by human standards would not qualify for sainthood because they fall short of moral principles and social norms, as demonstrated in their lives by certain actions (i.e. murder, the violation of basic natural laws like those of marriage, the violation of social laws, as in the case of medieval Orthodox rulers).

[15] Abba Daniel used to say about Abba Arsenius: "He never wanted to reply to a question concerning the Scriptures, though he could well have done so had he wished..." Abba Pimeon "does not readily speak of the Scriptures, but if anyone consults him about the passions of the soul, he replies." (*The Sayings of the Desert Fathers*, Abba Arsenius, 42 and Abba Pimen, 8).

[16] Simeon the New Theologian, *Catechesis*, 28.

[17] The "gnosiology of matter" is the epistemology that exclusively applies to categories of "nature" and to natural knowledge. Cf. Chapter II, 6 below.

[18] Besides this, there are cases in which great saints are temporarily "forgotten," neglected, even disputed, and their place in the church calendar is kept to a minimum, as with St. Simeon the New Theologian whose service was composed as late as the 18th century. "Even if allowance was made for the possibility that a much older service might have existed, the fact that it was lost in time is fairly significant" (B. Krivocheine, *In the Light of Christ: St. Symeon the New Theologian*, SVSP 1986, p. 394). There are cases of individual saints whose proper place in the calendar of the saints was later "expunged," like the Serbian Czar Uroš, the husband of Helen of Anjou).

If we take all of this into consideration, the answer to the question of apophatism of sanctity is as follows: since the glorification of the saints through the divine energies is within the power and is also subject to the *desire* of the personal God, it is not up to us, that is, subject to our human standards, to measure (judge) the content and quality related to sanctity. The tradition of the Desert Fathers explicitly teaches that *judgment* (over) of others is equal to "condemnation,"[19] which leads to self-condemnation. Since it is a unique manifestation, sanctity is not subject to classification, which will be discussed in section II. 3. J. Zizioulas gives the following edifying advice: "Let us not limit sanctity and sainthood only to those whom God has revealed to us by manifestly glorifying them. Our Church has wisely established the feast of *All Saints* and includes those that are known and unknown. It is only at the coming of the Kingdom of God that the entire community of the saints will be revealed."[20] Blessed is considered the one who will be found worthy to behold such a sight (cf. exclamation of one the apostles at Christ's description of the Kingdom: Luke 14:15).

However, the key criterion of knowledge and of sanctity is the experience of the *Cross*. The saints did not evade the Cross, for the Cross is impossible to escape; already St. Maximus explained how everything pertaining to creation "seeks" the Cross.[21] Christ went through much suffering and admonished his disciples as He brought to their remembrance: "How

---

[19] See Sts. John and Barsanuphius, *Letters* 17, 125, 453, 483, 561, 655, 759, 760. The problem consists in the appraisal of "good" and "correct," terms that are based on the ideas of moral and social laws—eternal ideas of good and evil. Since these eternal ideas lie outside the human person and are considered to be true, it follows that any behavior contrary to these ideas represents the decadence of truth. We face the following dilemma: a) we either emulate the eternal ideas through the repetition of examples from the past and, consequently, actual persons viewed from this perspective will remain merely elapsed phenomena; b) or we will make the effort to keep them in remembrance since they acted in harmony with the eternal ideas of good and evil, even if they no longer exist in reality and will neither exist in the future. Orthodox theology recommends a complete different approach that is discussed in this text. Bishop Ignatius (Midich) of Braničevo deals with this topic even more substantially in the lecture he delivered in honor of St. Simeon the Myrrh-bearer (National University of Kolarac, see pravoslavlje.org).

[20] J. Zizioulas, "Deification of the Saints as the Icon of the Kingdom" [original in Greek: "Η θέωση τῶν Ἁγίων ὡς εἰκονισμὸς τῆς Βασιλείας"] in: *Ἁγιότητα, ἕνα λησμονημένο ὅραμα*, Ἀθήνα: Ἀκρίτας, 2001, p. 40.

[21] "τὰ φαινόμενα πάντα δεῖται σταυροῦ": Maximus the Confessor, *Chapters on Theology and Economy* I, 67, PG 90, 1108b.

foolish you are and how slow of heart ... did not the Christ *have to* suffer these things and then enter his glory?" (Luke 24:26). The Church introduced the practice of baptismal immersion as a symbol of the Paschal *passing through* death of He who has passed through the Cross (Pascha). Furthermore, this applies to everyone who is in the fallen state—no one is to assume judgment over others or submit them to evaluation. Therefore, as a result, it becomes evident that the condemnation of someone else is nothing else than a deceptive knowledge, an imaginary consciousness of knowing the *other person,* which is contrary to the Holy Spirit (1 Cor. 2:10–11). If, however, this paschal passing through (suffering) is unavoidable, it then becomes necessary to empty oneself as much as possible of self-confidence and self-glory, which is not easy because *self-love* is the root of all passions.[22] The eradication of self-love frees the saint from all pretensions toward self-reference and leads him to the crucified love toward all creation. The contemporary Elder Porphryios would say that it is not the saint who works miracles but rather the one who has crucified himself together with Christ, which is most edifying for our topic.

II. Dogmatic knowledge as an ecclesiological event

Let us attempt to solve the riddle of the following question: if a clear formulation of the teachings is not a necessary *feature* of a saint, who then has the authority to teach in the Church? There is one simple answer to this: the fullness of the Church, the community of *many.* Indeed, in his epistle to the Philippians, the Apostle Paul says to the Christians that to know Christ and His love is not the work of an individual ascetic but the work of the community of *all the saints.* It is as if the Apostle wanted to say that God can be known only in communion with others: "...that you being rooted and established in love, may have the power together with all the saints, to grasp how wide and long and high and deep is the love of Christ, and to know this love that surpasses knowledge—that you may be filled to the measure of all the fullness of God" (Eph. 3:18–19). If sanctity consists of true knowledge of Christ's love, then it is a matter of ontology ("that you may be filled to the measure of all the fullness of God") and not of the faculties of knowledge (since "love surpasses all knowledge"). It is from this perspective that one should understand how from the be-

---

[22] Cf. J. Zizioulas, "Deification of the Saints as the Icon of the Kingdom," 38.

ginning private opinions contrary to the faith (δόξα) of the body of the community were called heresies and were not singled out by chance. As a result, sanctity and knowledge can only be experienced *within* the Eucharistic service, in the charismata.

Meanwhile, the idea that the fullness of the Church (the community of all the saints) has the authority to teach brings about the harmonious working of the diverse charismata within her: the bishop, the clergy, and the people. The dimension of the authority of teaching must coincide with the dimension of the community, of which the authority of teaching is vested in the episcopacy. It is interesting that this matter accurately expresses the necessary balance between the Body of Christ and the communion of the Holy Spirit in ecclesiology. Encroachments result in an increase of individuality, elitism, and various divisions; a tendency present in the Church throughout her history.[23] There is a fallacy that certain "spirit-filled" saints with special charismata (usually of the monastic order) exist who "are the preservers of the truth" in contrast to the "remnant" of the Church, the episcopacy, the clergy and the people. Central to this idea is the notion that, historically, the Holy Spirit is especially "concerned" with the inspiration of "worthy" individuals. Christ is left with the remnant, the organized Church, and history. This erroneous belief, which is not Orthodox and which appeared in the medieval West, maintains that Pneumatology applies to saints whereas Christology, the main and universal branch within which the Church moves and lives, is concerned with history. The history of the Church has shown how destructive the separation of Christology from Pneumatology is, both at the level of spirituality and ecclesiology.

Why then do we maintain that sanctity is not for a minority, as most people believe? From the hagiological point of view, that is, with regard to the subject of sanctity and sanctification, it has already been demonstrated that elitism in the form of a "pyramidal" structure, an aristocracy, and other exclusive "models" of holiness have not been substantiated. There is only one "ecclesial" aristocracy, completely independent of social status, namely: the affiliation with God's Church through charismata and service. Holiness is not reserved for an elite ("gnostics," "the initiated") but for all people, because there is more than ample

---

[23] See more about this in J. Meyendorff's, *The Byzantine Legacy in the Orthodox Church* (Crestwood, NY: SVS Press, 1982).

space in the Church for both strong and weak, for those who are "modern" and those who are "conservative"—it suffices that they begin to work for their salvation and sanctification. In the ascetic struggle for the acquisition of the "precious pearl" of holiness, there is no intellectual aristocracy (as in Neo-platonism[24]). The Church has shown that she values and acknowledges even those with impaired intellectual capacities (the developmentally disabled) as participants and champions. The only *sine qua non* is the mortification of one's "self-will" aimed at transcending self-love as one turns toward God. In view of this, St. Gregory the Theologian emphasizes that "for such is the Grace of the Spirit that it makes of equal honor those who are of one mind...divinely joined together."[25] Since holiness is associated with the Holy Spirit, it is accessible to every member of the Church and, according to the steadfast words of the Gospel (John 3:34), the Spirit is given "without limit" to all: the clergy and farmers, soldiers and animal breeders; to all. It is sufficient to have the desire to freely acquire it.

We now arrive at the question of the extent of participation of the human mind in a saint's relation with God. In what way is this existential-ontological relation experienced gnosiologically (by the human mind)? The answer to this question is probably best answered by the icon. For over two thousand years Christians have experienced a direct relationship and a profound personal closeness with the saints through the icon. Pious people experience not only the icon but also every aspect of the Orthodox Church life from the perspective of the Kingdom. The person "knows" or already anticipates[26] that the life of a saint evolves in his or her

---

[24] In the long run it is the Church that, thanks to her Catholicity and contrary to our human forgetfulness, preserves, resurrects and renews the memories of her members. Humble laypeople and monastics in Orthodox parishes and monasteries "preserve the memory" of the saints through constant services not allowing oblivion (which is a big passion) to claim its place in the life of the Church. The mention of names, diptychs, et al., eloquently testifies to the Church's self-consciousness. With this sober and prayerful attitude, the Church overcomes the psychological gap between the more "conscious" and "enlightened" Christian on the one hand and the simple faithful on the other.

[25] *Oration* 34, 6.

[26] "...Even if (man) reaches the highest (possible) level of virtue and contemplation during his lifetime, as long as he is still here, he will have knowledge, (the gift) of prophesy and a partial, that is, not a full pledge of the spirit. If he reaches the boundaries of this age in his measure of perfection when the Truth will appear face to face (1 Cor. 13: 12) to those who are worthy, he will no longer have (just) a part of the fullness but will be

union with Christ because the basic characteristics distinguishing holy people are their union with Christ in the Divine Liturgy, their love toward other people, and their forgiveness of the trespasses of others. The transcendence of self-love (mortality) is realized only through union in the Liturgy. As Zizioulas comments:

> ... the basis of the Orthodox consciousness is this relation with God that translates into the relation of the union of the saints and encompasses the material element of creation and all its concerns. When, for example, someone keeps their promise to God or to a saint and gives a donation to the Church, or lights a candle, the (church) preacher will say that it is of no profit unless he is also present with his mind in all of this. However, *what one thinks is not crucial* if one has relinquished his comfort zone in order to go to church to be with the community of the Saints. Even if he might not be present there gnosiologically, he is ontologically![27]

His point is not the emphasis of the individual approach to the Church, but the ontological presence that exceeds gnosiological illumination. At that particular moment, a Christian or saint is neither describing God nor his own experience, but is testifying to his relationship with God through his actions and revealing his knowledge of God through his attitude.[28] (Hence, a saint acts in a dogmatic-Eucharistic manner when he regularly treats nature ascetically; freeing it from mortality, and in this way expressing a dogmatic truth).

Here, we are just touching upon the central aporia of the aim of hagiographic texts: hagiographies are dogmatic texts (although inadver-

---

freed from suffering thanks to his participation in communion" (Maximus the Confessor, *Chapters on Theology and Economy* II, 87, PG 90, 1165c).

[27] Θέματα Ἐκκλησιολογίας. Θεσσαλονίκη (Μαθήματα Ἀκαδημαϊκοῦ ἔτους 1991–1992).

[28] One day some old men came to see Abba Anthony. In the midst of them was Abba Joseph. Wanting to test them, the old man suggested a text from the Scriptures, and, beginning with the youngest, he asked them what it meant. Each gave his opinion, as he was able. But to each one the old man said, "You have not understood it." Last of all he said to Abba Joseph, "How would you explain this saying?" and he replied, "I do not know." Then Abba Anthony said, "Indeed, Abba Joseph has found the way, for he has said: I do not know" (The Sayings from the Desert Fathers, St. Anthony, 17). Similar to a biblical and typological picture, the Archangel Michael, whose name signifies "no one like God," rises against rebellious Lucifer, and by so doing he reveals all his knowledge he has of God. "He does not describe God, he does not explain Him; he rises to the occasion and testifies. This name is the expression of the Archangel's overall radiance of God and is the measure by which this Archangel reveals this radiance," said Metropolitan Anthony Bloom.

tently) in which rational-irrational dilemmas are overcome without any imposition. For the ascetic fathers, God's "features," whose main epistemological term through which dogmatics are realized is *love*,[29] are not the object of faith. The ascetic fathers did not choose between rationality and irrationality, but rather pointed out a "third path": the path that leads to the knowledge of God. So, the saints (i.e. members of the Church) also witness unconsciously; they preach about their Lord both in silence and when speaking at assemblies. They confess Him with their minds, words, actions, and by their lives.[30]

All this most definitely determines the relation of *ontology* to *gnosiology* in the ethos of holiness. Holiness is not concerned with just any categorical, biological, social, moral or intellectual qualities or capacities (*abilities*). We frequently forget and begin to "compare" saints based upon subjective measures, personal "preferences" and the like; and like the Christians from the 11th century (the Three Holy Hierarchs) we too consider St. Basil to be "greater" than Chrysostom, and St. Silouan "greater" than Saint Justin, or that a certain saint is more "convincing" than others. Sometimes we regard holy men as "superior" to holy women. So, each time we form a judgment ("judging" in an evangelical sense) in such a way, we forget that *holiness is concerned with hypostases*, that is, with the confirmation of the uniqueness of a person in the absolute sense of the word. By the same token, however, we testify unconsciously that we are "trapped" by certain worldly standards: sexual determinism, functional roles, and even certain psychological experiences. As a result, it is not infrequent that some Christians give primacy to their "elder," that is, to their spiritual father, over their bishop. One forgets that the local Church has been gathered into one Body by the bishop and not by a spiritual father! The bishop has the ecclesiological primacy. The church

---

[29] Cf. the above-mentioned study of Bishop Athanasius, "A Prolegomenon to the Gnosiology of Hesychasm."

[30] In the Church, and according to Church Tradition, everything that is holy is sanctifying. "Holy" is not something neutral and inactive, instead as soon as it is holy it is sanctifying. Herein lays the dynamic, active character of Christian holiness—that is sanctifying as well, to those who desire it. There is another aspect of holiness that we should not forget: namely, its activity, or effectiveness. For in any case holiness gives birth to a certain ethos, to certain virtues, characteristics and attributes, like for example, the working of miracles (cf. St. Basil of Tvrdoš, the Miracle Worker of Ostrog). The fact here is a profoundly theological one that is associated with holiness.

cannot exist without the "first," that is, without the head of a local Eucharistic community, which is also testified by conciliar history. Throughout its history, in fact, it never occurred that outstanding spiritual fathers were sent to church assemblies in place of bishops,[31] even when their impact on dogmatic issues was invaluable as in the case of Maximus the Confessor.

How does this ecclesiological picture fit into our experience of saints as "perfect," their human weaknesses included? First, if we wish to follow a *hypostatic* path of knowledge contrary to nature, we should not base our relation with the saints exclusively[32] upon their "features" or on the basis of their "effect" upon us. When we observe them through the prism of shared "qualities" with others, their respective absolute uniqueness is lost.[33] Such qualities, which are otherwise of prime significance to the identity of the saint, become ontologically personal just by means of the hypostasis to which they belong. Given that the human hypostasis is tragic, and the "lives of the saints" describe nothing more than the *human reality in history*, this reality is nonetheless true because it reflects the *eschatological* uniqueness of man and redeems his very human nature. Since the hypostasis cannot be reduced to moral and psychological traits, we are able to accept the other person thanks to the hypostasis alone. If this were not the case, the "other" would be unacceptable, as demonstrated in experience outside the Church. This is the only reason, and I have found none other, why Christian Tradition disregards obvious "objective" human weaknesses and proclaims such people saints. Based on the practice of Byzantine icons, Stamatis Skliris has demonstrated in theory that this is possible because Christian iconographers regard saints as people and events from the perspective of the future,[34] that is, eschatologically.

[31] Fortunately, the ancient Church in which the ecclesiological and canonical relationship between universality and the Eucharist was established provides us with the answer to this issue. The synods were always hierarchical.

[32] Certainly, as people, especially as psychological beings, we search for ways of being united with persons psychologically. However, this should not dominate or determine our relation with saints, which should be free of psychological "prejudice."

[33] Cf. the instructive analysis of this problem by M. Proust in *À la recherche du temps perdu*: "Our social personality consists of the opinion of others" [notre personnalité sociale est une création de la pensée des autres]... "However even then... we are not a firmly established entirety identical to all (identique pour tout le monde) that anyone can get to know if he only wants to."

[34] See *In the Mirror*, ed. Sebastian Press, Los Angeles, 2007.

Therefore, not *all* saints are dogmatic teachers in an academic sense. (There is a category of saints called "teachers" and this designation is in fact reserved for the great dogmatic Fathers of the Church.) At times we may encounter unreliable and contradictory statements by them. Does this mean that they are no longer "holy"? To pose such a question involves once again a discussion within the context of some other, certainly not Orthodox, hagiography. Here, the observation of Father Meyendorff is worth mentioning. He maintained that every so often the spiritual teachings of certain ascetics led their contemporaries, even following generations, to forget certain dogmatic ambiguities and sometimes even explicit heresies of a particular ascetic. For example, Meyendorff cited the works of Evagrius, an anonymous author (most probably a monophysite), followed by St. Isaac of Nineveh (a Nestorian bishop), or—in the West—St. Cassian, all of whom remain among the classics of Christian spirituality, regardless of the formal condemnation of some of these authors.[35] On the other hand, when the *dogmatic* faith was in need of safeguarding, individual ascetics left their desert dwellings to defend the faith, as in the instances of St. Anthony the Great or St. Daniel the Stylite. The latter agreed to come down from his pillar because Vasilikus, the usurper, instigated by the monophysites, was violating Orthodoxy. His intervention in restoring the peace to the Church in Constantinople has been chronicled with many unusual details.

"A poor saint has no solemn office," i.e. a festive church service, probably not even a church dedicated in his honor. This "inconsistency" and antinomy of the Church in relation to this issue stems from her helplessness to historically "cover" and "include" all since as we have so far seen, the final judgment is in the Eschaton, in the hands of God. The truth of

[35] *Byzantine Theology* (NY: Fordham Univ Press, 1974), pp. 66–78. On St. Isaak, see L. Petit, "Isaac de Ninive," in *Dictionnaire de théologie catholique*, vol. 8, ed. Vacant and Mangenot, Paris 1903, p. 10. Fr. George Florovsky criticized the lack of concern for doctrine among the Orthodox ("A Criticism of the Lack of Concern for Doctrine among Russian Orthodox Believers," SVTQ 3 [1995]; also in The Collected Works of Georges Florovsky, vol. 13, pp. 168–70). Generally , great theological speculations matter little to the ordinary person. It is difficult to discern in them anything that relates to their own actual lives, i.e. the life of a normal mortal. A mediator is necessary... a great ancestor, saint or hero.

the above statement is confirmed in the example of many saints, even the apostles, like for example, St. Simeon the New Theologian, since his place in the Church services is very modest (not one church has ever been dedicated to him).[36] The analogy between Christ and a saint is absolutely appropriate. During His lifetime, the mystery of the Savior's messianic Person (the Person of the God-Man, the Redeemer of the world) was only gradually revealed to the world, step by step; the greater part was disclosed through predictions rather than explicitly and triumphantly. It was not until His death and Resurrection, until the descent of the Holy Spirit and the experience of the early Church, that His glory and fullness, "the glory of the Only-Begotten of the Father full of grace and truth," was made manifest. It was necessary for other eyes to recognize this, that is, the eyes of faith, as demonstrated at the appearance of the Resurrected Christ to His disciples and to the myrrhbearers. It appears that only the end of man makes the recognition of his person possible. Having this eschatological perspective in mind, the Apostle Paul said the following: "Remember your leaders... consider the outcome of their way of life" (Heb. 13:7). This is so because their evaluation of the truthfulness of their existence and, of course, of their holiness from the perspective that awareness of mortality provides is both crucial and significant.

---

[36] See about this further at B. Krivocheine, *In the Light of Christ: St. Symeon the New Theologian*, p. 394.

Is There a Biochemistry of Freedom?

Instead of an introduction

The topic of this study, with which I have been occupied for several years, is of great significance. I am, however, not able to adequately discuss it in this abbreviated presentation. I intend, therefore, to introduce certain fundamental hypotheses in the hope that these will raise further questions in subsequent studies. I am likewise aware that the manner in which they are described will seem unusual to some. Central to this topic are questions on the existence of theological propositions regarding medical therapy and on the proposition and possibility of medical asceticism.[1] Attempts at comprehending the genetic foundation of neuro-chemical processes, of which there are still no final results, have influenced modern man in his desire to discover a basic hormonal selection for taste, fashion, political choices, concerns and preoccupations, and finally, religiosity. However, to date, the genes and hormones[2]—those molecular transmitters of information from the glands to the cells whose final goal is to secure the optimal function of the homeostatic mechanisms—have not been examined in light of the anthropological experience of the Church, espe-

---

[1] Orthodox theologians adeptly enlighten this topic in several works. Among others see Irinej Bulović, "Duševne bolesti, strasti i vrline" [Irinej Bulovic, "Psychological Ilnesses, Passions and Virtues"] in the anthology of *Religija i duševni život čoveka*, Belgrade 1994, pp. 33–46. Atanasije Jevtić, *Pravoslavna asketika* [Athanasius Yevtich, *Orthodox Ascetics*], Belgrade–Srbinje–Valjevo, 2002 [in French: *Cours d'ascetique*, Paris 1986]. John Zizioulas, "Νόσος καὶ Θεραπεία στὴν Ὀρθόδοξη Θεολογία", in: *Θεολογία καὶ Ψυχιατρικὴ σὲ Διάλογο, Πρακτικὰ Ἡμερίδας, Ἀθήνα: Ἀποστολικὴ Διακονία, 1999, 133–156. ["Pristup lečenju sa gledišta pravoslavne teologije," *Vidoslov* 6/1994, pp. 21–32]. My study has been dependent in part on the suggestions from the council of professorial colleagues as well as students to whom I am thankful.

[2] Hormone derives from the word ὁρμὴ, which means stimulus, instinct, aspiration. This reflects the fact that the hormones act as a catalyst for chemical changes on the cell level, which is necessary for growth, development and energy.

cially not in association with her basic idea of freedom.[3] At the beginning of the third millennium since Christ, there is not a single inter-disciplinary medical-theological study of such a fundamental and fascinating topic. What we do find are, for the most part, speculations based upon positivistic knowledge, creating hypotheses and systems that are subsequently subject to validation through successful therapeutic practices. The authentic awareness of the Church, whereby man maintains homeostasis with nature and receives a foretaste of the Truth and supernatural *powers* (the grace of the Holy Spirit) through the eucharistic and ascetic life assisting him in his struggle for a wholeness against illness and sin, should be placed under the new scrutiny of a medical-theological approach. Together with this indisputable *transfusion* of powers, we emphasize that the Holy Eucharist, as πρᾶξις, an act and operation and as κοινωνία, the communion and participation of cosmic dimensions (since it is the gathering of the age to come), reveals the true *physical* and *moral* meaning of life. Thus one may say that a *genuinely* healthy man is he whose pulse is in harmony with the Church, i.e. with her Eucharistic life.

If we add to this non-existent field of medical asceticism the observation that theology and medicine have had an unfavorable relationship since the Enlightenment, we will be able to understand the kind of challenge we are facing.[4] As a result, numerous medical publications completely lack relevant theological references, while theological publications, which aspire to life's truth on the whole, have allowed a serious rift between evidence-based reality and theological rhetoric.[5] In view of this, both theology and medicine have not provided satisfactory answers to

[3] Cf. G. Gomez, "Free Will, the Self and the Brain," *Behavioral Science and the Law*, 2007/25, pp. 221–234.

[4] "A natural and reliable ally of Christianity exists, which the majority of Christians are not even aware of. This ally is—science. The history of the relationship between theology and science is tragic. The Church is to a great extent responsible for this clash. Whilst the Western Church insisted on imposing a strict control upon science, which led to the development of an anti-religious "scholarly nature" and to positivism, the Orthodox East was fairly inclined toward a contemplative, monophysite disposition. Why should we not acknowledge this? The East did not have the time to relate to this problem. Furthermore, modern science has been formulated in the European West and not in the Byzantine or Slavic East." (J. Meyendorff, "Teologija i nauka," *Logos* 4/1992, pp. 25–26)

[5] Theology ignoring the facts of science (the discovery of paleontology, geology, molecular and evolutionary biology, paleoanthropology, zoology, and ecology et al.) is one example.

numerous questions; for example: when are we responsible for our behavior and when are we under the influence of biological forces beyond our control? This intriguing question belongs to the scientific field of behavioral biology,[6] which studies the interactions of the brain, of conscience/awareness, of the body, and the environment, and their particular influences on our behavior. Love and falling in love, the intensity of our spiritual life, the degree of our aggressive impulses, are all examined in light of our cerebral system (brain structure), which determines our individual traits. Here, one can ask whether human identity is grounded exclusively in a biological hypostasis? If so, should it be this way? Finally, can the truthfulness of the theological statements of Orthodox asceticism be validated by observational methods of modern medicine?

In the year when Darwin's double jubilee—two hundred years since his birth and one hundred and fifty years since the publication of his celebrated work *On the Origin of Species*—is being commemorated world-wide, I will attempt to answer whether a biochemistry of freedom exists, and therefore, whether evolutionary laws exclude a transcendent cause, that is, a Personal God and His most intimate relationship with the world and history.

I. Fundamentals of the biochemical basis of anthropology

Since I do not have the boldness to enter deeply into the field of medical science, I will allow myself just a few remarks with the aim of somehow translating theory into practice regarding the theological implications of the aforementioned fundamentals. Namely, here I will examine some aspects of this problem, as perceived theologically and particularly according to patristic Tradition, and I will leave it to the medical field to form its own opinion on the extent of the significance this proposal may have on medicine.

At the beginning I want to ask the following questions:

a) Which phases has the relationship of theology and medicine passed through prior to arriving at this state in which we now find ourselves? Evidently, it is necessary to return to the past even if it is just for a short time in order to come to an understanding of the significance this problem has for us today.

---

[6] See J. Becker, M. Breedlove, D. Crews, and M. McCarthy, *Behavioral Endocrinology*, MIT Press 2002, 2nd ed. Also, T.J. Carew, *Behavioral Neurology: The Cellular Organization of Natural Behavior*, Sinauer, Sunderland, MA 2000.

b) What current conclusions follow from the study of the history of this relationship and which theological hypotheses concerning medicine can be made? To what extent do theology and medicine come into contact, either coinciding with each other or not, and to what extent can they interrelate?

c) What conclusions are we bold enough to draw given our present situation? Here, special attention is given to neurobiology and to the opportunities it may present to pastoral practice, education, spirituality, law, bioethics, et al.

I will deal with the historical background of the theology-science relation and associated problems in greater detail on another occasion. The discontinuity of the at-one-time more-harmonious relationship[7] between theology and medicine has led to the dichotomy within these two fields of human knowledge and creativity. As far as possible, new efforts should strive toward a greater *harmony* between the theological and scientific images of man,[8] by emphasizing both their differences and parallels. For instance, the daily struggle between the passions and virtues, joy and sorrow, consciousness and dreams, the particles and molecules, and the scientific images of atoms should be carefully recorded in their similarities, with the aim of greater congruence between the two worldviews. The task of a theologian is to conduct research into human nature with all its tangible facets (human physiology), but also to measure the same human nature in view of Christ's person, as shown in the works of the Fathers and by prominent Christian authors. The comparison of the positions of contemporary biologists on the status of human nature with the natural-scientific ("physiological") patristic data would be highly intriguing.[9]

---

[7] See Philip van der Eick, *Medicine and Philosophy in Classical Antiquity*, Cambridge: University Press 2005, especially pp. 343–378. Several chapters of this book offer a brilliant review of general topics, which are essential for anyone interested in the history of medicine and science in the old world.

[8] See W. Sellars, "Philosophy and the Scientific Image of Man," *Science, Perception, and Reality*, London: Routledge and Kegan Paul, 1963. Also, D. Bradnick, "Entropy, the Fall, and Tillich: A Multidisciplinary Approach to Original Sin," *Theology and Science*, 7, 2009, pp. 67–83. Theology should turn to multidisciplinary problems. As Matulić observes ("Teologija, evolucija i Darwin," *Bogoslovska smotra*, 79/2009, 2, 203–206), this encounter should develop within "the context of a friendly dialogue between natural science, philosophy and theology with a particular emphasis on God's creative working in the world of dynamic and evolutional processes."

[9] Hence, interviews of ascetics, Christians, and ordinary people, with the aim of obtaining a better insight into the neurobiological and physiological processes of *spiri-*

Since both b) and c) are sensitive points with regard to an exact interpretation of this relationship, I will address them here. The legacy of the
Holy Fathers is a treasury of knowledge about man and human nature that
requires, however, a new study in order to understand it in relation to our
current situation. A (co)relational comparison of patristic texts (associated with the etiology, development, symptomatology, and the healing of
human psychopathology and illnesses in general) with state of the art contemporary medicine, psychiatry and neurology in particular, would be a
significant contribution. Anatomy, physiology, and pathophysiological
mechanisms linked with the functioning of the human body, as well as the
most recent discoveries and research in the fields of immunology, endocrinology, and medical diagnostics are essential factors for such a project.
It would have as its aim a fresh vision of a *holistic* approach to the texts of
the Holy Fathers and to contemporary medicine. So, for instance, one
could enquire how knowledge emerging from the field of molecular biology can contribute to the struggle against the passions? To what extent
does endocrinology influence spirituality? Is there a hormonal basis for
prayer, virtues and passions? In neurology[10] the established link between
the superego (which includes internalized social norms, laws, "con-
science") (the old I) and the neuron raises the following question: is there
a role for medical therapy in the treatment of self-love? What would be
the risks of such therapy? And generally speaking, does a gene (or a molecule) exist for transcendence? In view of early and later Christian asceticism, I will attempt to answer the question of whether the saints of the
Church realized their personal ecstatic impulse toward freedom through—
unconsciously or consciously—controlling (supervising) their "eccentric"
molecules and "selfish genes."[11] Is there an answer to this question: to what

tual life, would be useful. However, caution is needed since sometimes even those who
often are at antipodes to the notion of "spiritual" are given the same epithet.

[10] See R. Sapolsky, *The Trouble with Testosterone and Other Essays on the Biology of
the Human Predicament*, Touchstone 1998, p. 24. Sapolsky suggests a theoretical model that would explain Freud's classic personality theory. J. Papez was the first to demonstrate (1937) that there is a specific and predetermined brain circuit responsible for the
experience and expression of emotions (Papez's circle).

[11] The concept of "selfish gene," introduced by Richard Dawkins (R. Dawkins, *The
Selfish Gene*, 1976) is not something autonomous but rather the blind tendency of the
genes (hereditary units) to prolong existence in future generations, whereby the concept
of "unselfishness" and "altruism" point to an "unconscious superficial behavior." On the
other hand, the modern biologist, Clark, developed a hypothesis about specific cells that

extent were they under the control of their DNA, or did they *epigenetically* influence their biochemical substrate? Is there justification for a "neurotheology"? The faith of the Church, expressed in the words of the Apostle Paul that God "who is able to do immeasurably more than all we ask or imagine, according to his power that is at work within us" (Eph. 3:20–21), is the therapeutic key, which points to the transcendent action of God in man. Meanwhile, diagnostics prescribes the need for us to comprehensively study man's complexity, which the Church Fathers did. Taking into account the many dimensions and the dynamics of the manifestations of man's psychological life—in those times they were rather fairly "modern" and progressive compared to the ancient philosophers,[12] and quite "contemporary" compared to our modern times[13]—the Fathers were proficient in differentiating the physical, psychological, and spiritual aspects of the human being and were thus able to offer a holistic approach to understanding the complete man.

Precisely because of this approach, an approach that has been validated by the ascetic practice and by the results of spiritual guidance in the acquisition of virtues through the healing from passions, I intend to consider human physiology. Human physiology attempts "to explain the specific characteristics and mechanisms of the human body that make it a living being. The very fact that we remain alive is almost beyond our control, for hunger makes us seek food and fear makes us seek refuge. Sensation of cold makes us look for warmth. Other forces cause us to seek fellowship and to reproduce."[14] The renowned physiologist Guyton, ob-

are programmed for death (*Sex and the Origins of Death*, Oxford University Press, 1996). Regarding the theological significance of this hypothesis see J. Zizioulas in *Communion and Otherness*, pp. 58–60.

[12] The great Aristotle, for instance, considered that the function of the brain was essentially for the heart, and that its function consists in the cooling of the blood. Aristotle, *On Sleep and Sleeplessness*, Part Three, trans. J.I. Beare.

[13] For instance, see Philip van der Eick, "Nemesius of Emesa and Early Brain Mapping," *The Lancet*, Vol. 372, 9th August 2008, Vol. 9637, pp. 440–441. Maximus the Confessor, Photius the Great, and many others read and made use of Nemesius.

[14] Guyton & Hall, *Textbook of Medical Physiology*, 2006, p. 3. There is certainly a group of proponents in the philosophy of science that assert that our mental processes can be explained entirely in neurochemical terminology. This position is akin to the assertion that mental states are nothing other than concrete chemical conditions of the brain, and the mind is nothing other than the brain. As a result, all selections and activities are fixated or determined by chemical laws (see below my note 98). In this case

serving from the medical perspective, notes: "the human being is actually an automaton, and the fact that we are sensing, feeling, and knowledgeable beings is part of this automatic sequence of life; these special attributes allow us to exist under widely varying conditions."[15] The hypotheses of the well-known British biologist Dawkins, which maintain that we, and all other animals, are machines made by our genes,[16] still enjoys a Darwinian reputation. However, most recent research appears to contradict these views by claiming that it is not our DNA that controls our biology, but rather DNA that is itself controlled by signals in the environment outside the cells, a topic belonging to the so-called field of epigenetics.[17] How can "patristics" contribute to the conversation ocurring right now within epigenetics?

From the biblical-patristic perspective, our actual biological state constitutes a) our fallen natural state (anthropologically and cosmologically defined), which as a result of the inevitable law of entropy, gravitates toward chaos, and b) a transcendent instinct toward an authentic existence, which does not desire to know death and decay. Therefore, experiential facts along with the most recent scientific data (biology and psychology) do not allow for the possibility that the human subject was made independent (as in fixation or objectivity) in an actual "moment," or in "midterm" of a lasting evolution of certain stable coefficients that organize both biological and psychological individuality.[18] Man as a being that dramatically moves within the amplitude of a two-fold way of

it would appear that we are incapable to act any different than we are already acting. For the ability to act freely (contrary to acting willingly) is based upon the assumption of having the ability to act differently. If this is not the case, then the existence of an authentic freedom is retracted. See a fairly recent study on this topic by N. Murphy–W. S. Brown, *Did My Neurons Make Me Do It? Philosophical and Neurobiological Perspectives on Moral Responsibility and Free Will*, Oxford University Press, 2007.

[15] Guyton & Hall, *Textbook of Medical Physiology*, p. 3.

[16] His well-known book, *The Selfish Gene*, from 1976, shook the scientific community worldwide, and is still controversial to this day. Since Darwin there have been very few who daringly stepped outside the interpretation of selection based on *genes* as the only mechanism of evolution. The most recent critique of this interpretation is presented by Fern Elsdon-Baker, *The Selfish Genius: How Richard Dawkins Rewrote Darwin's Legacy*, Icon Books, 2009.

[17] More on this in *The Biology of Belief* by B. H. Lipton, 2008. See most recent research on this topic: "Regulation of Histone Acetylation in the Nucleus by Sphingosine—1—Phosphate," *Science*, vol. 32–5/2009, 1254–1257.

[18] Cf. C. Yannaras, *Philosophie sans rupture*, Labor et Fides: 1986, p. 242.

existence, is, according to St. Gregory the Theologian, "an animal in the process of deification" (ζῷον θεούμενον) with all the implications this axiom infers.[19] Therefore, while medical science approaches the question of man introspectively and conducts its observations with the aid of technology, theology understands man as an "indefinable being which can be grasped only by being put in the light of his ability to relate to extra-human realities."[20]

In view of this, the following primary theological topics are formulated at the beginning of this study. 1. Proceeding from biblical facts (God's holiness, the mystery of Christ's person, the teachings of the Apostle Paul, etc.), questions concerning Baptism as a "new existence," the biological changes of man's hypostasis, and the purpose of the Eucharist should be first examined. 2. The Holy Fathers' legacy of their knowledge about man and human nature should be studied in its entirety; and the ascetic method of the Desert Fathers analyzed in particular (the *Gerontikon*, the *Ladder*, the Syrian Fathers, Maximus the Confessor, the *Philokalia*, and other relevant Eastern and Western patristic authors). 3. The differentiation of the three dimensions of the soul: the intellectual, the emotional, and the desiring-willing (λογιστικόν, θυμιτικόν, ἐπιθυμιτικὸν) aspects, should be examined in association with the passions and virtues, and, in light of that, the hormonal-molecular conditioning as well as the transcendental otherness of man should be examined, while preserving the otherness through an apophatic method (in which man's perceptions are considered relative so that the final judgment is left to God[21]). Consequently, this study is just the beginning

---

[19] Gregory the Theologian says that "man is an animal, a living being, organized here," but, "moved elsewhere," and through that, "deified through the aspiration toward God" (τῇ πρὸς Θεὸν νεύσει θεούμενον: *Oration* 38, 11; PG 36, 324b). Cf. P. Nellas, *Ζῶον Θεούμενον. Προοπτικὲς γιὰ μιὰ ὀρϑόδοξη κατανόηση τοῦ ἀνθρώπου*, Ἀθήνα 1995; English translation: *Deification in Christ: Orthodox Perspectives on the Nature of the Human Person* (Crestwood, NY: St. Vladimir's Seminary Press, 1987).

[20] J. Zizioulas, "Human Capacity and Human Incapacity: A Theological Exploration of Personhood," *Communion and Otherness*, p. 207.

[21] Cf. the most recent discoveries that emotions are "rational and intelligent," in *Passion—Philosophy and the Intelligence of Emotions*, by R. C. Solomon (The Teaching Company, 2008). Cf. also "Uloga pojedinih struktura mozga i percepciji i ekspresiji emocija" by M. Uljarević—M. Nešić, *Godišnjak za psihologiju* 6–7, 2008, pp. 41–62. Generally speaking, the apophatic position is valuable when the illusion of an "unquestionable" cerebral knowledge is imposed. Such a position has led Christian theology

of an attempt to arrive at the genetic basis of the human manifestations (psycho-neuro-biological) that are relevant to spirituality and human freedom. The genealogy of passions (whereby passion is the synonym for a) a psychosomatic disorder, and b) a state "against nature,"[22]) formulated by the ascetic fathers, can be complemented by research using the methods of molecular biology; the latter can also be applied in the study of the cause of both passions and virtues. St. Isaac the Syrian says that similar to the passions, the causality of virtues is defined by their reciprocal relationship: a passion (or a certain virtue) originates from another.[23] Therefore, every passion originates from some other passion or precedes another passion, and is at the same time the origin of another passion. According to the Fathers, passions follow upon each other and are either their mother or daughter.[24] (I believe that this kind of a study can shed some light on what could be considered the forerunner of bio-pharmacology: the observation of the healing of man's "natural" state and process in which our "pleasure seeking disposition and insensitive heart...become[s] God-loving and pure"[25]).

The obvious reason for such an approach is the need for a complementary and multidisciplinary approach. The main objection to an exclusively theological model is its "theologism" and its tendency toward downgrading the somatic and social dimensions of human existence. However, contemporary Orthodox theologians have observed that according to the Orthodox experience, the Christian life is understood not merely as a moral and spiritual reality—contrary to the somatic and physiological

to the practice of using poetic language and images rather than the conventional language of logic and representational concepts in its interpretation of the dogmas. The conventional (contemporary) logic of knowledge, along with the representational concepts through which this logic functions, impart the illusion of an unquestionable knowledge very easily acquired, that is taken full *possession* of, by means of the human intellect. On the other hand, poetry, by means of symbols and images, is also always able to express the meaning between the words and beyond, meanings, which basically fit concrete life experiences, and, to a lesser degree cerebral (rational) ideas. The monastic rejection of an epistemological or "gnosiological" absolutism has its origin in what is known as direct empirical spirituality, which focuses on elementary, essential, and the most direct insights of life.

[22] See J. Zizioulas, "Pristup lečenju...," p. 25.

[23] Cf. Homily 46 and 48, Athanasius Yevtich, *Pravoslavna asketika*, p. 99.

[24] Cf. Mark the Ascetic, "On the Spiritual Law," *The Philokalia*, Vol.1; A. Yevtich, *Pravoslavna asketika*, p.100.

[25] *The Ladder*, I.

reality—but as an all encompassing and complex reality, a God-given life in all its dimensions, beginning with the animal and somatic aspect and stretching across the psychological and spiritual planes to the cosmic dimension. Man and the entire cosmos are mutually connected in a mysterious way.[26] In the Orthodox experience, life is understood and experienced dynamically, which is adequately expressed in the Slavic word "podvig" (struggle, and in Greek ἀγών, ἄσκησις and ἄθλησις).[27] Man, created in the image of a perfect God, is continuously striving toward his Prototype, and does not rest on the horizontal plane of nature because the "infinity" of God's love incessantly calls out to the "infinity" of human freedom. It is for this reason that the biblical vision and the experience of man must also be the point of departure for observational studies of the freedom of biochemistry. How wonderful it is when we can behold that "man shall come and a deep heart (προσελεύσεται ἄνθρωπος καὶ καρδία βαθεῖα)," a man of psalmodic depth, of whom God ever "tests the hearts and minds" (Ps. 7:9), and thereby, we might add, testing his entire biochemistry!

Man, whose brain and nervous system is shaped by evolution, who is both restricted and boundless through his genes, is sealed by his early experiences, moderated by his hormones, and under a great diversity of other influences—is able to display a wide range of behaviors, some of which are abnormal. Our question is whether his current status, the epistemological picture of man, determines the theological fact of the revelation of God. Can the faculties of cognition access the intimate encounter between man and God, and eventually explain it in biochemical

[26] D. Bradnick, "Entropy, the Fall and Tillich: A Multidisciplinary Approach to Original Sin," *Theology and Science*, 7, 2009, pp. 67–83.

[27] In his aforementioned interesting and avant-garde study, *Pravoslavna asketika* [*Cours d' ascétique*, Paris 1986], Bishop Athanasius (Yevtich) says the following (in page 6): "Orthodoxy perceives the Christian life as an effort (entrainment), a physical and spiritual training, as an ascetical struggle. This struggle, this asceticism (=ascetic struggle, ἄσκησις) is certainly understood primarily within the context of the sinful, and fallen condition of man, the old Adam, that is, the old sinful man, and in his struggle to free himself from sin, the passions, the devil and death. It is from this condition that the word *ascesis* and ascetic struggle derives its negative attribute; in this case *ascesis* is the liberation from something. However, in the Orthodox understanding and perception of life, that is, in the theology of Orthodox Tradition, man is not perceived only as the old man, the sinful Adam. On the contrary, man is perceived primarily through Christ and in Christ, in Whom the old sinful Adam is renewed. He has returned to his primordial condition, and moreover, in Christ he has received much more."

terms? I believe that the answer to these questions will show a clearer picture of the comparative theological-medical asceticism in light of more recent scientific research.

II. The biochemical otherness and/or the transcendent existential otherness

The classic biblical-patristic differentiation between the image (εἰκὼν) and the likeness ("Let us make man in our image and in our likeness," Gen.1:26) is critical to the theology of medicine. Namely, together with his somatic-physical structure by which he is bound to the world within which he lives, man possesses an instinct toward otherworldliness, linked to the "image of God" within him. Even contemporary philosophical anthropology positively acknowledges the transcendent dimension of man and links it to his freedom. Man received his "icon" (image, picture) from the moment of his creation; however, he still has to attain his likeness; which is his eschatological designation and, in a certain sense, already now predetermines him. Thus his first structure, the psycho-physical one[28] (the entire genetics, biochemistry, neurology, physiology) points to the existence of a being that "naturally" reflects the image of God (λόγος τῆς φύσεως), but "supernaturally" (by means that nature does not provide), that is through his free will, becomes a being in the likeness of God. What he needs to attain through his will by modifying his "mode of existence" (τρόπος ὑπάρξεως) is that potential (ἐν δυνάμει, *in potentia*) inculcated in his being and realized through action. This is of great significance to man's eschatological status, wherein the "law of nature" does not undergo change, but rather the manner of its function does, in accordance with the Christological model following the Resurrection.[29] The Genesis account of man emphasizes that God did not only say "in the image" but added "in the likeness" which indicates that the "image" alone does not constitute the completeness and, therefore, the identity of man, too. St. Basil the Great says: "...by giving us the strength to re-

[28] See the remark below on the psychosomatic reaction to stress.

[29] More on that below. For now, we wish to point out that following His Resurrection, that is, eschatologically, Christ conversed with people in His physical body. It is interesting that this incorrupt body partakes of food and drink; the reason for this is for further participation with nature and people according to the human preconditions of communication, which is within a material-created context.

semble God, He gave us the freedom to create the likeness to God so that we would be rewarded for our toil and so that we would not resemble those portraits, inert subjects originating from the hands of a painter...In truth, the rational being (λογικὸν) possesses the image (icon), but he attains the likeness by becoming a Christian."[30]

Let us leave aside further particulars of patristic interpretations of the divine image and likeness, and presently attempt to comprehend the relationship of man's somatic aspect with his otherworldliness; that is, let us attempt to observe the interaction within the medical-theological framework of an Orthodox ascetic anthropology.[31] First of all, let us say that a Christ-centered anthropology in Eucharistic-ascetic theology views man as a complete psycho-physical being, who according to the words of Irinej Bulović, "is intended to resemble God; this can be achieved within the boundaries of history already here and now through the cooperation with the Holy Spirit and with man's freedom and love, in expectation of the fullness of well-being and perfection in Christ, following the passage from this age into the future Age, from time unto eternity, from history unto the Eschaton."[32] It is precisely because of likeness to God that the phenomenon of man, given the freedom that shapes him,[33] is unthinkable without his pursuit of transcendence in his endeavor to surpass his given reality (his given biological substrate). This leads to the existential question about God, an inevitable element in dealing with the question of man. Ancient spiritual authors, such as, for instance, John of the Ladder or Mark the Ascetic, are not dreamers who entertain fantasies about man with the parameters of infinity, but are knowledgeable of the authentic and tangible human being with all his miserable emptiness and

---

[30] In Athanasius Yevtich's *Pravoslavna asketika* on page 7, the word λόγος certainly has that meaning for the Church Fathers and even much more than what the word "rational" denotes. And yet the word λογικὸς, which derives from λόγος, is mostly connected to the word Logos, that is, Christ, the Creator and the eschatological prototype of man, according to the Apostle Paul (see Col. 1:15–28; 3:9–11).

[31] Actually, this dynamic movement (κίνησις, asceticism) from the image to the likeness represents the foundation of Orthodox ascetic anthropology, that is, man's growth (αὔξησις, Col. 2:19) and fullness (πλήρωμα, πλήρωσις, Eph. 4:13) from the image to the likeness of God.

[32] Bishop Irinej Bulović, "Duševne bolesti, strasti i vrline," p. 34.

[33] See W. Pannenberg, *Anthropology in Theological Perspective* (T&T Clark 1999). From the patristic viewpoint, the human being is the only one free in all that is materially created, and this is what sets him apart from all other animals.

the fullness of his magnitude: "...and in addition, they always speak with experience, like shepherds, with fatherly love, and finally soteriologically, by offering and wishing both to themselves and to their neighbors salvation as the fullness of life."[34]

Why is all of this relevant to the problem of the freedom of biochemistry? It is because the interaction of the psychosomatic aspect with otherworldliness constitutes the fullness of man's life. The following is how a contemporary elder describes this necessary interaction between medicine and spirituality in practice:

> Whenever someone came and told me about a bodily pain, I made it a matter for prayer. This fact also incited me to study. When I "saw" a sick part of the body, I wanted to know its scientific name and the position of all the organs in the human body, the bile, the pancreas, etc. And so I bought medical textbooks on anatomy, physiology, etc., in order to study and understand. For a time, indeed, I attended classes at the Medical School to acquire a fuller knowledge.[35]

We can see in the above section how this conscientious elder dealt with human physiology by means of a *holistic* approach to anthropology and contemporary medicine. Whoever speaks such words as those quoted above has undoubtedly studied the physiology of homeostatic mechanisms, having observed the control mechanisms and the systems of the body. In his papers, one reads his studies in the fields of immunology, neuroendocrinology, and medical diagnostics, which helped him to medically recognize the beginning, the development, the manifestation and treatment of man's psychopathology with the eyes of a spiritual father. All those who are used to the simplified schematic separation of "soul-body" may be amazed at the elder's insights, which testify to a strong connection between molecular biology and the struggle with the passions, and to the existence of an *interaction* between the hormones and the nervous system, and therefore, to the influence of endocrinology on spirituality and vice versa. This short review demonstrates—although Elder Porphyrios represents an exception in recent times—that today we

---

[34] Bishop Irinej Bulović, A speech delivered for the promotion of the book by Vladeta Jerotić, *Učenje svetog Jovana Lestvičnika i naše vreme*; http://www.rastko.rs/filosofija/jerotic/drugi_o_jeroticu.html#_Toc490719491.

[35] *Wounded by Love: The Life and the Wisdom of Elder Porphyrios*, Limni-Evia, 2009, p. 58.

are still following the trails of the Holy Fathers' holistic approach in the area of medical insights.[36]

However, it is exactly here that we need to ask *whether the biochemical identity of man allows us to reduce his existential otherness to a mere biological hypostasis.*

Here, we touch upon the identity of man, that is, to what extent is man in the image and likeness of God, and to what extent is he the sum of chemical elements? Which one (if any at all) prevails and can they be observed separately? By looking at the problem synthetically, we arrive at the following significant conclusions. Despite the *universal* principle of human nature, every human body differs biologically from one another in an absolute sense. This is primarily manifested in the unique *shape* (in its physiognomy, the individual iris, fingerprint), in its *function* (for instance, the body tolerates but never assimilates a transplanted tissue or organ from a foreign body), and also in its *genetic properties* (each genetic DNA code is unique and unrepeatable in its chromosomes which constitute the physical and psychological aspects of our subject of research).[37] Psychiatrists observe that every situation affects both body and soul simultaneously. This is distinctly manifest in borderline states and in some

---

[36] Holistic also because the image of the human being is not only connected with one of his parts, but at times is connected with his soul, at times with his spirit, at other times with his intellect, and at times with his self-governance. All these examples show that the Holy Fathers do not perceive the human being simply as nature, but as a person who possesses nature, and, that a person cannot be reduced to a part of a human being, be it soul or spirit, intellect or freedom, or any other human part. A human being is above all a personal unity, a singular and unique person, and this is why St. John Damascene says: "It is not only the soul, or the body that is called a (human) person, but both are called a hypostasis (ἐνυπόστατα), for only that which is created from one and the other is a *person* of both" (PG 94, 616). St. Gregory Palamas says the same: "We cannot call a man only his soul or only his body, but both of them together; for the Holy Scriptures say that God created precisely such a man" (PG 150, 1361). Even prior to these Fathers, St. Irineus said that God's image in man is understood to be both man's soul and body, which are also created in God's image (*Contra Haer.* V, 6, 1). As we hear the following in the funeral rite of a deceased person: "I cry and lament when.....I see our beauty created in the image of God motionless," it becomes clear then—in the words of Athanasius Yevtich—"that the Church also considers the human body as the image of God; however, here we are touching upon the Christological notion of the divine image in man" (*Pravoslavna asketika*, pp. 21–22, and footnote 9).

[37] Cf. C. Yannaras, *Philosophie sans rupture*, pp. 238–244. As the sum of the hereditary factors of the individual, the genotype is determined at the moment of insemination and remains unchanged during the whole course of a lifetime.

less acute conditions. In a situation of acute danger, in a so-called stressful situation, a group of stress-related hormones is released, resulting in a series of changes that affect the body. Somatically, this leads to mydriasis, hypertension, tachycardia, hypoglycemia, a redistribution of the blood, so that the pupils enlarge, blood pressure increases, the heart's function changes, the distribution of the blood cells shifts, and the blood sugar level alters. Psychological changes are registered as hypertenacity, hypovigilance, a heightened state of alertness; further changes are manifest in concentration difficulties, anxiety disorders, slowing of or racing thoughts, a decreased level of consciousness... Modern psychosomatic medicine rightly insists on freeing us from Cartesian duality by asserting that, both psychologically and physically, there is always *a simultaneous reaction in response to certain external and internal stimulations.*[38] St. John Damascene writes along the same lines with regard to this subject:

> Since we are twofold, created with a soul and a body, *our soul is not naked but is covered by a veil, and so it is impossible for us to attain to spiritual things independent of the body.* Therefore, just as we hear sensory words through our bodily ears and comprehend spiritual things, in a similar way, we arrive at spiritual sight (contemplation) through our bodily sight. Christ took on a body and a soul because man had a body and a soul. This is why everything is twofold: Baptism—with water and the Holy Spirit, the Eucharist, prayers and chanting; everything is twofold, bodily and spiritually, even the lamps and icon candles.[39]

The aforesaid certainly does not give us the right to execute a platonic-ontological incision through the body and the soul, that is, along a somatic and spiritual segment. In view of all the biological and psychological elements, man's existential otherness cannot be reduced to the function of bodily organs or "centers" that are determined by their biochemical com-

---

[38] St. Gregory the Theologian makes a distinct emphasis as follows: *"no matter how much the mind tries, it is powerless to depart from its corporeality"* (Oration 28,13, ed. Gallay, 128). In his *Critique of Pure Reason*, Kant says something very similar. "Space and time" are our tools, instruments of comprehension and observation of this world, a "frame of reference" which is not based on experience that leads to "transcendental idealism." The object of the *Critique of Pure Reason* is the reasoning about the world, which claims to be "pure," that is, unstained by experiences of the senses. Kant criticizes pure reason by arguing that pure reasoning about the world always leads us into a mess of antinomies. Consequently, the *limitations of the experiences of the senses are also the limitations of all sensible reasoning about the world.*

[39] *Three Treatises on the Divine Images*, III, 12.

position. This is the reason why biochemistry, even in its most concrete and analytical particulars, does not cease to be an entirely phenomenological science. Its assertions and descriptions of the primary organic chemical compounds, the "elements," or of the most complex functions, are certainly statements about the hypostatic otherness of each being.[40] However, biochemistry cannot penetrate into the interpretation of the *manner* of the existential otherness, namely, into the personal "tropos of existence": how it functions and manifests itself within concrete chemical structures and through the function of individual organs and organic "centers." Christos Yannaras observes that personality is discovered through its personal energies, which can be biochemical or psychological; however, the energies do not "cover" the entire ontological reality of the existential otherness of the human subject.[41] Here, we find the authentic spiritual experience of freedom "beyond the reach" of objective investigations; it eludes experimental research.[42] Biochemistry is concerned with the basic, irrational aspect of human nature's self-determination, which is contrasted with the rational— *self-governing* (αὐτεξούσιον)—aspect; the latter is not in the realm of biochemistry. In contrast to the Fathers, the main stream of ancient Greek philosophy did not make use of the term "will" (the idea θέλησις never had a terminological status in Greek philosophy). The Fathers understood that only when we take into account the transcendent impulse and instinct of the free person and also comprehend the importance of the *personal* energies (*tropos*), would we then arrive at a satisfactory philosophical (theological and medical) interpretation of human complexity.

[40] St. Maximus writes that every being has a hypostasis, but that it is genuinely *actualized* only as freedom toward Christ. Cf. *Epist*. 15, PG 91, 549bc. This does not revoke the patristic notion of the person in terms of freedom and transcendence; see J. Zizioulas, *Communion and Otherness*, pp. 24–25, particularly footnote 36.

[41] *Philosophie sans rupture*, p. 242. Lipton's approach (*The Biology of Belief*, 2008, chapter 4) is deficient because it draws the existential otherness from the energies (as understood in quantum physics terminology). However, the energies themselves are not the answer to the ontological question. Rather, the question of being is resolved through the personal relations between subjects.

[42] Consequently, biochemistry and the neurological processes in the organism (λόγος τῆς φύσεως) also encompass the human will as the "basic" part of human nature, which can even be "measured" in a laboratory (the process of human decision-making causes psychophysical changes; see remark in footnote 96), whereas freedom (self-governance) as a transcendental impulse, is not subject to biochemistry and cannot be measured. Cf. the study of C. Shantz, *Paul in Ecstasy. The Neurobiology of the Apostle's Life and Thought*, Cambridge, 2009. In this study Paul's ekstatic experience is examined by different disciplines, neuroscience in particular.

Such an interpretation would not ignore the status of biochemistry in the community of the Church, given how central the liturgical experience is in the life of saints—those who have resolved the internal conflicts occurring within the body and, thereby, acquiesced in the transcendence of the complexity that, to others, lingers as an irresolvable philosophical quandary. Following in their footsteps, how do we overcome the entropy of biochemistry in view of the fact that spiritual life is observed through the ascetic and Eucharistic experience? Let us have a closer look.

III. Biochemistry behind the ascetic ethos

No other aspect in the life of the Church can deal with this question more appropriately than the one the Church has historically demonstrated through the ascetic ethos that is nurtured by monastic spirituality. The ascetic feat of expectantly enduring the Cross and, consequently, experiencing the Resurrection encompasses the whole person and, consequently, defines the ascetic ethos as one based on the brutal struggle for humanity's wholeness and health. One of the fundamental characteristics of the ascetic struggle is that the monastic is the slayer of passions and not the slayer of the body (οὐχὶ σωματοκτόνοι, ἀλλὰ παθοκτόνοι[43]), whereby the term *slayer* should not be taken literally. One contemporary ascetic elder summarizes man's neurobiological status and offers the following directives for his transformation:

> Man is a mystery. We carry within us an age-old inheritance—all the good and precious experience of the prophets, the saints, the martyrs, the apostles, and above all our Lord Jesus Christ; but we also carry within us the inheritance of the evil that exists in the world from Adam until the present. All this is within us, instincts and everything, and all demand satisfaction. If we do not satisfy those internal impulses, they will take revenge at some time, unless, that is, we divert them elsewhere, to something higher, to God.[44]

We say that man is formed through the evolution of inherited and acquired behavioral patterns, which prompts us to ask the following question: which behavioral patterns, required to overcome "selfish genes" (egotism), does spirituality offer? Does such an ethos exist?

---

[43] The *Gerontikon* or the *Apophthegmata Patrum*; Abba Pambo, 183.
[44] *Wounded by Love*, p. 134.

Without a doubt, spirituality, too, generates an *ethos* as a behavioral habit. The verb ἐθίζομαι (from which a number of terms etymologically derive, such as ethos, ethics, etc.) means "I become *acquainted* (here: with my psycho-somatic being); in the Church this training is applied to the "law of the Spirit in Christ" (Rom. 8:2). In the 4th century, Nemesius of Emesa, who succinctly expounded this topic, wrote that "*habit is second nature (i.e. an acquired nature).*"[45] But he also considered *what is really under our control*, and our *relation to our freedom of power (will)*,[46] since we know that God created us as free beings and that He certainly had a reason for that. So, the author acknowledged that we do not decide what occurs *by nature*, as in the instance of the appearance of gray hair in a sixty-year old, or a beard in a twenty-year old youth.[47] He further added: "nobody incites us to be hungry or thirsty or not to fly because those things do not depend on us."[48] Those are things that occur independent of man's consciousness, will, and consent. Consequently, since man cannot be the cause of any natural action, his decision-making ability is then futile. Why then would he make use of decision-making if he cannot be the master of any situation?[49] In search of the answer to the question for what is God-given freedom, we arrive at the following claim: we have power over the *energies*, which have their corresponding virtues—therefore, we have power over the *virtues*. Everyone completely agrees that the practice (exercise) of the virtues lies within our power. This practice also encompasses the origin of habits, since "*habit is second nature (i.e. 'an acquired nature')*" Nemesius does not stop at this idea, but continues: if the practice of a certain virtue is the beginning (origin) of a habit, and if the practice is within our power, then the corresponding *effects* of those habits are under our control, since the effects correspond to the habits.[50] Vice (passions) is not engendered by abilities (energies) but by habits, and habits are established by

---

[45] Chapter 39, in he most recent English translation: Philip van der Eijk and R. W. Sharples, *Nemesius On the Nature of Man*, Liverpool University Press: 2008, p. 196. Also see Morani (ed.), *Nemesii Emeseni De Natura Hominis*, 114, pp. 3–4.

[46] Chapter 39, pp. 194–197.

[47] Chapter 34, p. 181.

[48] Chapter 39, p. 197. See also Morani (ed.), *Nemesii Emeseni, De Natura Hominis*, 114, pp. 3–4.

[49] Chapter 39, p. 195.

[50] Chapter 41, p. 201.

choices.[51] So, it follows that natural forces do not generate a life of immoderation or lead to the telling of lies, but our choices do.

With the help of Nemesius, we can conclude the following: He who gave us the power is not the cause of our sinfulness. Instead, our sinfulness results from the habit we developed, which we ourselves have acquired because of ourselves. Furthermore, there is a distinction between power and habit inasmuch as the former is natural (innate) while the latter is acquired. One cannot acquire power through learning, whereas habits are formed through their acquisition and custom.[52] Therefore, we are left to acknowledge that man himself who acts and generates action, is the foundation of his own effects and has the capability of self-determination.[53]

On the spiritual path of virtues toward the authentic person, it is not the autonomous[54] or utilitarian approach to God that prevails, but rather the blessed consequence of a lasting and loving relationship that becomes a "second nature." Thus St. Isaac the Syrian boldly says that Christ does not ask a Christian "to fulfill the commandments but to redirect (διόρθωσις) his soul" (*Homily* 37). St. Isaac explains that "the redirection of the soul necessitates the soul to love the Lord with all its might (precisely the first commandment of love of God), but the soul cannot love God the same way as when it is healed and healthy once again; and the health of the soul is impossible without observing and fulfilling the commandments."[55] A contemporary theologian observes:

> God's commandments bestow new grace-filled gifts of life and what is more: according to the words of the Apostle Paul, they are the 'law of the Spirit' of the new life in Christ (Rom. 8:2), or the 'rules' of the new creation in Christ, according to the words of the same Apostle (Gal. 5:25; 6:16). The holy Apostles, the holy martyrs, and all the great ascetic saints existed this way and lived such a life. However, it is precisely these great saints who have always spoken of the need for a change of mind for all people (cf. 1 John 1:8–10 and others) and the need of repentance after Holy Baptism. This is so, because man still lives in this world, which lies in evil (cf. 1 John 5:19), and be-

[51] Chapter 41, p. 203.
[52] Chapter 41, pp. 203–204.
[53] Chapter 39, pp. 195–196.
[54] This is a controversial point of view of whether Nemesius supports the autonomy of man or not. See Philip van der Eijk and R. W. Sharples, *Nemesius On the Nature of Man*, p. 14–15.
[55] St. Isaac, *Homily* 4; A. Yevtich, *Pravoslavna asketika*, pp. 74–75.

cause man together with all of creation 'has been groaning right up to the present time' (Rom. 8:22), and because all of us, or almost all of us, have soiled our white garments of Baptism in our struggle against sin and the demons on account of the many temptations in this life. The abyss of our human weaknesses must incessantly call out in repentance to the abyss of divine mercy. This is why in the Orthodox Church we always pray: 'Open the door of repentance to us, O Giver of life... with your compassionate mercy.'[56]

There is no need, however, to ascribe any magical effect to the baptismal experience. The dying of the old man with all his wisdom, habits and deeds, signifies the permanent "immersion" of his being "in Christ" and the dwelling in the environment of the Holy Spirit. This occurs through the grafting onto the Vine of life, and by being fed with its life-giving sap. Repentance, μετάνοια, is an all encompassing act—it conquers the wisdom of man according to the flesh (Rom. 8:7)—which consists of an entire neurological complex (*milieu interieur*), intricately connected with emotions that are intelligent and are most intimately connected with the nervous system, which in turn is under the strong influence of the environment (*milieu exterieur*).

At this point for lack of space, methodologically speaking, it is necessary to include psychiatric research that relates to the key issues of the "theory and practice" of the tradition of the Holy Fathers, like for example, the *Philokalia*, the *Gerontikon*, the *Ladder*, the Letters of Barsanuphius and John, the writings of Maximus the Confessor, Macarius of Egypt, Isaac the Syrian, Peter Damascene, Photius the Great,[57] Nemesius of Emesa,[58] the classical Western authors with Augustine at the head, the more recent elders (Porphyrios, Paisius, Sophrony), and others. Although not medical professionals, the medical precision with which these authors relay the experience of the struggle with the passions—the experience of good, of beauty and of sanctity, the experience of the presence of the image of Christ in us and among us—is simply astonishing. Let us

[56] A. Yevtich, *Pravoslavna asketika*, p. 75.
[57] St. Photius availed himself of his medical knowledge in the care of sick patients as well as in the concoction of appropriate medicines. He has been compared to Galen and Hippocrates.
[58] His text, *De Natura Hominis*, deals for the most part with physiology, anatomy, and what in contemporary times is called experimental psychology. See the aforementioned study of Philip van der Eijk, "Nemesius of Emesa and Early Brain Mapping," published in *The Lancet*, Vol. 372, 9; August 2008, No. 9637, pp. 440–441.

look at just one aspect for a moment. The Holy Fathers' list or "classification" of passions and virtues emphasizes, above all, the reciprocal and close relationship that exists between them. For example, the argument that the most primitive passions of the body are closely linked to the most refined and spiritual ones (for example, the passions of debauchery and pride are closely interconnected) is worthy of attention from medical specialists.

In view of this, can one inquire about the neuroendocrinology of the ascetic ethos? Medical research would have to begin by inquiring into the manner with which the brain regulates the body through the autonomous nervous system (ANS). First of all, enquiries should be made into the manner of how the limbic system regulates the body through the release of hormones. This should be followed by a study of individual hormones and the specific influence each exerts; for instance, how does the reciprocal influence of brain and hormone work, wherein the brain regulates the hormones and the hormones regulate the brain? How do the hormones change the homeostatic function of the brain? The key issue of this research is the refutation of the hypothesis that hormones "cause" certain behaviors (for example, the assertion that testosterone "causes" aggression, or that there are specific hormones responsible for religiousness), and instead explain how the hormonal *interaction* with the nervous system changes the probability of certain behaviors in certain situations.[59]

Other texts further elaborate on the question of causality. In speaking of the hormonal consequences of the life in Christ, Elder Porphyrios says the following:

> When we surrender ourselves to Christ our spiritual organism finds peace, with the result that all our bodily organs and glands function normally. All these are affected. We become well and cease to suffer. Even if we have cancer, if we leave everything to God and our soul

---

[59] The legal age of eighteen has its biological basis; namely, the frontal layer of the brain, responsible for social behavior, reaches maturity during this developmental stage, although there are many exceptions to this. The frontal gyri and sulci of the average human brain have matured by then. It is during this period of life, the medical experts inform us, that the hormones are instrumental in turning children into adults. Bearing in mind the role of the hormones in the associative region of the cortex, above all their dominance over the conscious, active and willful actions, which are linked to social activities (responsible to others and in front of the law)—this period is legally sanctioned.

finds serenity, then divine grace may work through this serenity and cause the cancer and everything else to leave.[60]

As the Elder continues his thought, he speaks even more explicitly about the effects of spiritual manifestation on the biochemistry of the human organism:

> Stomach ulcers, you know, are caused by stress. The sympathetic system, when it is subjected to pressure, is constricted and suffers harm and so ulcer is created. With stress, pressure, distress, anxiety, an ulcer or cancer comes about. When there are confusions in our soul, these have influence on our body and our health suffers.[61]

Prayerful vigilance over our somatic and psychological condition (the equivalent of regulating the biological, psychological, and hence the hormonal functions) is difficult, but is worth the effort. Thus, for instance, John of the Ladder emphasizes the importance of not surrendering to eccentric somatic desires, which is the basic pre-condition of spiritual health.[62]

Isaac the Syrian is well known for his insights into the connection between gnosiology and therapeutics. According to him "love of the body—φιλοσωματία—is a sign of unbelief." Here is how Justin (Popovich) of Chelie renders his text:

> Faith frees the mind from the category of the senses; the latter becomes sober through fasting, constant mindfulness of God, and vigils. The lack of abstinence and a full stomach brings the mind into a state of confusion and dissipation, and distracts it through fantasies and passionate lust. The knowledge of God does not dwell in a pleasure loving body. A healthy and wholesome mind—τῆς σωφροσύνης— blossoms from the seed of fasting just as licentiousness and impurity blossom from the seed of satiety. Lustful thoughts and greed create a destructive fire in man; its remedy is the immersion of the mind in the ocean of the mysteries of the Holy Scriptures. If one does not divest oneself of all attachments to things, the soul cannot free itself from the confusion of thoughts nor can peace prevail in its mind if it

---

[60] *Wounded by Love*, p. 229.

[61] Ibid., p. 229.

[62] Young people should not listen to the enemies, the demons, who advise: "Do not exhaust your body so that you will not become sick or troubled." He says that especially in our times, "it is difficult to find anybody who is determined to mortify his body," "although there are some who are ready to deprive themselves of excessive and tasty food" (*The Ladder*, Hilandar Monastery, 2008, p. 24).

does not mortify the senses. The passions darken the thoughts and weaken the mind. The turmoil of thoughts stems from satisfying the stomach.[63]

The given examples show that Orthodox *asceticism*, this ascetic and grace-filled life in the Holy Spirit, is closely linked to the Orthodox dogmas of the Church, which according to Church hymnography, have a *therapeutic* effect while the canons act as *medicines* since they are concerned with Holy Communion.[64] The Fathers identify this therapeutic effect as the soteriological motive animating dogma, confirming that there is no true life without true faith. Once a person's process of being born in Christ along with his growth in the Holy Spirit has begun, it turns into a holy triune fabric of his god-like nature, intended for deification and for the everlasting perfection in the fullness of life eternal. "While maintaining the general biblical conception of the ontological unity of man's composition, St. Gregory Palamas had no desire to dogmatize about any physiological system, and so left full freedom for scientific research. Revelation was only concerned with eternal verities necessary to salvation, and not with physiology."[65]

"If we ask how the mind is attached to the body," Palamas writes, "where is the seat of imagination and opinion, where is memory fixed, what part of the body is most vulnerable and so to say direct to others, what is the origin of the blood, whether all the humours are quite pure and without admixture, and which organs serve as receptacles for each of them, in all such matters each man may speak his opinion... it is the same...with all questions of this sort about which the Spirit has given us no plain Revelation; for the Spirit only teaches us to know the Truth which penetrates everything. Therefore, even if you find that on such a point we contradict the holy and wise Gregory of Nyssa, you should not attack us for that."[66]

The human being is an intangible reality and eludes one's own control; this is a universal human experience. Medicine and asceticism are in agreement when it comes to the importance of maintaining the bal-

---

[63] Justin Popovich, "Gnoseologija Svetog Isaka Sirina," *Put Bogopoznanja*, Manastir Ćelije, 1987, p. 112.

[64] Cf. A. Yevtich, *Pravoslavna asketika*, p. 9. It is said that certain saints "heal by means of the dogmas" (e.g. the office of St. John the Theologian). It is also said that the canons are *medicines*, although this has not been sufficiently made clear theologically.

[65] J. Meyendorff, *A Study of Gregory Palamas*, SVSP 1964, pp. 148–149.

[66] *Triads* II, 2, 30, at J. Meyendorff, *A Study of Gregory Palamas*, pp. 148–149.

ance—homeostasis of the human body. They are at variance, however, in regard to its purpose. Unlike medicine, the ascetic approach maintains that its purpose is aimed at the good of the whole community of saints rather than the individual only, of which the former is suggestive. This perception is of paramount importance for the establishment of an Orthodox *social biology* which, however, I will not address further at this time. John of the Ladder emphasizes the need for control in relation to the body, although the question about the hormonal reaction to such a "harsh" ascetic perception still needs to be examined. "The narrow path is recognizable through the control of the stomach, all night vigils, drinking limited amounts of water, the lack of bread, being purified through shame, scorn, ridicule and reproach, by cutting off one's desires, through the endurance of insults, and scorn without complaints—one can recognize it *if you are not angry when you are slandered, humiliated; if you are humble when someone rebukes you.*"[67]

If a faulty function of the hormones, that is, if their pathology leads to the appearance of passions, theology and medicine could concur on the diagnosis of *passions* as "incorrectly programmed hormones," which are in actual fact false substitutions. They are moreover demolishers and parasites of man's energy and possibilities, with which God endowed man and with which he can strive toward Him and participate in the divine life. Our Savior came purposely to save us from the "curse of the law," from the law that governs the "selfish genes" and from the power of sin, death and the devil (cf. Gal. 3:13; Heb. 2:14–18), to grant us true life.

We have now arrived before the facts relevant to the relationship between theology and science. Independent of our opinions about man's fall and the resulting introduction of entropy into the cosmos, and consequently into biochemistry too, or vice versa, the fact remains that both medicine and theology are confronted with a very complex topic. The concept of entropy, first used in physics (thermodynamics), became useful in the explanation of the behavior of biological systems, particularly of the evolutionary characteristics (e.g. all of the human homeostatic systems). Can this concept be expressed in theological terminology? For

---

[67] The aspect of the "hypostasized energies" that are representatives of nature may be one way of solving this question. The function of the homeostatic systems and the state that surpasses their scope, like in the case of some saints-people, can be explained by means of the ascetic synergy through grace.

now, let us say that entropy confirms the theological fact that truth cannot exist when the entire development of creation—biological and physical—can be diagnosed as having "increasing chaos in the system," which is to say, death and decay.[68] *Senescence* (aging) is also a process introduced by the evolution of the genetic essence of an organism; an organism can live in optimal health up to the time of its reproduction, after which it slowly and gradually dies.[69] This unpleasant feeling of bondage engendered by the chemical-biological conditioning of human "nature," inherited by the person, has been sufficiently studied both in medicine and in light of the ascetic experience of the Church.

IV. Is there a physiology of spirituality?

Neurobiology[70] and other associated sciences support the conviction that spirituality has a biochemical basis. However, this does not hold true unconditionally, especially when the faith and theology of the Christian Church are concerned. The evolutionary theory developed by the natural sciences gives an account about the entire phenomenon of biological life based on the principles of *chance*, *mutation* and *selection*, and as such does not make any assumptions, nor is it required to make assumptions, about a transcendent cause in terms of God's creative actions. This, however, only confirms its phenome-

---

[68] "In view of this basic understanding and of the application of entropy, the theological understanding of the natural chaos within creation can be explored, particularly its link to the Fall" (D. Bradnick, "Entropy, the Fall, and Tillich: A Multidisciplinary Approach to Original Sin," *Theology and Science*, 7, 2009, 71).

[69] See the aforementioned book by the biologist, Clark (*Sex and the Origins of Death*, Oxford University Press, 1996, pp. 79–104), on the phenomenon of aging (senescence). Each somatic cell is inherent with a self-destructive program, the "death gene," which is activated at a specific moment resulting in the standstill of cell division and in suicide.

[70] In contrast to the biochemistry of freedom, it is interesting to note that there are many references to the existence of the biochemistry of love. In the latter process, lust is identified as the instigator of sexual desire that stimulates procreation, and the release of hormones such as testosterone and estrogen, which have an effect only for a few weeks or months. The attraction is the "romantic" phase of love during which chemicals that include dopamine, phenylethylamine, norepinephrine, and seratonin are released. The action of these chemical processes, released in the bloodstream, is similar to the symptoms of stress, i.e. an increased heart rate, clammy palms, heavy breathing, etc. In contrast to attraction, proximity entails a longstanding relationship, monogamy and loyalty, which are linked to oxytocin and vasopressin; a period of mature love.

nological character (that is, a biological view that does not have a holistic picture).

I wish to commence with the physiological, neurological, and biochemical basis of Christian asceticism. Every human movement, and therefore, the ascetic struggle, too, requires a psychological and a physiological condition, an organization of energy, which, as is well known, unfolds on the level of simple cells. What does this look like?

> Although the many cells of the body often differ markedly from one another, all of them have certain basic characteristics that are alike. For instance, in all cells, oxygen reacts with carbohydrates, fat, and protein to release the energy required for cell function. Further, the general chemical mechanisms for changing nutrients into energy are basically the same in all cells, and all cells deliver end products of their chemical reactions into the surrounding fluids.[71]

While biochemical synergy is sufficient for physiological functioning, the result of an asymmetric synergy of grace and effort is the *sine qua non* of any spiritual achievement, which will be dealt with further on.

Before addressing the patristic *neurobiological* notions, which are of significance to medical science, let us first turn to the role and significance of the nervous system. The nervous system consists of three main parts: the *sensory (afferent) division*, the *central nervous system (or the integral part)*, and the *motor (efferent) division*. We could assert that each one corresponds to the three aspects of the human psychological make up, which the Holy Fathers often speak of: the desiring, the intelligent and the aggressive aspects. The constant concern for and the study of man have led the Fathers to certain views, which are still relevant in our day from a medical point of view. The Fathers have indeed produced solid scientific knowledge. For instance, the sensory receptors, which receive information about the condition of the body and the environment, correlate with the desiring aspect and with the will, or with what Maximus the Confessor terms "the gnomic will."[72] Furthermore, on the somatic plane, the receptors are situated in the skin and are stimulated every time an object comes

---

[71] Guyton & Hall, *Textbook of Medical Physiology*, 2006, p. 3.

[72] I support the view that (see section below: Biochemistry and the Eschaton) the teaching of Maximus the Confessor on the gnomic will (which is clearly distinct from the authentic will, from freedom) is the theological key to the comprehension of biochemistry and neurobiology, as well as his inexorable teaching on the logoi of beings which direct them toward their ultimate goal.

into contact with the skin. This is reflected psychologically, too. The eyes, that is, the sensory organs that provide a picture of the environment, "inform" the cortex (this also applies to the ears, which are also sensory organs). The *central nervous system* includes the brain and the spinal cord; the brain deposits information, produces thoughts, ambitions and determines the reaction of the body to various sensations. Is this perchance that "organ" ("logistikon" or the mind) to which the Fathers refer when they emphasize the need for "control" over the senses? Once the sensory stimuli have been received, the cortex conducts corresponding impulses to the efferent motor division, leading to the activation of the desired function. This applies to the sympathetic system. Naturally, the greatest part of the nervous system is autonomous, and is called the *autonomous system*. It functions on the unconscious level and controls many functions of the internal organs, including the function of the heart as a pump, the movements of the gastrointestinal tract and the secretion of the glands.[73] There is the example of a man who had the highest intelligence level although he had a tiny brain.[74] This feature, nonetheless, gives us the right to "defend" and to support the intangibility of the *theological-spiritual* experience within the framework of biochemistry and neurology.

Of course, we cannot speak of a high level of support for this finding in patristics. Despite many obvious implications, they do not provide us with any explicit evidence for this relation. However, a number of indirect allusions, found in the works of Maximus the Confessor for instance, encourage us to reflect upon this relation in order to gain a better understanding of the significance of contemporary neurobiology; Maximus testifies to the relationship between the spiritual and the physical:

> Of the things contingent upon those given us by God, some are in the soul, some are in the body and some relate to the body. Those in the soul [=cortex] are spiritual knowledge and ignorance, forgetfulness and memory, love and hate, fear and courage, distress and joy, and so on. Those in the body [=limbic system] are pleasure and pain, sensation and numbness, health and disease, life and death, and so on. Those relating to the body [projections] are having children and not having children, wealth and poverty, fame and obscurity, and so on. Some of these are

[73] Cf. Guyton & Hall, *Textbook of Medical Physiology*, pp. 3–9.
[74] The journal *Science* ("Is Your Brain Really Necessary?," *Science Frontiers*, No. 15/1981) provides such an example. See Bruce Lipton, p. 131.

regarded as good and others as evil. Not one of them is evil in itself. According to *how they are used they may rightly be called good or evil.*[75]

Following this insight, we ask ourselves how does the cortex exert restraint on attachments, or on the programmed "misperception," that is, on a passion? St. Maximus offers us the following picture:

> The intellect receives impassioned conceptual images in three ways: through the senses, through the body's condition and through memory. It receives them through the senses when the senses themselves receive impressions from things in relation to which we have acquired passions, and when these things stir up impassioned thoughts in the intellect; through the body's condition when, as a result either of an undisciplined way of life, or of the activity of demons, or of some illness, the balance in the body is disturbed again and the intellect is stirred to impassioned thoughts or to thoughts contrary to providence [God's]; through the memory when *the memory recalls the conceptual images of things in relation to which we were once made passionate, and so stirs up impassioned thoughts in a similar way.*[76]

Let us look at Maximus' genealogy of passions in light of the medical observations we have mentioned.

> The passions lying hidden in the soul provide the demons with the means of arousing impassioned thoughts in us. Then, fighting the intellect through these thoughts, they force it to give its assent to sin. When it has been overcome, they lead it to sin in the mind; and when this has been done they induce it, captive as it is, to commit the sin in action. Having thus desolated the soul by means of these thoughts, the demons then retreat, taking the thoughts with them, and only the spectre of the idol of sin remains in the intellect. Referring to this our Lord says, *"When you see the abominable idol of desolation standing in the holy place (let him who reads understand)..."* (Matt. 24:15).

Continuing this brilliant thought, Maximus says: "For man's intellect is a holy place and a temple of God in which the demons, having desolated the soul by means of impassioned thoughts, set up the idol of sin."[77] Since the passions have become settled in the soul (the habit of ex-

---

[75] Maximus the Confessor, *On Love*, II, 76. One should mention here that the cortex registers the feelings while the feelings are registered by the neuroendocrine section of the human heart, for the associative centers of the cortex lead to the projective fibers which proceed from the heart.

[76] *On Love*, II, 74.

[77] *On Love*, II, 31.

citement as a response to the impulse has been formed), they are in a state of constant "arousal" (in expectation of an impulse). Then the mind (here: the frontal cortex) aroused by the demons seeks a connection with the passions, and is thus led into sin by means of the thoughts. After that happens, sin is followed by action. This is how the "idol of sin" is formed within us. Fleeing this idol, St. Silouan the Athonite[78] said that following his first sin on Mt. Athos he never again allowed his mind to be defeated by impassioned thoughts but only "tolerated" them.

Maximus' astounding diagnosis is not without a corresponding therapy. We shall easily be convinced of this if we immerse ourselves in his subsequent explanation. To begin with, the Confessor says: "He who drives out self-love, the mother of the passions, will with God's help easily rid himself of the rest, such as anger, irritation, rancor and so on. But he who is dominated by self-love is overpowered by the other passions, even against his will..."[79] As long as self-love exists, an entrance to the other passions will also exist. However, a perception is not necessarily evil on its own, as long as there is *attention (vigilance)* as a prerequisite: "When the intellect turns its attention to the visible world, it perceives things through the medium of the senses in a way that accords with nature. And the intellect is not evil, nor is its natural capacity to form conceptual images of things, nor are the things themselves, nor are the senses, for all are the work of God." The question, then, of what is *evil* is answered as follows: "Clearly it is the passion that enters into the conceptual images formed in accordance with nature by the intellect; and this need not happen if the *intellect keeps watch.*"[80] Having said this, Maximus clarifies the term *passion*: "Passion is an impulse of the soul contrary to nature, as in the case of mindless love or mindless hatred for someone or for some sensible thing. In the case of love it may be for needless food, or for a woman, or for money, or for transient glory, or for other sensible objects or on

[78] Archimandrite Sophrony, *St. Silouan the Athonite*, St. Vladimir's Seminary Press, 1991, p. 22. "His first 'fall' in his thoughts made him soberly cautious until the end of his life; and the extent of his caution can be judged by the fact that since the day his confessor directed him never to withhold a sinful thought, he never permitted a single perverted image in his entire forty-six years of monastic life."

[79] *On Love*, II, 8.

[80] *On Love*, II, 15. The attentive reader will find this to be another example, from the *Gerontikon* (the Elder Abraham), which testifies to the fact that not a single passion is uprooted during a human being's lifetime, historically speaking.

their account. In the case of hatred, it may be for any of the things mentioned, or for someone on account of these things."[81] Therefore, mindlessness (unreasonableness) and inattention allow sensations to arouse and overcome the entire will and desiring aspect of man.[82]

How can a passionate thought become a dispassionate thought and, therefore, free from passion, that is, separated from a wrong perception? An impassioned conceptual image is "a thought compounded of passion and a conceptual image. If we separate the passion from the conceptual image, what remains is the passion-free thought. We can make this separation by means of spiritual love and self-control, if only we have the will."[83]

A very important conclusion from the above passage is that the separation of the passions from the thoughts is possible only through love, restraint (i.e. self-control), and free will. For, it follows from this analysis, that the natural impulse of man cannot produce a passion if man's "ego" does not *desire* it. Consequently, self-love (along with the superego, narcissism = love of self) is the root and cause of all problems, and also of the capricious passions, because in the fallen state they appear as a separate self (in psychology: a detached self) that is concerned only with "itself." As such, it pertains to the *soul* and subjects everyone and everything to its *own* judgment,[84] nurturing the deceitful idea of its own idealized image. This causes a strange law in human behavior. "For I delight in the law of God after the inward man: But I see *another law* (ἕτερον νόμον) in my members, warring against the law of my mind, and

---

[81] Some exemplified passions speak about this. For instance, "The demon of unchastity is powerful and violently attacks those who struggle against passion...With the lubricity of sensual pleasure he imperceptibly steals into the intellect and thereafter persecutes the hesychast by means of the memory, setting his body on fire and presenting various forms to his intellect. If you do not want these forms to linger in you, turn again to fasting, labor, vigils and blessed stillness with intense prayer" (*On Love*, II, 19).

[82] Ibid.

[83] *On Love*, III, 43. On some other occasion, I will present a comparative chart (tabella genealogica passiones) for the illustration of these processes from a theological and medical perspective. The similarities are conspicuous and close to identical.

[84] There is an example in the Gerontikon of a monk who gradually rejected everybody, including his elder and finally even the Lord. Abba Isaac of the Thebaid said: "Take care not to judge anybody in the future before God has judged him" (Abba Isaac of the Thebaid in *Gerontikon*). Abba Theodore of Pherme said: "There is no greater virtue than not to judge" (*Gerontikon*).

bringing me into captivity to the law of sin which is in my members" (Rom. 7:22–23). For Maximus the Confessor, the ability to desire includes both the rational and irrational aspects of the human soul's self-determination (self-governance). Self-love appears in a "vacuum," according to the testimony of St. Maximus, "when the passions cease to be active in us, and this whether they are inactive because their causes have been eradicated or because the demons have deliberately withdrawn in order to deceive us."[85]

It is important to know that genuine ascetics perceived a victory over themselves by means of a humble understanding and a perception of their *self* as their greatest enemy, knowing through experience that the self gives birth to and nurtures individualism. Accordingly, the search for "formulas" for the harmonious functioning of the human biochemical structure can also denote a concern over oneself, which, though, entails the withdrawal from individualism and from self-sufficiency that are obstacles to a true encounter of man with God and his fellowmen. Contemporary civilization promotes in all things a culture of self-preoccupation in the pursuit of happiness and well being.

If we apply these truly elementary insights to the neurobiology of man, who has entered into communion with the Church, a very interesting picture emerges.

V. Biochemistry in the community of the Church: the conquest of the selfish genes

With regard to the biochemical hypotheses of anthropology, I straightaway want to exclude representations of an individualistic and dualistic spirituality. At times such a picture prevails in patristics; however, this subject matter should not be understood in terms of an introduction of the spiritual "primacy" favored over the biological-somatic aspect. The position that I am working on stipulates that the *transcendent aspect constitutes man who at the same time is also constituted from the immanent reality.* The somatic and spiritual aspects are inter-dependent; they converge but are not identical, just as historical existence is dependent on the eschatological existence, that is, on the true existence.

---

[85] *On Love*, II, 40. Bishop Athanasius used to say to the author of this study that the danger starts when we least expect it, that is, in a vacuum.

In fact, one must acknowledge that all of medicine is psychosomatic, because every disease manifests somatic and psychological factors. Since every disease is a disease of a given person, both factors are intertwined and form a unique psychophysical organism. If there is a psychosomatic link to space and time, to what is the transcendent spiritual linked? Through the action of the Holy Spirit, the somatic aspect is freed from the negative restraints of the space-time of history and from its own pathology, although ultimate freedom is attained only at the Eschaton. However, the impulse toward transcendence, which is given to man as part of the gift of freedom, responds to the call from *above*, to the grace of the Spirit.

In order to discover the roots underlying this somatic and spiritual convergence, we first need to understand that in the patristic writings about the somatic aspect, the negative statements about the body are not a negation of the body *as such*. Instead, the somatic can make for a "fortress of individualism" and an armor of the self, and is, therefore, problematic (e.g. Gregory the Theologian[86]). St. Maximus explains the convergence of the somatic and psychological aspects in his teachings about the will. "Only in harmony with it (the will) do we naturally desire (ἐφιέμεθα) to exist, to live, to move and to think (νοεῖν), to speak and to feel (αἰσθάνεσθαι), to partake of food, sleep and rest, not to be ill, not to die, and, simply, to have all that which strengthens nature and avoid all that which destroys her."[87] Once again we repeat: the function of the *natural* will, which brings together all the attributes of the human being, occurs more or less instinctively, i.e. independent of human reasoning and of any of his rational decisions.[88] As we have previously seen in Nemesius, this also applies to the *desire* for self-preservation, the desire for food, drink, the avoidance of death, etc. This appears to apply not only to the human but to the animal nature as well and is characterized as predominantly instinctive. However, this instinctive desire is not relevant to self-determination. The rational will, that is, freedom plays a role here, and a self-determined motion (νοερὰ) is characteristic of a rational will (αὐτεξούσιος κίνησις).

[86] For instance, Gregory the Theologian, *Oration* 43, 19; SCh 384, 162; PG 36, 520d–521a. Cf. A. Theodorou, "Αἱ περὶ ἀνθρωπίνου σώματος ἀντιλήψεις τοῦ ἁγίου Γρηγορίου Ναζιανζηνοῦ," ΕΕΘΣΑ 21 (1974), pp. 83–122.

[87] *Opusc.* 16, 19. See D. Bathrellos, *The Byzantine Christ. Person, Nature, and Will in the Christology of Saint Maximus the Confessor*, Oxford University Press, 2004, p. 123.

[88] Cf. D. Bathrellos, *The Byzantine Christ*, p. 123.

This problem is of such significance that it cannot be circumvented and the answer is found in Christology.

Compared to us, Christ's hypostasis is not a hypostasis derived from a biological existence, but rather from a free and divine existence, and therefore, it is possible for Him to have a body and to be the Savior of the world. With Christ, we learn what a transcended biological existence is. His "mode of existence" is such that it modifies the requirements of the "law of nature" without abolishing the body and its instincts, but redirects the same toward the truly Desired one. Whoever is grafted onto that hypostasis (is "hypostasized into") inside His Body, has the opportunity to "immerse" his biochemical and psychological individuality in a new life of freedom and grace. Since Christ is in an indivisible union with the Holy Spirit, which according to Paul's ecclesiology signifies the *community*, this communion results in the "communion of the Saints" who, though experiencing the tragedy of existence within the framework of history, overcome it through the foretaste of Truth encountered in the Holy Eucharist.

In the communion of the Church, the Holy Eucharist offers the only occasion in history where individualism is healed in such a radical way. In the Eucharist, the "Body of Christ," both individually and ecclesiologically, is the *gathering* that is irreducible to its basic elements.[89] Hence, *soteriological assumptions in anthropology cannot be made outside the Holy Eucharist.* This represents a revolution in the history of thought

---

[89] "The Church is present in the Holy Mysteries (the Eucharist) not in symbols but as members of the heart, and as the branches of the root of the tree, and as the Lord Himself said, like the grapevines in the vine. For this is not a fellowship in name only, or some similarity by analogy, but this is the very same (identical) thing. For these mysteries are the Body and the Blood of Christ, and they are the real food and drink of Christ's Church...And if someone could see Christ's Church through the extent of one's unity with Christ and through the communion with His Body, he would see none other than only the Body of Christ... It is also obvious that everything that takes place in this divine service is communal for both the living and the departed (i.e. the entire community of the Saints)...What causes all the joy and blessedness for the departed saints (in Heaven), call it Paradise, or the bosom of Abraham, or the place of those freed from every pain and sorrow, a place full of light, freshness and refreshment, or the Kingdom itself—is nothing other than this Cup and this Bread (the Eucharist)...This is why the Lord called the delight of the Saints in the Age to come [to] the Supper, in order to demonstrate that there is nothing greater (in the Kingdom) than the Feast (the Eucharist)." N. Cabasilas, *Commentary on the Liturgy* 38, 43, 45. PG 150, 452–3, 461–5.

because the human subject is not regarded as a separate subject (a detached self) but an "I" who loves and is loved by the community, "the first born among many brothers" (Rom. 8:29). The grace-filled consequences of "being in communion" for man's true life are assured.[90] Love and freedom, the two key components of an authentic therapy, can overcome one's own pathology only in a deeply involved relationship, where love overcomes the biological selectiveness and narcissism and freedom becomes freedom for the other.[91] As a result, the Holy Eucharist, which is for the healing and for life eternal, eliminates our desire for death by not allowing the fusion of being and non-being, life and death, which is characteristic of our biochemical existence.

It is interesting to note that such spiritual teachings did not develop into "elitism." St. John of the Ladder says: "God is the life and salvation of all who are endowed with freedom: the believers and unbelievers, the righteous and unrighteous, the pious and impious, those who are dispassionate as well as those who are passionate, monastics and laypeople, the intelligent and the foolish, those who are healthy and those who are ill, the young and the old—just as the light, the sun and the air is for everyone without distinction. *For God does not show favoritism* (Rom. 2:11; cf. Eph. 6:9)." The very nature of the Eucharist cancels out divisions, which dictate nature, philosophy, sociology et al.

Accordingly, we can perceive that man's new ecclesial—his biologically transcended—hypostasis is actualized in a *kenotic* (suffering) way, and in an *anaphoric* (relational) way, leaving the last word to the Eschaton, that is, to the future true state of existence. The answer to the question: what kind of experience regarding the true person does the ecclesial hypostasis give us, is as follows. By becoming a member of a com-

---

[90] The following is written in the *Didache* text: "Search for a holy person each day, so that you can find peace through their words" (IV, 2; see also *Barnabas' Epistle* 19:10), In his commentary on this section, Athanasius Yevtich says: "Here the saints are the faithful=Christians like further below in H, 6, and in accordance with the New (Matt. 18:20) and the Old Testament (Sirach 6:28–36) and with St. Polycarp (*Philip* 12:3), and *Hermas Shepherd* (Vision 3:8)." Also, the Ladder and Ecclesiastes provide a very significant maxim, an antidote to individualism: "But pity the man who falls into despondency, or indolence, or idleness, or despair, and has no one to help him up!" (Eccl. 4:10). "For where two or three come together in my name, there am I with them," the Lord said (Matt. 18:20).

[91] "If you love those who love you, what credit is that to you? Even sinners love those who love them" (Luke 6:32).

munity of relations—the Church (which supercedes the exclusiveness of nature, social, racial, gender, and other aspects), man *learns to love and to extend his love beyond nature* (aesthetics, eros, class), that is, he is free from the law of his biological nature (individualism). He is not free only in respect to death.[92] As long as death has not been finally overcome, the ailing biochemistry will continue to last.

VI. Does a biochemistry of freedom exist?

Whether there exists a biochemistry of freedom depends on whether the anthropology of which we are speaking is "open" or "ekstatic." Next to the assumption of the complex structure of human nature, based on molecular and hormonal characteristics, man's otherness cannot be questioned, which remains transcendent and, for the greater part, not determined by a chemical hypostasis. "For who among men knows the thoughts of a man except the man's spirit within him" (1 Cor. 2:11); therefore, the very nature of the transcendent relation with God is unknown and, in the least, is certainly not obvious. Analogous to the problem of the so-called probability approximation of the evolutionary theory, where many evolutionary claims are not based on experimental validation but on reasonable and all the more justified hypothetical assumptions,[93] so too, the transcendent impulse cannot be experimentally validated. To put it simply, there are limits to natural knowledge and any biochemistry of freedom is conditional upon these limitations.

It is well known that contemporary genetic engineering can reduce the human *personal otherness* to a "chemical otherness," based on a chemical series of genetic information for the programming of living beings. An Orthodox approach to medicine rejects the pretense of a scientific-technological compilation and a chemical programming that can create

---

[92] The reason for this was successfully answered by Zizioulas in his study "Personhood and Being," *Being as Communion: Studies in Personhood and the Church* (London: Darton, Longman & Todd, 1985), pp. 27–68.

[93] These assumptions are followed by "this" or "that" interpretation, which without a doubt reveal a metaphysical view of the world. The epistemological naturalism, with its absolute exclusion of all transcendental interpretations of evolution, is in fact, epistemologically inconsistent because it establishes an *a priori* metaphysical view of the final purpose and meaning of the origin and development of the world and of life. Cf. T. Matulić, 205. Atheistic proselytism can readily be ascribed to Dawkins, which is otherwise uncharacteristic of a scientific method or position.

man-made identities and personal particulars independent of God. In fact, our approach with regard to genetic engineering[94] should lead to a "biochemical ecology" that bypasses the rock of scientific materialism (wherein man is defined as a complex of molecules; a biochemical "storehouse") and the whirlpool of theological spiritualism (a reduction of man to purely spiritual functions and moral behaviors). Man is a *twofold* being; he is not only of this immanent reality nor is he entirely transcendent; consequently, ignorance of neurobiological functions may prove to be very risky for pastoral psychotherapy, just as medical anthropology untempered by theology will fail to realize the difference between man and nature in its diagnosis. Although the fundamental difference between the Person (freedom) and Nature (unchangeable laws) should never be jeopardized, it is ironic that modern scientific research can lead to the virtual abolition of these differences.

Theologians are almost always faced with competing and different goals. Namely, how can one present a real but, objectively inaccessible dogma of Church life, and transform it so that it remains accurate, yet is comprehensible and relevant for those who have not experienced it?

Prior to any modern biochemical "explanation" of spirituality, biblical spirituality refused the ascription of a mechanical role through the introduction of the notion of "grace."[95] Grace, neither conditional to biochemistry nor anything else, points to God's free, uncoerced gift of Himself, and to His unreserved regard for man's freedom. Grace is the divine action within us, free of coercion and awkwardness. It is a personal call, an embrace of our most intimate and innermost chords, which opens us for His visitation, and brings about our restoration in the joy of our Bridegroom. It is an action that, as the bishop prays in the prayer of ordination, "*heals infirmities and covers deficiencies.*" The "spirituality" that emerges from this grace-filled relationship is, therefore, precious within theology because it points to the *supra*-biochemical reality of this relation, to the non-determinism of the encounter and communication. Therefore, the concept of grace, as developed in Eastern patristics, rests on the concept of absolute freedom, an uncoerced and unconditional

---

[94] See Thomas Eisner, "Chemical Ecology and Genetic Engineering," *A Symposium on Tropical Biology and Agriculture*, St. Louis, USA, July 15, 1985.

[95] With regard to this notion refer to New Testament encyclopedias, also Lampe Patristic Lexicon, et al.

gift, and not on the excess of man's nature, like a *donum supranaturalis*.[96] Grace does not act upon human freedom in an overwhelming way (cf. θεαρχικὴ ἀσθένεια).

The teaching of Maximus the Confessor on the *gnomic will* (which is clearly distinct from the real, or free, will, that is, the free will) is the theological key to understanding biochemistry and neurobiology; and so is his teaching of the *logoi of beings*, those eschatological movement "navigators" that direct beings toward their final goal.[97] The freedom of choice (St. Augustine's "libertas minor") implied by the gnomic will (θέλημα γνωμικὸν) could be explained biochemically since biochemistry employs a duality and ambiguity when describing the activity level of the brain stem, where specific recorded chemical reactions take place. However, freedom "for" is an affirmation of a being in communion with God, and is therefore not subject to psychosomatic processes.[98] Christology

---

[96] Not only is human nature not at variance with grace, but quite the contrary, it ne-cessitates grace and lives normally only with the help of grace. Divine grace is not some kind of a "surplus" (the scholastic "*donum supranaturalis*") which nature can live with or without by means of its "pure nature" ("natura pura"). On the contrary, in Orthodox an-thropology, divine grace is precisely the life of the human being's soul and of his entire nature, to the extent that, if deprived of that life, the soul dies. The person whose life is deprived of the grace of the Holy Spirit, becomes dead; his apparel turns into an apparel of mortality, debauchery and corruption" (A. Yevtich, *Pravoslavna asketika*, pp. 45–46).

[97] Refer to *Ambigua* 7 (Maximus' interpretation of *Homily* 14 by Gregory the Theologian).

[98] Freedom, or rather the feeling and state of freedom as the *process of willful decision-making*, can be measured in two ways that correspond to the chief manifestations of our thoughts and feelings. They are a) the electrical impulses of the nervous system, primar-ily the brain, and b) the metabolic rate, that is the consumption and production of spe-cific molecules, which can be measured indirectly. The electrical brain activity can be measured by the EEG or MRI techniques on a live human being (which was not possible several decades ago), whereas the rate of metabolism is best measured by PET, which es-sentially records the consumption of glucose in certain parts of the body. This method is able to measure some of the other molecules, too. The MRI is also indicative of the blood circulation, which in turn is indicative of its activity. It is also important to know that the electrical and chemical manifestations of our activities are essentially the same; they are interconnected. The electrical transmission of information is stronger and quicker, how-ever, both at the beginning and at the end there are chemical signals, by means of the neurotransmitters and molecules, which activate various metabolic processes within the cells. These processes regulate primarily the activity of the genes, which leads to an in-creased or decreased synthesis of the essential metabolic substances, which can ultimate-ly be measured, and there are some that separate from each other and these represent the impulses from the environment. This explains how often our intuition is more accurate

can perhaps best solve this problem, where a real relation exists between the vital, instinctive, rational, and self-determining (self-governing) aspects of the human will. Christ's prayer to His Father in Gethsemane is an ideal example. Thus D. Bathrellos emphasizes, "Christ's aversion to death is viewed by Maximus as an expression of His human will. But His decision to obey the will of the Father, a decision that plainly relates to the rational, self-determining aspect of the will, is seen as an expression of Christ's human will too, and obviously the latter [rational] had the power to counteract the former [instinctive]."[99]

Thus grace, as the personal visitation of God, awakens one's freedom, which now renewed and sanctified (and filled), opposes the "will of the flesh"—to those absolute natural desires resistant to spiritual life—that had overpowered the free will by conquering one's internal space.

In view of the significance of this personal grace, that is, the hypostasized energies of God, one can offer a more definite answer.

Every man has an *otherness* with regard to his psychological and physical aspects (earlier on there were fingerprints, presently there is the biometry[100] of the eye and DNA). It appears, namely, that every human being is also unique in his physical form of existence, which is contrary to the opinion that man's uniqueness applies only to his soul.[101] On the other hand, let us assume that the human being shares more than 98% of his genes with the chimpanzee. While some consider that the distinction between man and the chimpanzee lies in the fact that the former is a linguistic being, others see man's freedom in the differ-

than "objective and logical knowledge" (which is based only on external facts). However, as our study suggests, these techniques and measurements register only the *consequences* or *results* of willful decision-making, not the freedom itself. The difference is immense. For further reading see the following studies: Bernard J. Baars, "How Brain Reveals Mind. Neural Studies Support the Fundamental Role of Conscious Experience," *Journal of Consciousness Studies*, No. 9–10/2003, pp. 100–114; Dhamala et al. "Measurements of brain activity complexity for varying mental loads," *Physical Review E*, 65/2002, 041917; J. Schwartz, Jeffrey M., *The Mind & The Brain: Neuroplasticity and the power of mental force*, Harper Collins Publishing, New York, 2002.

[99] *The Byzantine Christ*, p. 126.

[100] There are, for the most part, the optically–based biometric techniques; retinal scanning and iris–recognition are the most familiar ones.

[101] This is the teaching about the continued existence of the soul while the body undergoes decomposition. Thus the soul prevails not only axiologically but ontologically as well. The modern Orthodox "theologian of the soul" must take into consideration this physical uniqueness.

ence between the two, which points to the fact that DNA does not determine man! We share almost everything and yet the *differentia specifica* proves to be so radical and solid![102] The Holy Fathers observed much earlier that the only difference lies in man's *freedom*. Yannaras observes with great discernment how the new field of chronobiology seizes the opportunity to set aside a "biological clocked-timed rhythm" of the bodily functions, whereby each *individual is unique in his biological clock* (the biological functions of each individual follow a separate and special "clock"). But even if next to this exceptional periodic rhythm, we choose a time "constant" for the subject's biological otherness, this constant does not represent an objectification of hypostasized identity. Instead, it is just another proof of the otherness in the dynamic and periodic occurrences of biological functions.[103]

Nevertheless, the recognition that the greater part of human consciousness is a natural-biological product does not cancel out the truth that God is able to "touch" the existential chords of man that are beyond neurobiological processes. Now, the question to be asked is about the nature of God's action in man, both psychologically and physically. What happens to the individual genes, to the hormones and neurotransmitters when God touches our existential chords? When, for instance, according to John of the Ladder, "Jesus...will come to uproot the wall of coarseness from the heart and free the mind from the attachment to sins," will the hormones then be "disturbed"; will they be "happy"? To this provocative question we encounter a tantalizing answer within a single sentence from the works of St. Maximus, wherein it appears that the action in question is not linked to neurobiology or to biochemistry but to freedom, which God "sets in motion" in an *uncreated* way: "the Divine itself is subject to movement since it produces an inward state (σχέσιν ἐνδιάθετον) of intense longing (erotic force) and love in those receptive (τοῖς δεκτικοῖς) to them; it moves others since by nature it attracts the desire of those who are drawn toward it."[104] Thus God actually sets in motion our relation to

[102] As the paper "Sense and Sensibility" by H. McCabe in *God Still Matters* (2002) demonstrates.

[103] *Philosophie sans rupture*, p. 243.

[104] *Ambigua*, PG 91, 1260c. Therefore, it is up to us to make an effort, but it is God who decides. St. Agathon was asked the following question: "Is it possible that you are afraid, too, father," whereupon he answered: "Until now I have made an effort with all

Him in a manner of absolute freedom; every other existing relation (natural, human, or "religious") represents a kind of "threat" to our freedom, which is exemplified in friendly, marital, social and similar relations. The human subject can attain this free communion and become God-like only when he is led into this divine relation. In this relation the genes, directed by the hormones and neurotransmitters, no longer control our bodies and minds. It is this transcendent relation and *tropos* which controls our bodies, minds, and hence our lives.[105] The philosopher Sartre once said that it is not physiology that affects our emotions but *vice versa*.[106]

In view of the above realization, it is no wonder that Maximus the Confessor was able to explain the physiology of the will and its role in overcoming fragmentation and death through the example of remembrance of wrongs. He writes that the state in which we call to mind our past sins occurs when a memory lingers in our mind, gradually fragmenting the "nature willingly" because remembrance of wrongs brings one into conflict with another who shares the same nature. This process stands in stark contrast to the love for one's enemies leading to true union of the free will with the logos of nature. Through such love, nature ceases to rebel against itself through the action of the free will, which leads to reconciliation with God Himself.[107] The only authentic way out of the vicious circle of this biochemical predicament is by connecting it with Christology and ecclesiology, that is, with the life of the Holy Mysteries of the Church.

VII. Biochemistry and the Eschaton

In the final analysis, the relation and tropos between God and man determines the life of man and, thereby, fashions the skein of history

my might, but I do not know whether my effort is pleasing to God; for God's judgment is one thing and man's is another" (*Gerontikon*, Novi Sad, 2008, pp. 85–85).

[105] Cf. B. Lipton, *The Biology of Belief*, xxvi. Cf. the saying: "Jesus the Conqueror, lift up my mind to Your Divine heights, so that it will reason with Your reason and not with the madness of sin and death" (Bishop Nikolaj of Žiča, *Akathist to Christ the Conqueror of Death*, Irmos 1, 2nd Ode).

[106] R. Solomon, see aforementioned work, section "Are Emotions 'in' the Mind?," pp. 186–195.

[107] For, "if the free will unites itself with the logos of nature then he who has established this unity will not rebel against God" (PG 90, 901). Cf. J. Zizioulas, "Eucharist and the Kingdom of God," *Sourozh* 60/1995, p. 41.

threading through the lives of many; yet it is not history, but the age to come that determines the last word on biochemistry and ascetic theology. How does biochemistry appear in light of the Eschaton, that is, in light of the future true existence? Are we willing to study the biochemical status of man in light of his future condition and not restrict ourselves only to those factors that define man as a biological being?

The Eschaton, as the true state of existence, sheds light on the problem of the human chemical substrate in a decisive way, through the perception of man as the "law of nature" (λόγος τῆς φύσεως, genotype[108]) that does *not* change the human body as a biochemical mechanism. However, there is an *epigenetical* change, that is, the "mode of existence" changes in a radical manner. In patristics, the general rule applies, according to which all God-given *forces* (including those that appear to be negative, such as anger and lust) are positive as long as they are in accordance with God. The moment they cease to be so, they become passions. Their aim is no longer the Desired One (God); instead they become an aim unto themselves. According to St. Maximus, when they become goals unto themselves, they remove the central Desire as the most exalted goal of complete fullness; they become contractions and, as such, they require transfiguration.[109] The Eschaton will show—Orthodox patristics and asceticism bear witness to this—that nothing of all that exists is created unto perdition but rather for a *change* in its mode of existence. Thus eros becomes an authentically insatiable loving desire, aggression (anger) a fiery zeal for the Truth, the mind (reason) assembles all the λόγοι into one,[110] and the soul becomes inhospitable to faintheartedness and unbelief...God transfigures us by His personal presence according to our desire and receptiveness, respecting our otherness, and changes the mode of be-

---

[108] The genotype is internally coded, hereditary information intrinsic to living organisms. This deposited information is used as a "pattern" or as a set of instructions for the development and maintenance of a living being. These instructions are in (the internal part of) almost every cell, are genetically coded, and are copied during the reproductive phase of the cells at which time they are transmitted onto the next generation of cells ("inherited").

[109] "The state of eternal movement is the continual and uninterrupted *enjoyment in the Desired One*" which further means "participating in the *supranatural* Divine realities" (μέθεξις δέ τῶν ὑπέρ φύσιν θείων) Maximus, *Ad Thalassium* 60; PG 90, 608d.

[110] Therefore, in St. Maximus's fashion, by uniting his free will unites with the *logos of nature* he who has established this unity will not rebel against God, man and the nature but live and act in a manner that gives space to his highest Desire.

ing. The hardware remains the same whereas the software undergoes a change. History, human nature, and culture become a "burning bush without being consumed."

It is possible to arrive at this *tropos* only because the human person has a reference; a reference *pointing* to a factor outside the human being, and hence to an uncreated ontology, that is, to the existence of God. This tropos cannot be realized within the framework of history without suffering (πάθος). Namely, since the human psychophysical structure is in a "fallen" state, man inevitably has to go the way of the Cross, through the *narrow gates* that lead into the Kingdom. Freedom from "selfish genes" and "narcissistic-like molecules," achieved by the saints, is only possible by not avoiding a *martyrium* and by the honest acceptance of human limitations and weaknesses. At the same time, this also proves to be a golden opportunity in the life of a human being for the action of the Holy Spirit and his grace to become manifest. Sooner or later, every saint recognizes, through his own painstaking experience, that it is not our personal struggle against the passions and the overcoming of our fallen biochemistry that leads to salvation; this is accomplished by Him who sees our efforts (it is not he who reaps or he who sows but it is up to the Lord). By experiencing their own infirmities through the foretaste of the gift of the Kingdom, the ascetics experienced such love that it could be celebrated as "the greatest of all" (1 Cor. 13:8–13).

The Church has offered both Baptism and the Eucharist as two Mysteries through which we can overcome our fallen biochemistry. In Baptism, the person is immersed into Christ's death, that is, the actual death of the old man and of his "methods of knowledge"[111] and natural passions. Resurrecting as a new man with Christ, continually renewed and transfigured in the image of Christ, the God-Man, and, according to the Apostle Paul, acquiring a *new mind*, the *"mind of Christ"* (1 Cor. 2:16), the person emerges from the baptismal font free to fully participate in the life of Christ through receiving the Holy Eucharist.

The Eucharist does not only give a foretaste, but what may be even more important, gives a *warranty* for eschatological health and healing!

---

[111] St. Diadochos of Photiki emphasizes that "natural love of the soul is one thing and love that is generated by the Holy Spirit in the soul is another," *Gnostic Chapters*, 34; A. Yevtich, "Metodologija bogoslovlja," [The Methodology of Theology] *Pravoslavna teologija* (a collection of studies and articles), Belgrade, 1995, p. 210.

"We have seen the true light, we have received the Holy Spirit, we have found the true faith..." is not *licentia poetica*, words that exude poetic freedom, but is the fruit of the free gift of communion, belonging to the future, and, containing a pledge of fidelity to the same. The Eucharist, administered correctly,[112] is a place of healing, not because it offers immediate "alleviation" but because it is a "medicine of immortality" which has a long-term effect—as a warranty of future health—and which is received as a gift by the community and persons therein. By virtue of being the *place* of healing, it is the means and *manner* by which one arrives from self-love to the love of God and to brotherly love.

Unfortunately, the eschatological dimension of this problem cannot be satisfactorily studied and is beyond the scope of this presentation. I will have to postpone this task to another time.

VIII. Implications

I will now attempt to present a few implications significant to theology.

Educational consequences. In the works of the Holy Fathers, education is concerned with the ethos, that is, with the creation of psychological and physical lifetime habits, and with man's correct response to the complexities of the cosmos, and to social and cultural relations. From the earliest developmental stages of its life, the habit formation of a "young" biochemical entity in response to specific situations, patterns, rituals, forms et al., attains its true purpose by responding to God's call. This call is in the voice of Christ's evangelical Eucharist, in His Church, and above all in the heart of man, that inner spiritual sense by means of which the Apostles and Martyrs recognized the source of life and of salvation; in the heart of an unknown and, by all appearances, ordinary and inconspicuous man whom God has invited us to follow.

Implications for pastoral practice. Priests, spiritual fathers, and ascetics should at least be acquainted with the basic neuro-biochemical features

---

[112] It is, therefore, a tragic hypocrisy of our times that following a liturgical dialogue between the priest and the faithful—a dialogue of which the main topic is *communion*—the communion of the faithful is missing. Following a series of affirmative answers (from "Amen" to "Take, eat...," "Drink of this *all of you*...," and further on "With fear of God ....come forth," "Blessed is he who comes...," "Having received the Divine Mysteries...," "Lord have mercy" and "We thank Thee...," "Amen") one should ask who is deceiving whom and what is the purpose of such dialogue, when its main subject (=communion) is ultimately left out in practice?

of human nature and know that the complex actions pertaining to life (particularly "theoretical" ones) are the result of the work of millions of neurotransmitters. In addition to that, they should have a personal experience with evangelical therapeutics. Our Savior's story about the sowing of the seed (Matt. 13:10–23) and its interpretation are indicative of our topic within the context of pastoral care. The disciples asked Christ, "Why do you speak to the people in parables," to which He answered, "the knowledge of the secrets of the kingdom of heaven has been given to you, but not to them." A personal insight into the secrets of the Kingdom is given to the friends of the Bridegroom, whereas regarding the others, He "speaks in parables ... for though seeing they do not see; though hearing they do not hear or understand." What the prophet Elijah spoke of occurs outside a personal encounter: "You will be ever hearing but never understanding; you will be ever seeing but never perceiving. *For this people's heart has become calloused; they hardly hear with their ears, and they have closed their eyes. Otherwise they might see with their eyes, hear with their ears, understand with their hearts and turn, and I would heal them"* (cf. Acts 28:27). Afterward our Savior added for those who knew Him personally, "But blessed are your eyes because they see and your ears because they hear." This is followed by the important explanation of the story about the sower, although it is actually man's relation to his transcendent cause that is emphasized: "When anyone hears the message about the kingdom and does not understand it, the evil one comes and snatches what was sown in his heart. This is the seed sown along the path" (verse 19). This stands for what God Himself has pledged and placed as a "connection," which man loses through his own negligence. This is what happens to he who does not understand the invitation: "The one who received the seed that fell on rocky places is the man who hears the word and at once receives it with joy. But since he has no root, he lasts only a short time. When trouble or persecution comes because of the word, he quickly falls away" (verses 20–21). What happens to those who are weighed down by the worries of "this world"? "The one who received the seed that fell among the thorns is the man who hears the word, but the worries of this life and the deceitfulness of wealth choke it, making it unfruitful" (verse 22). "But the one who received the seed that fell on good soil is the man who hears the word and understands it. He produces a crop yielding a hundred, sixty or thirty times what was sown" (verse 23).

Toward a *synthesis of a person-energy-orientated approach to theology.* The notion of hypostasized energies accurately portrays what happens in life. Human nature is steadfastly engaged with this world through its "energies" (emotions, consciousness, intellect etc.), but the character of that relation is dependent on the person (τρόπος ὑπάρξεως). The human genotype is manifested in the energies—a smile, joy and sorrow, anger—and the energies are the manifestation of the person. (Biochemical or psychosomatic disorders may be the result of genetics, the environment or learning). In contrast to established opinion, the energies by themselves are not the key to the solution of anthropological and cosmological questions. The Protestant world has a tendency to view energies, that is, the positive actions (mostly thoughts) of man as an influence not only on his soul but on his biological makeup as well, which is clearly an anthropocentric approach.[113] Even if it is true that there may be a biochemistry of a free will (see sections 2 and 3), one should not forget that biochemistry, too, is under the control of the person, that both the biochemical phenomena and energies are personal, that they point to the personal otherness, and actually demonstrate it, and, of course, that they do not exist without the person. One should also know that in Christology (and, therefore, in the other branches of theology) the hypostatic unity, in which the person possesses the energies of nature, is of crucial importance, not the interaction of the features and energies (*communicatio idiomatum*).

Consequences for missionary work. As a result of this, Orthodox missionary work emphasizes that God calls upon every man without exception. He knocks on the door of the heart ("Here I am! I stand at the door and knock. If anyone hears my voice and opens the door, I will come in and eat with him, and he with me," Rev. 3:20). Sooner or later, at a certain moment in one's life, everyone without fail has the opportunity to open his or her door and to meet with our Lord Christ. While one is at work in the boat of one's life, mending the various torn nets of one's plans, hopes, expectations, anxieties and worries, enthusiasms, and all the rest that make up the fabric of our lives in this world, there will come a moment when he or she will leave all at the beckoning of Christ. Mis-

---

[113] This is the key issue in Bruce Lipton's book presented here: *The Biology of Belief,* 2008. On bookstore shelves are appearing an increasing number of popular books on spirituality, describing many ways of influencing human life through positive thoughts via energies.

sionary work starts from this very belief that every human being experiences such an encounter, in ways so manifold, wonderful, and mysteriously impossible to enumerate or describe and least of all to explain through biochemistry.

Risks. There are risks to medical therapy in the treatment of human passions, *self-love* as the chief one in particular. If a molecular basis for the passions and virtues exists, what conditions would have to be established in the case of molecular screening in diagnostics and what would reduce—if not altogether eliminate—risks associated with the human person? It is important to know that the *Human Genome Project* is still in the research phase (until recently led by Francis Collins). The problem in determining a hereditary pattern of behavior, of which many are pathogenic, lies in their polygenic basis. The multiple-factor hypothesis, which explains the different levels of genetic integration, should be one of the primary points of interest here. John Zizioulas is perhaps the only Orthodox theologian who has set up a list of conditions that society should insist upon as a minimum guarantee for the protection of the person. In the case of administering such a therapy, he poses vital questions. For instance: "is the knowledge of someone else's genetic defects in actual fact going to lead to the prevention or to the cure of a potential anomaly or terminal illness? How great is the risk for an individual, left with his or her health information, to be deprived of the possibility of a scientific follow-up?"[114] The collection of information on the kind of grand scale the Project entails is of great concern because, if the sequentialization of entire genomes becomes a routine procedure, it is not clear who will guarantee the privacy of DNA donors to the so-called "biobanks." On the other hand, those individuals who donate their genotype and phenotype to databases for research are considered "health information altruists."[115]

Legal consequences. If the genetic manipulation of the hormone and molecules could successfully change the "status quo," human freedom would have to face fundamental challenges. First of all, such changes would be engendered by people themselves, which is a much more seri-

[114] J. Zizioulas, "Ličnost čoveka i nova naučna kretanja," [Human Person and the New Scientific Developements] *Vidoslov* 21/200, pp. 51–52.

[115] David Gurwitz et al. "Children and Population Biobanks," *Science*, 14 August 2009, Vol. 325, pp. 818–819.

ous challenge, perhaps even unacceptable, in comparison to the inevitability imposed upon the person by nature. For example, God did not impose immortality upon the human being, but made it subject to his or her freedom of choice; in effect, granting humanity the freedom to choose to be enslaved to nature, and hence to mortality.[116] Even if science was able to offer immortality to the human being against his will, man as a person should have the freedom to reject it and to choose mortality if he so wills. This, in fact, is precisely what Adam chose, and what God held in utmost regard.[117]

The Holy Fathers say that "nature" bequeaths man's free will an "unpleasant feeling" of bondage, leading to its final mortality. Zizioulas asks the following interesting question: "What difference is there between the bondage to nature and the bondage to other people?" In any case, is the person a slave to nature, even without any scientific interventions and manipulations? In answer, we observe that the human person, although reluctant and not without frustrations and protests, has adapted to the limitations imposed by nature. Bondage to people, though, represents something altogether unacceptable to the person.[118]

Consequences for bioethics. The impatience of science to explain each atom, molecule and hormone can easily turn into an arrogance depriving life's mysteries of their enchantment. Scientific research can be productive only if it does not deprive the wonderful meaning—deeply hidden in biochemical substrates—of its mysteriousness, and does not ascribe to it erroneous attributes et al....If science trespasses the boundaries of the species, the human person will establish his or her otherness with regard to nature not on the basis of given distinctions as beings, but on the basis of particularities, drawn up by science by means of its crude interventions, held in common. Science, in effect, could limit humanity's ability to transcend its fallen state.

The threat of such science gone awry applies even when man is understood as an immaterial soul-entity, separated from the body, or when it is located in physical characteristics and processes (the condition of the

---

[116] It is altogether another question why God gave mankind another chance in the New Adam, i.e. Christ, in spite of man's free will and of his freedom to choose life outside of Life (=God).

[117] The entire argument in this passage belongs to J. Zizioulas, "Ličnost čoveka i nova naučna kretanja," p. 50.

[118] Ibid., p. 49.

brain, memory, etc.). Since the meaning of salvation, as we shall see further on, is already articulated in the revelation of the personal God, the same cannot be *verified* through scientific epistemology. The genetic and hormonal basis of man is the precondition of his natural function, but a part of it can influence his *freedom*, that constitutive and transcendent aspect of the person. As a result, an interesting question is whether changes in the characteristics of the person, attained by means of genetic engineering, can lead to the complete destruction of the freedom of an individual, and to the ultimate nightmare of the creation of human beings whose characteristics and particularities are determined by the will of others.

IX. Conclusions

These are the basic conclusions that can be drawn from the study of ancient tradition and applied to neurological assumptions of asceticism. Let us summarize them.

In this study I have tried to document the compatibility, the incompatibility, and at times also the complementarity of the ancient ascetic authors with contemporary approaches in psychiatry and psychotherapeutic schools. This was done in the form of comments, observations, descriptions and some proposed therapeutic methods as well. In addition, this study points to something much deeper and broader, that is, to the truthfulness of Orthodox Christian anthropology, and to the solid and healthy framework of the salvific and therapeutic approach it offers to every man. A sober, careful and empathetic approach of an ascetic elder toward his novices along with his consideration of the external (environmental), internal (psychological) and somatic (neuroendocrine) circumstances of the human condition, are actually indicators of the correct approach to man, which entails a concern for the entire human being. The question as to why a monk was so insensitive, depressed, or even despondent on a particular day or moment can be answered in more than one way; however, hormonal explanations should not be overlooked.[119] The extent to which the hormonal contributions evoke a greater or lesser

---

[119] Modern science contends that there is a very strong connection between depression, the cortex and the limbic system. Sapolsky describes depression in a simplified manner. "Your cortex takes on those abstract and sad thoughts and induces the hypothalamus to assent, and, that is like an elephant grabbing you with its trunk. Simply speaking, this is an overgrown diseased cortex that regulates the limbic and hypothalamic regions" (R. Sapolsky, *Why Zebras don't get Ulcers*, Holt/Owl, 2004, p. 286).

sensitivity to a specific "trigger in the environment," causing the brain to manifest specific behaviors and not others is a vital line of reasoning. The hormones, evolution, the genes and behavior, certainly do not operate in a vacuum but are exceptionally sensitive to nature and to the social environment. Human nature has an immediate involvement with the world through its "energies" (emotions, consciousness, intellect, etc.); however, the nature of that involvement depends on the person (τρόπος ὑπάρξεως) and on the character of that person.

These theological conclusions, translated into the language of church therapeutics, demonstrate that the wholesomeness of man depends on the following conditions:

One can acknowledge the existence of a biochemistry of the natural *will*, but not a biochemistry of *freedom* since the latter evades biochemistry in a manner that is both mysterious and experientially real, mainly because of God's salvific action and His transforming presence in us and among us.[120]

Consequently, a hopeless determinism that reduces freedom to impulses and instincts does not exist.

Orthodox theology needs to develop an ethos of freedom and love in order to create a *bioethical culture* that acknowledges the soteriological motive behind dogma; within such a culture, transcendence would be implicit in the very notion of true freedom and complete healing would be understood as possible only through Jesus Christ. Until the development of this culture, human freedom remains a mystery, even though it is revealed, and although—paradoxically—consciousness of it is not self-evident. After all, it is an illusion to believe that the task of biology is the establishment of what a living organism is; biology is oc-

---

[120] The next passage from St. Maximus indicates how important freedom and synergy are: "For the grace of the Holy Spirit does not effect wisdom in the Saints without the mind that grasps it; nor knowledge without the power of the reason that is capable of it (τῆς δεκτικῆς τοῦ λόγου δυνάμεως); nor faith apart from the fullness of the mind and reason concerning the things that are to come, and which until now have remained hidden from us; nor the gifts of healing apart from natural philanthropy; nor any of other gifts apart from the faculty and power of grasping each (gift) (χωρὶς τῆς ἑκάστου δεκτικῆς ἕξεώς τε καὶ δυνάμεως)" (*Ad Thalassium*, 59; PG 90, 605b). And concludes the Confessor: "On the other hand, none of the things listed does a man acquire by its natural powers, apart from the Divine power that bestows them" (οὔτε μὴν πάλιν ἕν τῶν ἀπηριθμημένων ἄνθρωπος κτήσεται κατὰ δύναμιν φυσικήν, δίχα τῆς χορηγούσης ταῦτα θείας δυνάμεως) (Ibid.).

cupied with what we are able to say about the living organism. Our statements though are limited without exception.

Regarding the topic of freedom and love, the following question will always need to be answered by anthropology: to what extent is man determined by his genetic code? Is his freedom the result of elementary biochemical processes, as modern biology (neurobiology) suggests? Is our functioning dependent on "exercised" and "trained," that is learned, suggestions, whether using a theistic or an atheistic approach? To what extent is our consciousness entirely a natural-biological product?

In the spirit of contemporary neurobiology, we can claim that the natural view a religious man has of this world is always *selective*. So, he always searches for his beforehand selected object, his appointed goal and interest, since the angle of his observation is determined on the basis of his biochemical and neurobiological "habits," which define his theoretical interests, assumptions and anticipations, that is, his point of reference and his expectations. However, it is not possible to decipher the transcendent aspect of man by means of mathematical models or chemical elements. Since faith is a gift ("...flesh and blood hath not revealed it unto thee but my Father which is in heaven"—Matt. 16:17), its path is evidently different from, for instance, the path of emotional anxiety or sorrow, which can be chemically "described" and "dismembered." Paraphrasing Heisenberg, when a neurobiologist develops a scientific formula for the description of the biochemistry of love, in reality, he does not describe a genuine love but the love that was exhibited to his method of scientific research. God as well as God's action will never lend itself to neurobiology as an *objective subject matter*, since He is always the Subject, the Initiator and the Originator of communication with man. With His logos He "penetrates even to dividing the soul and spirit, joints and marrow; it judges the thoughts and attitudes of the heart" (Heb. 4:12). This fact prevents Him from being the object of "ascertainments," let alone, to be "under the control" of or dependent upon cognitive abilities and techniques. In contrast to the natural sciences, the object of investigation in theology *cannot* be controlled (something which is necessary in a setting of repeated experimental trials in order to obtain the same results) because "God is not a cat that scratches you when you pull it by its tail."[121]

[121] Bishop Athanasius (Yevtich), "O apofatičkom i katafatičkom bogoslovlju," [On Apophatic and Cataphatic Theology] *Filosofija i teologija*, Vrnjci, 2004, 181.

When He appears, and this depends *solely* upon His will or "caprice," it is then that we can speak of God's revelation and only then do we have the possibility for an empirical epistemology and gnosiology, which is once again dependent upon His wish to be known if He so desires, and only according to the measure and in the manner of that desire. The revelation and knowledge of God cannot be approached through the formulation of basic models, which describe and predict an event in an identifiable manner. A scientist cannot penetrate uninvited into the intimate relationship between God and man no matter what kind of cognitive capacities, techniques, or disciplines may be at his disposal. "*The Personal God in communion with man as a person—is the alpha and omega of the Orthodox knowledge of God.*"[122] By the same token, because empirical validations of any characteristic of God are unobtainable apart from the personal relation, the encounter and faith[123] (as an experience of freedom), there are established boundaries to theological research.

Although God constantly sends us His loving, transcendent invitation, He does not have the pathos of a forceful bestower of happiness, instead "the Spirit himself intercedes for us with groans that words cannot express" (Rom. 8:26) and only He has the key to the riddle of the mystery of salvation, of healing, and of the purpose of man's existence in history.

---

[122] V. Perišić, "Nad Ljubostinskim Stoslovom" in *Sveti Vladika Nikolaj Ohridski i Žički*, Žiča–Kraljevo, 2003, pp. 401–404.

[123] "Divine contemplation is given to man not at the time he has specifically set this as his goal but when the soul has descended to the hell of repentance and truly recognizes that it is worse than any other creature. Contemplations achieved through the effort of one's reason are not true contemplations but imaginary. When the imaginary is accepted as true, a certain state within the soul is created, which obstructs the very possibility of the action of grace, that is, of true contemplation" (Archimandrite Sophrony, *Starac Siluan*, ed. Hilandar, 1998, p. 151). Karl Barth, also, sees the foundation of theology not in epistemological techniques but in faith corresponding to the other teachings of the Christian West, including Roman Catholicism and the Reformation.

Lord Jesus Christ
(icon by Andrei Rublev, 1410)

An Existential Interpretation of Dogmatics

Theological Language and Dogma in the Face of the Culture of Pluralism

"There is no dogma of our Church that does not have something to say about the actual problems of humanity" (J. Zizioulas)

I. Introductory remarks

"No man has seen God at any time; the only begotten Son, who is in the bosom of the Father, He has *explained* (ἐξηγήσατο, made known) Him" (Jn 1:18). The contents of theology are quite complex, mostly because they are related to the great mystery of the existence or *the way* (τρόπος) of God, and therefore of man and the Church. As we know, theology is not about whether or not God exists; its theme, rather, is *how* He exists (cf. 1 Jn 3:2). Other important questions depend on this main and crucial question: Can one participate in God personally, or not? Is He in communication with the world, or not? Such fundamental questions, which go beyond dry academic inquests and their answers, have immediate consequences for man's general attitude toward the world and life. It is in such a spirit that I propose to submit for your consideration certain reflections on the way I understand the challenges for Orthodox theology and Orthodox theological education in the twenty-first century.

Our Orthodox Church, which is none other than the One, Holy, Catholic and Apostolic Church, being in the image of the Holy Trinity[1]

---

[1] See the incomparable interpretation of the Eucharistic Liturgy in the *Mystagogy* of St. Maximus the Confessor (PG 91, 657–718). The "ecclesia" of the *Mystagogy* can be considered as a type of the providential action of God, and moreover as a reflection of God's relational being on His economical work. St. Maximus and the Cappadocian Fathers see the relational ontology of Trinitarian personhood as the source of the communion of the Church and the very basis of anthropology.

is relational and inescapably of an *incarnational* (and not *docetic*) nature, which is why it actualizes Truth *hic et nunc*, by accepting human history and culture. From the very beginning, the Church could not live and go on simply "as if" Christ had been incarnate, as the docetists would believe.[2] As the servant of Truth, with her all-embracing vision of the recapitulation of the world, the Church *had* to affect the cultural milieu. However, it is my strong belief that without theological awareness, sensitivity and criteria, the transmitting of the message of the Gospel into the world and time (the so-called "inculturation") can be a very hazardous endeavor. The acceptance of history and culture emerges through a *critical*, prophetic approach. As the late Fr. Georges Florovsky said, "Without sober guidance, without the stable element of sound doctrine, our feelings would but err and our hearts would be blinded."[3] If the twenty-first century is going to be a century of Orthodoxy,[4] as the renowned British Byzantinologist S. Runciman has said, then our theological education and schools have an immense responsibility placed on their weak shoulders to witness to the Truth.

The close of the twentieth century and the arrival of the new millennium have brought changes of fundamental significance for Christians. Modernity—that heady combination of science, learning and democracy, with its latest form: globalization—has been replaced by post-modernity, in which everything is *relative*, even the sense of ultimate reality and of existence itself. Happily, as a counterbalance, a flourishing Orthodox theology has in recent decades rediscovered its patristic sources, has recognized the magnitude of the *"lex orandi"* grounded in the *Eucharistic* experience of God, and has revived the spirit of the Desert Fathers in and through a genuine monastic revitalization of remarkable dimensions. Yet, a creative encounter is to be had with a world that has experienced marvelous achievements, but whose culture is dominated by the greed of utilitarianism and self-justification. Caution is necessary because culture,

---

[2] V. Thermos, "Ecclesiological Docetism," *Synaxi* III, Alexander Press 2006, 137.

[3] G. Florovsky, "A Criticism of the Lack of Concern for Doctrine among Russian Orthodox Believers," *SVTQ* 3 (1995); also in *The Collected Works of Georges Florovsky*, vol. 13, 168–70.

[4] At least, it will be a century of religion. And while European liberals sneer about American theocracy, American conservatives claim that secular, childless Europe, through a continued descent into Godlessness, is turning into Eurabia (a takeover by Islam). We rapidly move into a religiously pluralistic world.

as a very complex matter, is impossible to differentiate from the world-view it expresses. Thus, in the new millennium a *proper* inculturation of Christianity will be vital for the Church's existence. Orthodox theology and Orthodox theological education have to articulate the meaning of salvation in such a way as to prevent it from being falsified by accommodation to the demands of culture.

Our task in this presentation is to identify certain realms (disciplines) in the Church's life and to see how they relate to existential human needs.[5] The Church Fathers had marked success in interpreting the Gospel in existential terms by entering into a deep dialogue with the surrounding culture. I will also attempt to identify certain dichotomies that I believe are responsible for the failure of our theology to accomplish such a task. Furthermore, I will try to explain why I believe it is so important to interpret the Gospel in such existential terms. Orthodox theological education must help determine how to unify the Bible and the dogma of the Church, how to overcome the separation of dogma from ethics, and how to bring closer the *lex credendi* (faith) and *lex orandi* (devotion), whose dichotomy provokes a significant crisis in our days, as well as clarifying other similar dichotomies, such as dogma and canon law, ecclesiology and Church administration, or ecclesial and modern art and emphasizing their unity. Also requiring clarification is how Church institutions (bishop, synod, priesthood, etc.) are connected with the doctrinal substance of the Church, how to demarginalize theology from ordinary life, even from modern Church life, and how to incarnate the Gospel in different cultures and,

---

[5] The bibliography on this subject is somewhat limited. For our very summary treatment of it here, we have used the following articles: G. Florovsky, "A Criticism of the Lack of Concern for Doctrine..."; Idem, "Patristic Theology and the Ethos of the Orthodox Church," *Collected Works*, vol. 4, 11–30; J. Zizioulas, "The Being of God and the Being of Man," *Synaxis* 1, 100; J. Meyendorff, "Historical Relativism and Authority in Christian Dogma," *Sobornost* 5 (1969), or *SVTQ* 84; V. Thermos, "Ecclesiological Docetism"; Athanasios N. Papathanasiou, "The Language of the Church/The Language of the World. An Adventure of Communication or Conflict?" http://www.myriobiblos.gr/texts/english/papathanasiou_language.html; David Tracy, *Christian Theology and the Culture of Pluralism* (New York: Crossroads, 1981); J. Zizioulas, "The Orthodox Church and the Third Millennium," *The One and the Many*, Sebastian Press: 2010, 388-401; Ch. Yannaras, The Freedom of Morality, SVS Press 1996; S. Skliris, *In the Mirror, A Collection of Iconographic Essays and Illustrations*, Sebastian Press, Los Angeles 2007; A. Yevtich, *Christ—The Alpha and Omega*, Sebastian Press, Los Angeles 2007.

at the same time, introduce peoples, together with their cultures, into the local ecclesial community.

We cannot develop any further these profound issues, for one chapter is not sufficient for such goals, and only some of them can be addressed in this short space. However, without providing answers to such questions "with boldness and without condemnation," I believe our theological education will not be able to adequately face the challenges of the post-modern, pluralistic world. I would ask you to consider whether this could indeed be our specific gift to the world in the twenty-first century. I also strongly believe that "theology must provide the Church with the fundamental guidelines that will enable her to judge in a given case *which cultural forms embody the Gospel faithfully*, and which express, in fact, 'another Gospel.'"[6] Since culture is a human creation and is consequently marked by imperfection, it too needs to be *eschatologized*, i.e., "healed, ennobled and perfected." As we shall see, this *embodiment* must in no way compromise the distinctiveness, the basic existential outlook and integrity of the Christian message. At the same time it must emerge from a strengthened and deepened theology, as opposed to religious agnosticism or relativism.

II. Descriptive and interpretative dogmatics in its encounter with the modern mindset

An Unquestioned Faith in Dogmas
and the Methodology of Theology

It is not by accident that our Faith is based on dogmas. The Church is a Eucharistic and "dogmatic" community in the sense that it cultivates faithfulness to dogma[7] and to the true *kerygma* of the Apostles in order to fulfill the soteriological motive. The Church's unquestioned faith in the value and authority of dogmas is commensurate with her adamant insistence on preserving the apostolic message in its original purity. However, this is not the case simply because dogmas rationalize and set forth

---

[6] J. Zizioulas, "The Orthodox Church and the Third Millennium," p. 395.

[7] "The interpretation of dogma cannot be done without explicating old concepts and terms by means of contemporary concepts, just as happened with the Church Fathers. It is precisely this faithfulness of interpretation that should be the criterion in each case, and not the attempt at interpretation *per se*" (J. Zizioulas, "The Being of God and the Being of Man," *Synaxi* 1, p. 100).

certain truths or the truth. It is rather because dogmas have become *symbols, icons, expressions* and *signs* of communion within the Church community. Throughout the centuries, the Church succeeded in expressing even her art in *dogmatic* ways, so that even iconography became "the most perfect dogmatic language expressed in and through colors";[8] V. Bolotov aptly appreciated Orthodox icons as "dogmatic monuments." Similarly, "some of the greatest hymns of the Eastern Church are simply paraphrases of dogmatic definitions," as Fr. Georges Florovsky recognized.[9] However, if Christian art does not have a connection with the present culture, it functions unfruitfully. Its fidelity to dogmas must be combined with openness to the culture, and not restricted to a historical, legal or confessional context. At the beginning of the twentieth century, there was a return to Byzantine art through the teaching and artistic work mainly of Photis Kontoglou. But this return to the Byzantine has led to a situation where Byzantine art does not relate at all to our present Western culture. On the other hand, Orthodox "dogmatic monuments" such as icons and frescoes were in their times (the fifth to fourteenth centuries) first-class artistic achievements. Christian art has always had to exist within contemporary culture.

Orthodox theology has its *methodology,*[10] and a discipline known as the history of dogma. However, given the fact that theology is not mere *historical* research but also an *interpretation*, two things should be underlined here as *sine qua non* for our theological education. The first necessity is a precise knowledge, through *historical research,* of the content given to a dogma in the period when it was formulated.[11] The sec-

---

[8] S. Skliris, *In the Mirror: A Collection of Iconographic Essays and Illustrations* (Alhambra, Calif.: Sebastian Press, 2007). "And if one can be instructed by Orthodox hymnography and icons, this is precisely because a very definite 'theory of Christianity' is embodied and expressed there" (G. Florovsky, "A Criticism of the Lack of Concern...," p. 169).

[9] G. Florovsky, "A Criticism of the Lack of Concern...," pp. 168–70.

[10] See more in A. Yevtich, "The Methodology of Theology," *Κληρονομία* 14 (1982), pp. 163–85.

[11] "This task is essentially one of historical research, so at this point dogmatics really coincides with the history of dogma" (J. Zizioulas, "The Being of God and the Being of Man," p. 100). As A. N. Papathanasiou points out, "In no event should she [the Church] alienate herself from the linguistic treasures gathered through the ages. After all, a good knowledge of the original language of the ecclesiastical texts is of vital importance for serious theological studies. Her language should neither be reminiscent of an exhibit in a museum, nor a fossil.

ond is an attempt to find a creative link between dogma and modern times. This twofold task of theology—i.e., its descriptive and interpretative character—leads one to question how our modern theology relates to dogmas. Do we believe in these dogmas simply because that is what an Ecumenical Council has decided or because, *actually*, they *reveal* a truth upon which our existence depends? If the first is the case, then we are doing a disservice to theology. Fr. Florovsky observes that "It is really embarrassing that there is so little concern for 'dogmatic systems,' as well as for the Doctrine of the Church, in various circles and quarters of the Orthodox society of our day, and that 'devotion' is so often forcefully divorced from 'faith.'"[12] As Metropolitan John Zizioulas points out, "Theology does not just have the obligation to *describe* dogmas, presenting the form they took in the past. It also has a duty to *interpret* them, so that it becomes apparent how and why our existence depends on them."[13] This leads us to the assertion that no methodological absolutism is permissible within this interpretative transmission of the Tradition. While such absolutism lasts, it will be impossible to instill Christian values in the culture, and *vice versa*.

However, this theological "cultural" epistemology, as the inculturation itself, has an "incarnational" basis. "For the Word of God (Christ) and God wants always and in all things to accomplish the mystery of His embodiment."[14] Inculturation involves inevitably the Incarnation of Christ, be it in forms other than and in addition to the historical one. *"Always and in all things"* (continuously and everywhere) indicates that there is no race and no culture to which the Word of God can be unre-

---

Its roots lie in the distant past, but its branches must blossom in the present and prepare the fruit for tomorrow" (A. N. Papathanasiou, "The Language of the Church").

[12] G. Florovsky, "A Criticism of the Lack of Concern."

[13] J. Zizioulas, "The Being of God and the Being of Man," p. 100.

[14] Βούλεται γὰρ ἀεὶ καὶ ἐν πᾶσιν ὁ τοῦ Θεοῦ Λόγος καὶ Θεὸς τῆς αὐτοῦ ἐνσωματώσεως ἐνεργεῖσθαι τὸ μυστήριον, St. Maximus the Confessor (PG 91, 1084cd). Seen in this perspective, the incarnation is not an event locked in the past, but a procedure that started almost 2000 years ago and continues through history mystically and uninterruptedly. In order to save the world, the Son of God assumed the human nature, lived in certain human societies, spoke the language of His contemporaries. Ever since, Christ has been inconceivable without His body, the Church. The Church is the continuation of the incarnation in history: she is not a spiritualistic sect indifferent to the outer world, but a workshop where the world is constantly transformed into the flesh of Christ (A. N. Papathanasiou, "The Language of the Church").

lated. It is critical for the *Logos* (both the eternal Word and the theological word) to regain existential meaning and purpose. Yet, Christ relates to the culture of the people by the Holy Spirit, because Logos is inseparably connected with Pneuma, and there are *not* two economies, not even complementary ones. The Holy Spirit is a divine Person, who, working with Christ, makes Him an *inclusive corporate personality*, that is, eschatological Son of Man. "The Spirit allows Christ to enter again and again in every culture and assume it by purifying it, that is, by placing it in the light (or one might say under the judgment) of what is ultimately meaningful as it is revealed in Christ."[15] All this allows for a variety of cultural expressions of the one Christ, since the Pneumatological mission always respects the freedom of the people to express the faith in their own way. The Gospel of the Church remains always the same, but every culture is welcomed to become its flesh, so that the message of salvation is conceivable "*always and in all things*" (in every society, in every nation, in every epoch). Otherwise, the idea of a "cosmic Christ," who is the recapitulation (*anacephalaiosis*) of all things, is inconceivable. The Holy Spirit blows, pointing to Christ, in order that He can be inculturated in all places and at all times. In order to have a profound (and not merely an extraneous) effect on public life, theology must not simply speak about God, but *invite* people to His Body, for Christ is not an individual conceivable in isolation: He is "the firstborn among many brethren" (Rom 8.29). Such a Christological vision demands an intrinsic unity between Pneumatology, ecclesiology and eschatology. Communion with the personal being of God through Christ in the Spirit is the primary service that the Church can render to every person and to all humanity in the modern world.

III. A brief look at the patristic method of inculturation

The Holy Fathers provide us with the interpretation of the Gospel, whereas our dogmatic theology provides us with the interpretation of the biblical-patristic tradition. Dogmas have always been interpretative commentaries on the truth of the Gospel, with the intention of shaping the deepest assumptions of Christians. This interpretation has helped the Church to have an impact on culture wherever she has found herself. This

---

[15] J. Zizioulas, "The Orthodox Church and the Third Millennium," p. 394.

was clearly evident already in the fourth century, when the Church had long since established herself beyond her Palestinian cradle and throughout the Mediterranean. The encounter "face-to-face" with the dominant Greco-Roman culture of that world and time was inevitable. The Church found herself before a crucial dilemma: *Jerusalem* or *Athens*, i.e., to remain restricted to the Jewish context, or to open herself to the wider world? Although the Greco-Roman culture implied a way of life, a mode of thinking and a *language* different from those of the Jews, the Church Fathers chose to have the Church address other nations, making use of their languages and of their way of thinking.[16]

History, of course, clearly testifies to a great deal of antagonism between Athens and Jerusalem. Here we will not pursue the details of this complex relationship or of its historical development. However, if we look back in Christian history, we will see that the Fathers had a "dynamic, free and critical attitude toward Greek philosophy, which characterized the patristic period" (Meyendorff). Today, we find ourselves in a position not unlike that of the Apostles and Fathers, who did not hesitate to employ contemporary terminology to proclaim the Gospel of the Kingdom. This transmission and explication did not betray the spirit of the Gospel, for it was certainly interpreted faithfully.

As noted above, this process of transmission is commonly known as incarnating the Gospel in the people's culture, or *inculturation*. The term "inculturation" is used in Christian *missiology* to refer to the adaptation of the way the Gospel is presented for the specific cultures being evangelized.[17] All through the Church's long history—*as* and *when* necessary—the message of the Gospel was inculturated, but with certain *criteria* and theological guidelines. This does not necessarily entail a marriage of the Gospel with all cultural forms. If we look back at the two thousand years of Christian history, we see that problems[18] arose due to a lack of discern-

---

[16] For more about this, see A. N. Papathanasiou, "The Language of the Church."

[17] Our present use of the term "inculturation" is resonant—but not identical—to the use of the same term in sociology. The term was popularized by the encyclical *Redemptoris Missio* of Pope John Paul II (1990), but predates that encyclical. In fact St. Paul's speech to the Greeks at the Areopagus of Athens (Acts 17:22–33) could rightly be considered as the first inculturation attempt.

[18] In his text "The Orthodox Church and the Third Millennium" (pp. 389–391), J. Zizioulas, indicates a few disappointments and failures in the history of inculturation, among others the fact that Orthodoxy has mixed up the Gospel with the national and

ment concerning *which cultural forms embody the Gospel faithfully*. We also see problems when attempts were made to stop this natural inculturation movement, as for example when Latin was made a quasi-sacred language, or when the translation of the Bible in the vernacular languages was condemned. However, history testifies to a significant number of successful post-Apostolic practitioners of inculturation throughout centuries of missions, among them St. Patrick in Ireland and Sts Cyril and Methodius for the Slavic peoples of Eastern Europe.

The patristic method of inculturation demonstrates on many levels (ethics, philosophy, worship, institutions, art, asceticism, etc.) that there was not a radical split between the Gospel and culture. At the level of ethics, Christianity influenced society so deeply that most of the Christian principles of moral behavior became the humanitarian and moral values of contemporary society. On the level of philosophy, all the questions raised by the Greek mind (though to a great extent alien to the Bible) were regarded as legitimate, above all the ontological concerns, while philosophical terminology was unhesitatingly borrowed and used in theology.[19] At the level of worship, many customs were accepted and Christianized, such as native feasts, "slavas," rituals of all kinds, etc. At the level of art, all the great Greek achievements were evaluated and incorporated into the Christian artistic heritage, which displayed a boundless richness and diversity of color, form and expression.

It will be of interest to bring to our attention the question of whether or not, and how and to what extent, certain "realms" of theology (Triadology, Christology, ecclesiology, etc.) can be translated *existentially* into the new cultural context of today—into a particular society with its cultural-philosophical milieu. Although the Church is not of the world, She lives in the world. Patristic theology (not reduced only to that of Byzantium or of the Middle Ages in the West) offers important elucida-

cultural values of a particular time. We have failed to achieve a true inculturation of the Church due to an infiltration of the Church by nationalism and sometimes by ethnophyletism. He also observes that the idea of autocephaly has become *autocephalism*, that is, a means of serving national or phyletic interests by using the Church for that purpose. Furthermore, he states that the situation of the Orthodox Diaspora in the twentieth century is in direct and open violation of Orthodox ecclesiology, concluding that we should obviously not be proud and happy with such a situation, although unfortunately we seem to have blessed it in the most official way.

[19] J. Zizioulas, ibid.

tion of existential questions. It allows us to place our own existence in the light of our faith in the Triune God and His Church. The fact remains that, in the so-called patristic era, theology (Trinitarian ontology and Christology) had its implications for Church life, for modern culture and for theological epistemology. The inculturation of the Gospel in the patristic era did not produce the loss of the Church's identity; on the contrary, it saved her from withdrawing from the world into a ghetto-like existence.[20] The essential point here is that, *in this process, history and culture are accepted not so as to remain as they are, but so as to be eschatologized* ("healed, ennobled, perfected"), in such a way that the Truth is not subjugated through being incarnated in history and culture.

This cultural incarnation of the Gospel is inherited from the first millennium of Church history, and offers us patterns and inspiration for our own era. The Church can truly benefit from looking backward as well as forward. But today, when for example we say to contemporary man that God is Trinity (*Triadology*), what are we really saying to him? Does this throw any light on problems such as those created by individualism, universalism, etc., which mark our present culture? What does an *ecclesiology* of the catholicity of the local Church have to say to the issue of globalization, which dominates the world's agenda? Therefore, the question is: How do we enter more deeply into the contemporary culture and establish creative links with its premises? We can attempt this cultural resynchronization of ecclesiology if we not only place the Gospel in a critical attitude toward modern culture but also propose alternatives to the culture. Today the Church cannot stand vis-à-vis with her surrounding culture because She has, to some extent, contributed to the creation of the culture; she must cease from being alien to the agonizing questions of contemporary man. Inculturation is a two-way exchange: it means the "intimate transformation of genuine cultural values through their integration in Christianity, and the insertion of Christianity in the various human cultures."[21]

When the Church Fathers were teaching, they did not have dilemmas over such issues. In preaching as they did, as fisherman (ἀλιευτικῶς)

---

[20] Even such an institution as monasticism, which with its ascetical ethos reminds the Church that she does not belong to the world, has had a deep impact on the culture of Orthodox people. Together with the Liturgy, our theological education must appreciate the monastic tradition, i.e., the ethos of the Desert Fathers.

[21] *Redemptoris mission* 52.

rather than according to the methods of Aristotle (Ἀριστοτελικῶς), they were embodying their experience of our Savior's message of truth, which is convincing when it reaches the existential chords of the human heart, not when it merely answers philosophical and academic demands. The Christian message is what frees us from the constraints of the created world; hence, the way of theology corresponds to existential human needs. As a complete "philosophy of life," Christian theology (and of course the "neo-patristic synthesis," too) is inconceivable without tracing out existential problems. Church history teaches us that the Church never "dogmatized" without reference to the Person of Christ,[22] and this is because *dogmatics* is always connected to *salvation*. Theology communicates with people, not by shouting out mottos but rather by addressing the existential needs of man. Furthermore, theology should emphasize the Church as the way of life and as the way of redemption from both death and decay. Allow me to paraphrase what Christos Yannaras brilliantly said: The freedom that interests the Church is the one that frees us from the constraints of the created world. For instance, Jesus called the overwhelmed and frightened disciples to walk on the water on the rough lake of Gennesaret, and Peter stepped out of the boat and began to walk on the water. Yannaras remarks that at that moment Peter derived his existence not from his own nature but from his relationship with the Lord. This is the freedom that delivers us from death.[23]

IV. "Καινοτομεῖν τὰ ὀνόματα" — explicating old concepts with contemporary concepts

By the end of the previous century, it became clear that Orthodox theology is called to answer the questions of the non-Orthodox world from the depths of its catholic and uninterrupted experience, and to face

---

[22] This is Fr. Florovsky's observation.

[23] C. Yannaras, "Towards a New Ecumenism," http://www.orthodoxytoday.org/articles/YannarasEcumenism.htm: "*The Church calls us to realize our existence not on the basis of our created and mortal nature, but on an immediate relationship with Him who called us from non-being into being. This is the definition of the person: the person is found in the freedom of an immediate, existential relationship with God....* We exist according to the mode of an ecclesial existence when we are able to walk on water, and the whole life of the Church is an ascetic struggle designed to teach us to walk on water." There is no biochemistry of freedom; the existential chords of a man touched by God cannot be reduced to a strictly biological level.

that world not with accusations but as a witness—to witness the truth of Orthodoxy. This can occur when theologians revise the cultural and linguistic means of expressing, not dogmas, but the *language* of our faith— or, as St. Gregory the Theologian would say, by "innovating the terms and concepts" (καινοτομεῖν τὰ ὀνόματα). This is what is known as the neo--patristic synthesis, with "neo" entailing new images and terminology, and "patristic" entailing the spirit and intention of the Fathers. On the subject of this existential relationship between dogmatics and life, we may say that the linguistic sensibility of the Church has to do with the very *being* of the Church. As A. N. Papathanasiou points out, this "existential relationship enables a local Church to be truly local and truly Church. It enables her to express herself, to produce her own texts and a new transplantation of the Truth into a new field, in a new cultural context, in a particular civilization, in a particular society."[24] We should not refer to the Fathers literally, but rather try to *comprehend their pulse and their message* and to interpret it consistently with their inner logic. As long as its meaning reaches human needs, a saying (dogmatic formulation) can be both historic (patristic) and current (modern).

The transmission of the dogmas cannot be done without their interpretation, i.e., through explicating old concepts and terms by means of contemporary concepts. This is something beyond the mere translation of texts from one language to another. Meyendorff and Zizioulas have traced many answers that have been offered over the centuries, showing how the meaning of many theological terms has changed and expanded far beyond the original (Platonic or Aristotelian) conception. They illustrate this with certain terms and concepts the Church borrowed from Greek culture for dogmatic purposes. Zizioulas takes, for example, the terms καθολικὸς, πρόσωπον and ὑπόστασις, while Meyendorff writes about ὑπόστασις and φύσις in connection with the Chalcedonian definition. Historically and culturally, they are Greek words. "Would Aristotle have understood their meaning, had he been given the Nicene Creed to read?" inquires Zizioulas.[25] In the same spirit, Meyendorff asks: "Would Aristotle himself understand Basil of Caesarea?"[26]

[24] A. N. Papathanasiou, "The Language of the Church."

[25] "Truth and Communion," *Being as Communion: Studies in Personhood and the Church* (London: Darton, Longman & Todd, 1985), p. 118.

[26] J. Meyendorff, "Historical Relativism and Authority in Christian Dogma," *Sobornost* 5 (1969), or *SVTQ* 84. "Did Aristotelian terms like *hypostasis* and *physis* keep their

The conclusion is that they would have, had the words been linked sole-ly to history and culture. If they would not have understood, as one has the right to suspect, then something crucial must have happened to these historical and cultural elements through their being associated with the thought-structure and life of the Church.[27]

The advantage of this resynchronization is existential, not ethical. Orthodoxy must begin to answer cultural questions not with ethics (which has proved unsuccessful) but with dogmas.[28] However, in order to achieve this, it must interpret its dogmas existentially.[29] According to the very tradition of Orthodoxy, language signals to the human being realities that cannot be restricted or fully described by words. Every word out of the mouth of the Church is not only a declaration of the Truth but also an invitation to a free, wholehearted, personal encounter with the Truth, since the Truth is not something, but Someone: Christ Himself incarnate."[30] This has been expressed especially through hymnography (St. John Damascene was not a systematic theologian but primarily a poet!) and iconography.

full original meaning in the Chalcedonian definition?" And Meyendorff concludes: "The new Christian meaning of these terms remained basically unacceptable for those in the ancient world who rejected the historical Christ of the New Testament. The dynam-ic, free and critical attitude toward Greek philosophy which characterized the patristic period and which implied an often painful process of discrimination as well as many in-dividual mistakes can be studied with great profit in our challenging days of change."

[27] Ibid.

[28] Fr. Florovsky of blessed memory acquired this viewpoint from the Greek Church Fathers. "Chrysostom was a witness of the living faith, and for that reason his voice was so eagerly listened to, both in the East and in the West; but for him, the faith was a norm of life, and not just a theory. Dogmas must be translated into experience. Chrysostom was preaching the Gospel of Salvation, the good tidings of the new life. He was not a preacher of independent ethics." (St. John Chrysostom: The Prophet of Charity, http://www.orthodoxytoday.org/articles4/FlorovskyChrysostom.php). This approach of Fr. Florovsky emerged from his conviction that the Greek Church Fathers have always been contemporaneous.

[29] As Metropolitan J. Zizioulas asserts, "In any case, the Church must apply theo-logical and not simply ethical criteria, which can often be identical with cultural ones. Questions for example of whether or not magic or polygamy, and its opposite monog-amy, constitute ethical matters in the cultural context of Africa, or relate to the basic outlook of the Gospel, are possible to decide only if we know what this outlook consists in. This is something that the theological consciousness of the Church can provide us with" ("The Orthodox Church and the Third Millennium," p. 395.

[30] A. N. Papathanasiou, "The Language of the Church."

V. Challenges for neo-patristic theology through the new process of inculturation

Theological Education and the "Neo-patristic Synthesis"

Of course, the proper inculturation of theology can be only within the "neo-patristic synthesis." Since Fr. Georges Florovsky, the exposition of the theses of the Fathers must always be followed by a search for their significance (implications), for only by so doing can one accomplish a neo-patristic synthesis (and not simply a "patristic synthesis"), i.e., something more profound and more creative then the mere copying of the Fathers. The generation after Florovsky set the first principles and laid the foundations of this ecumenical and neo-patristic Orthodox theology. In new and perhaps unforeseen conditions, these theological criteria will play a critical role, but only when dogmas are understood in their soteriological and doxological character.

Right now, all this is important because modern times demand much reconsideration of our past. We started this article by saying that "there is no dogma of our Church that does not have something to say about the actual problems of humanity." There is a long list of examples that need to be reconsidered. For instance, today the dogmas of the Holy Trinity, of Christ, etc. (rather than the deistic idea of divinity, or the Slavic idea of "*vsecelovek*"), may be of great help to people in their search of personhood, of freedom, of community, and survival in an age of acute anxiety. Christian theology has the duty to reveal and to show all of this, because Christological docetism leads to ecclesiological docetism. As a consequence, "a Church that rejects the incarnational view expressed by St. Maximus—that is, a Church that refuses to speak to the world and with the world—is not simply a silent Church; she runs the danger of ceasing to be a Church at all!"[31] If the Church is to avoid marginalization, she must avoid the danger of historically disincarnating

---

[31] Ibid. He adds: "In the event that she does not introduce the world into her life-giving Body, she abandons the world to the realm of death. It is as if a local Church refuses to accept the bread of the world and thus finally becomes unable to prepare the Holy Eucharist!" For instance, St. Gregory of Nyssa, when opposing the heretic Eunomius, who claimed that God reveals certain words, argued that God reveals the meanings and man invents the words. "God's voice," says Gregory, "is neither Hebrew, nor expressed in any of the ways known to the nations." Indeed, while human languages can become the flesh of the truth, they are not truth of themselves. As Orthodox, we must search for *inspiration in our own Tradition!*

Christ and must play a leading part in a dialogue with the prevailing culture at the deepest level.

Furthermore, this "neo-patristic" synthesis has theological elements. Therefore, we are not to cultivate and "do" patristic theology in the sense of quotation or copying;[32] rather, we are to cultivate a theology that will be a "synthesis," which means to gather into one—in a creative way—all the theses and positions that are developed in relation to contemporary problems.

To determine the characteristics of the new millennium, we can call to mind the theories of many secular intellectuals who claim that the real "clash of civilizations" is not between different religions but between superstition and modernity. S. Huntington sees in the new millennium a period of what he describes as "a clash of cultures." Theological education in the new millennium will be challenged by certain factors, which the Church must take into account. In the years to come, complex social and moral issues, issues arising from medical and technological advancements in the biological sciences, issues of inter-religious and political dialogue, together with other issues such as pluralism, globalization and the ecological crisis—all these will change with alarming rapidity, and this will make it necessary for clergy and church workers to be provided with a high level of balanced education. It means little to say that the alarming news concerning advances in biology and genetics requires mere theological reflection. Indeed, these developments will make God indispensable. Again and again, the image of God, the human person, will be endangered, as well as the freedom, uniqueness and the indispensability of every human being—as well as of nature itself. A succession of best-selling books has torn into religion: S. Harris's *The End of Faith,* R. Dawkins's *The God Delusion,* and C. Hitchens's *God Is Not Great: How Religion Poisons Everything.* This reactionary attack against religion already evinces a religious intensity, which immediately leads us to the conclusion that the main problem we will have to face will be that of *inculturation.* Dawkins has set up an organization to help atheists around the world. As is evident from the reaction of modern scientists and philosophers such as Dawkins and Hitchens, the modern mind cannot absorb the historical

---

[32] On the return to the Fathers being a creative one, with elements of self-criticism, see G. Florovsky, "The Ways of Russian Theology," *Collected Works,* vol. 4, p. 191, and "Patristic Theology and the Ethos of the Orthodox Church," *Collected Works,* vol. 4, pp. 11–30.

outlook that Christianity brings with it, including faith in God's incarnation and the resurrection of the dead. In any case, what the Church should note today is that she must be able to establish a positive relationship with science and to interact with it. The next generation of Orthodox theologians should build upon the biblical/neo-patristic foundations, after intensive studies and an in-depth understanding and evaluation of modern science.

So, if we take these things into consideration, we are faced with the question: Will our seminaries with their programs be able to answer this problem beyond a mere ethical[33] or moral discourse? By embracing the fundamentalist approach (copying and repeating the Church Fathers' sayings, an easier solution), Orthodox theologians in the past cast themselves into a scientific wilderness. Whatever the exact cause, this is hardly surprising: many theological schools do not have in their curriculum any reference to the scientific approach. Theology stands at a distance not only from the scientific world, but also from ordinary life. In other words, it seems that the language of theology and the language of the world are not conducive to dialogue.

VI. A holistic approach: theology is both dogmatic and liturgical

A renewed organic bond with modern man's life requires unusually creative abilities, a gift for synthesizing and a kind of forward-looking-ness. What must theological discussions do in order to obtain this? I think that the answer of Orthodox theology cannot be established on anything less than the following foundation:

First, theological discussions should proceed with a renewed effort to draw knowledge from the Church's dogmas, just as the Holy Fathers did in their time. However, in order for the dogmas to be significant for people's lives today, *they need to be interpreted so that their soteriological meaning may come to the surface*. Dogmas are not logical propositions to be accepted or refuted, but truths that are experienced in the Eucharist and life. We need to show the world that our Orthodox faith (being the true and authentic way of life) does not propose an escape from nature

---

[33] In going beyond the ethical categories of society, theology will not stay conservative at any price. Being cautious of not betraying ethical norms, which were later abandoned easily by the next generation, our "moral" theologians only rarely displayed any prescience.

and does not avoid the confrontation with life and death. Preaching Christ without living within His Body is not of any profit. Christ as the God-man answers the ultimate existential questions, specifically with regard to those issues that preoccupy every person, such as death, love, freedom. Referring to such topics, our theology will once again find its contact and communication with life.

Secondly, theological *logos* (discourse) needs to become *Church* discourse, and most certainly a *Liturgical* and a *Eucharistic* one as well. An examination of the *theological* understanding of the Liturgy might bring some new, welcomed insights, in an era where the Church has in many ways been reduced to an association, the Holy Eucharist to just one among many other mysteries, and the Liturgy to a ceremony. Without the liturgical and sacramental life of the Church, Christ simply remains a name, deprived of any possibility of experiential knowledge. The only way to experience Christ and for Him to give life and answers to people with agonizing existential problems is through the Church, as a "gathering at one place." The Gospel, then, "the good news of salvation," is what mankind expects to hear from the Church and the Church's theologians.

This brings the Eucharistic Liturgy into the debate concerning new cultural problems. If we believe that the Eucharist is the summing up (*anacephalaiosis*) of the entire reality of the salvation of the world, then the Liturgy and the Sacraments represent the methodological tools fundamental to a theological approach to the culture. The Orthodox Church must draw more and more from her liturgical life, particularly the Eucharist. Recent discussion in Serbia alerts us that we must first pay attention to the way we celebrate the Eucharist and worship if we are to offer anything to the world of existential significance.[34] Additionally, we must interpret our Liturgy in existential terms. *Lex orandi* is so often forcefully divorced from *lex credendi*. "There is too much concern with 'the vessels' and too little concern with the Treasure, which alone makes the vessel precious."[35]

---

[34] More on this see, A. Yevtich, *Hristos Nova Pasha, Bozanstvena Liturgija* I–II (Vrnjacka Banja, 2007). See also A. Schmemann, "On the Question of Liturgical Practices. A Letter to My Bishop," http://www.jacwell.org/Supplements/liturgical_practices.htm.

[35] G. Florovsky *Collected Works*, ed. Richard S. Haugh (Belmont, MA: Nordland), Vol. XIII, *Ecumenism I: A Doctrinal Approach*, pp. 168–170.

Finally, theology should adopt a holistic approach, emphasizing *integration* rather than "fragmentation" in its educational programs. As we know, the idea of "university" presupposes *the cooperation of different disciplines so that these could make their way into one Truth.* Through its holistic approach, Orthodox theology has to bring doctrines together into their appropriate interconnectedness. The word "hologram," which is derived from the Greek words, *holo*, meaning *whole*, and *gram*, meaning *message,* can be used to help illustrate this idea of interconnectedness. As a metaphor for perfect communication, hologram theory has been used as a language to describe our universe (physics), our brain (neurology), metaphysics, medicine, psychology and communication. If we take this hologram theory in a metaphorical sense, then a holistic theology is what is needed. The idea of "a whole in every part" corresponds to an idea that St. Justin Popovic developed in his works, where he notes that the whole of dogmatics is contained in ethics, the whole of liturgics in dogmatics, and so on, just as we might observe that height, width, depth, and motion-time are all recorded in a holograph. However, the *sine qua non* for this is life "with all the Saints." This holistic approach gives us many indications that several theological methodologies and theses need urgent revision. Theological epistemology is grounded not on apophaticism, but on the experience of the Eucharistic event. Our theological schools should become the place where every discipline refuses its own autonomy and self-sufficiency in a most positive manner. It will be hard to confront the theological schools with this fact, let alone kick start the process overnight. We may have to be cautious and systematic about it, and just wait for this to come to fruition.

VII. The experience of the cross and theological education

In celebrating the feast of the Universal Elevation of the Holy and Precious Cross, Orthodox theology today, as in the apostolic times, preaches the victory of the *foolishness of the Cross* ("a stumbling block to Jews and folly to Gentiles") in a non-Christian cultural context. And this will continue in the coming century. The Cross is an event of salvation in history celebrated liturgically in the feasts of our Church. Perhaps some are unaware of the fact that here, in the Church, dogmatics (the teaching on the Cross) is understood and expressed liturgically (the feast of the

Cross). This is what Metropolitan John Zizioulas calls *liturgical dogmatics,* or *dogmatics understood and expressed liturgically.*

Some will say that we do not have any guarantee that we will succeed, and this is true because our theology is *kenotic* and *anaphoric.* Let us not deceive ourselves: in our present time and in the times to come, Christ will be more than ever a "sign which shall be spoken against" (Luke 2.34). Yet, through "kenotic" (in the image of Christ[36]) self-examination and self-criticism, we will be able to recognize our failure to succeed in the language of love, in the cross of self-emptying, and in understanding, all of which contemporary man is so much in need of, in his tragic and hopeless predicaments. To criticize is easy, but the real test comes when words are turned into deeds.

The Orthodox Church has entered the third millennium in a condition of perceived weakness before secular society, in danger of appearing nameless and pointless. Theology has been reduced to producing books as a substitute for an inspired witness, to recall St. John Chrysostom. By our insistence on keeping the Tradition (taking refuge in passivity) and producing only books, even as our presence in the world diminishes, we just postpone the inevitable. Hamlet's dilemma of inaction should be replaced by an active application of theology. First of all, the so-called self-explanatory ideas in dogmatic theology need to be challenged and re-examined, and their contemporary meanings must be communicated. This can only be done, first, if we are well-acquainted with dogmatics. At one time, Fr. Florovsky criticized the disinterest in dogmatics among Orthodox. Furthermore, it is a sad truth that there is a tendency in Orthodox theology to underestimate that which is *modern* in history. Disappointments and failures are an occasion for reflection and even self-examination and self-criticism, in spite of faithfulness to the Tradition. The fact that we, Orthodox Christians, are not aware of the new challenges—this is our principal problem. In the depths of his soul, an average Orthodox person is detached from the world in which he lives. He voluntarily and fanatically severs himself from the West, underestimating the great achievements of Western civilization because of his hang-up. The achieve-

---

[36] "Christ Jesus, who, though He was in the form of God, did not count equality with God a thing to be grasped, but emptied Himself, taking the form of a servant, being born in the likeness of men. And being found in human form He humbled Himself and became obedient unto death, even death on a cross" (Phil. 2:5–8).

ments that have come from the West, whether we recognize them or not, have brought about a change in the mentality of the entire world, including ours. We, however, do not wish to acknowledge this, as if the same God has not created all people: them and us. What is more, it would appear that what we do by virtue of being Orthodox should be correct because the Holy Spirit enlightens us, whereas what Westerners do would be, so to speak, devoid of anything Orthodox because they do not have the Holy Spirit.

VIII. Theological disciplines and soteriological needs

Our modern theology should not be hesitant in introducing new terminology that is not found in the Holy Fathers. It suffices to safeguard the faith of the Holy Fathers from a false understanding. "It is *conservatism* of the wrong sort to reject *a priori* any transmission of the old in a new form."[37] The Councils and Fathers certainly did not exhibit such conservatism when they introduced the term *"homoousios"* (in the Nicene Creed), or apophatic theology,[38] or the Cappadocian distinction between person and nature, or the hesychastic distinction between *essence* and *energies*, or the complex philosophical vocabulary of Maximus the Confessor, to mention a few. Their attempts could not be justified by the spirit of conservatism exhibited today by those who reject *a priori* any use of contemporary philosophical terminology in theology.

The outcome of the dynamic neo-patristic dialogue is impressive. In the field of Christology, Fr. Florovsky contributed in various ways, chiefly with regard to the two natures of Christ, introducing the term "asymmetrical Christology":[39] an attempt to articulate how the Incarnation of Christ did not produce a new Person, being that the union of the nature is "on the basis of the Hypostasis" and that Hypostasis is the Divine Logos.[40] All such endeavors are very edifying examples for all those who

---

[37] J. Zizioulas, "The Being of God and the Being of Man," p. 100.

[38] The Areopagite and other representatives of apophaticism linked their theology with categories used by Neoplatonism, but this did not *necessarily* mean selling out to Neoplatonism. Knowing that Truth is not "comprehensible" and thus cannot be objectified and defined, they did not want to make dogmas, "formulations" or "definitions" of the truth captive to the bonds of historical and cultural forms.

[39] Already in 1933, in his work *Byzantine Fathers from the 5th to the 8th Centuries* (in Russian).

[40] There are other instances of asymmetry in theology: "asymmetrical" Christology, asymmetrical synergy, etc.

presently maintain that we should simply repeat the words of the Holy Fathers without interpreting them in our contemporary language. All patristic terms and concepts, such as love, freedom, eros, ekstasis, other, self, person, etc., have to be seen from a new angle and in a fresh light.[41]

Furthermore, these offerings should not be made outside of the *anthropology of the person* and the *ontology of ecclesial communion*, because they could become lifeless teachings imposed by dogmatists on the human mind. Raising, therefore, the fundamental or ultimate questions concerning the way of theology, which Orthodoxy translates into experience, will be extremely important in the new millennium, when the inculturation of Christianity will be once again crucial for the Church's existence. The Church is a place where theology is translated into experience through liturgical and sacramental life.

What does the Triune God have to do with anthropology? Does the Triune God belong in ecclesiology? For, surely, the significance of dogma, such as the dogma of the Holy Trinity, cannot be simply and only as a concept to be accepted for mankind to be saved. Nowadays, we witness how discussions provoke attempts to describe a trinitarian shaping of ecclesiology and anthropology. According to the representatives of neo-patristic theology, the attitude as well as the content of the thought of the Greek Fathers possess a breadth that makes them attractive to the investigation of Western man. Although the dogma of the Holy Trinity is crucial and essential to the Christian faith, difficulties begin to occur in connection with the manner in which this faith is expressed, especially the dilemma with regard to the transposition of our concept of person to the being of God (a new kind of anthropomorphism) or to the possibility of God's way of being to reveal to us true personhood.[42] One way of bring-

---

[41] A good example of dialogue between patristic theology and contemporary philosophy is Ch. Yannaras who doesn't see a sharp dichotomy or conflict between the two. See his *Person and Eros*, Holy Cross: 2007.

[42] For a further discussion of the subject, see J. Zizioulas, "The Father as Cause," *Communion and Otherness*, New York: T&T Clark, 2006, pp. 140–41: "The first thing we must underline is that our way of being persons cannot be transferred or projected onto God. Existentialist philosophy can only help us to appreciate the limitations, the antinomies and the tragic experience of personhood, and this in itself is important in order to make it clear to us that, *as human beings, we are not content with what we actually are as persons, and long for true personhood*. But it is precisely because we realize the tragedy of the person and of our personal existence that we cannot transpose our concept of the person to the Being of God. It is the reverse that

ing the dogma of the Holy Trinity closer to people today is to recognize that we are not satisfied with our momentary condition because we long for authentic personhood. The Holy Trinity, our model through the relational event of the Eucharistic, transforms our being into true personhood in the image of Christ.

Like Trinitarian theology, Christology can also be communicated more effectively. According to the biblical tradition—as interpreted by the Church Fathers of the past and in the same way by present-day theology—Christ is the only authentic "perfect Man," who—as "perfect God"—shows the way out of the tragic condition humaine. The Church never established dogmas (or "dogmaticized," if you will) without referring to the Person of Christ, because dogmatics is always connected to salvation. We might ask, however, how Christology can be helpful in this modern condition? Only insofar as the Church and her theology explains Orthodox Christology and emphasizes its existential aspects—specifically within the context that we are discussing—will modern man perceive that "there is no salvation outside of Him" (Acts 4:12). Christ should be of interest to contemporary man, whose life is permeated and affected by acute anxiety and nothingness, because He can help him out of his miseries and tragic failures by establishing him as true person.

In the present period of cultural transition, ecclesiastical art has to answer man's needs. Iconography should, even today, become the most perfect dogmatic language expressed in and through colors. Given the fact that culture is a means through which existential human needs are expressed, contemporary Orthodox iconographers must reveal to modern man the icon today, not by copying icons from the fourteenth or twelfth centuries. We need more examples of this synthetic approach in order to enter into a deep dialogue with modern culture.[43] Therefore, the modern iconographer *should articulate a dialogue with modern art* by evaluating, for example, the brush strokes of Van Gogh and Cézanne, the colors of Monet, the forms of Matisse, even the cubism and post-modernism of Pi-

---

we should do, namely *allow God's way of Being to reveal to us the true personhood."* The same author has dealt with this matter more extensively in his article, "The Trinity and Personhood: Appreciating the Cappadocian Contribution," *Communion and Otherness*, pp. 155–177.

[43] Fr. Stamatis is an example of this synthetic approach because he has entered into a deep dialogue with modern culture. See S. Skliris, *In the Mirror.*

casso. This was a feature of ecclesial art during times when the Orthodox Church had the ability to shape culture. She has not been as irrelevant to human culture as some people have wanted her to be. Also, Orthodox artists should not hesitate to be *authentically post-modern*, if they employ purely artistic criteria and do not adopt ready-made solutions from the iconographic past. It is desirable that they research everything anew, with a strong experimental sense at their disposal, while combining strictly traditional elements with those that are modern.[44] Orthodox theologians should combine essential faithfulness to tradition with the accurate and fruitful transmission of this tradition to modern times.

IX. A few closing remarks

One of the striking messages of Fr. Florovsky and other founders of neo-patristic theology is that we have to go beyond self-preservation and move out of our autarky (self-sufficiency), which developed after the Schism. All Orthodox Churches are in difficulties, and they will be more so in the future. But, however great the risk of this undertaking might be, the profit will be even greater. The strength of Orthodoxy is in its biblical-patristic Tradition, both dogmatically and liturgically, *but only on the condition that this Tradition is interpreted in a way that makes it relevant to the existential needs of humanity.*

Theology is and will be more and more the *sine qua non* for the survival of the Orthodox Church in the new millennium. Since the Logos became incarnate and became our interpersonal *dia*-logos between God and the world, Orthodox theology should not fear dialogue with any culture. It is the only way for it to assert its uniqueness, importance and indispensability. Thus, if we take these things into consideration, we can much more easily answer the question of how our Orthodox theological education can say anything to and have any relation with our culture. Our theological education and culture must exist within this culture, for the benefit of humanity. This coexistence, however, must have some positive

[44] See for example, Stamatis' icon *The Mighty Protectress* (Theotokos), which is strongly traditional; but Christ has the movement, the colors, and brush deposits of modern, expressionist art. Although Stamatis basically employs a dark Byzantine underpainting, adding to it light "accents" (illuminations), he still plays with colors in such an impressionist manner that his work gains a *"non-determinism of color"*; he leaves sections of his painting uncolored and then treats these sections in an unpredictable manner with an eagerness to play and not to make use of the calligraphy that is usual in iconography.

elements. Through interrupting the Orthodox monologue, we have to find ways of not making theology simply an esoteric thing that has to do with certain exotic people, but rather we must *relate* it to the culture of our times, in a manner both traditional and innovative. Our great achievement will be if we contribute to the marriage between Orthodox tradition and our times. We need that very much in the Orthodox Church, and this is not as radical as it might sound.

On account of this, the main goal of our theology in the new millennium will be the "neo-patristic synthesis," which signifies a deeper search for the existential meaning of the theology of the Holy Church Fathers and, furthermore, a synthesis of the same. And if Fr. Florovsky set the first principles correctly and clearly, laying the foundations of this ecumenical and neo-patristic Orthodox theology, we are obliged to develop them further. This entails an encounter with both the ancient and modern mind. This is not an easy undertaking in the current theological confusion we are experiencing, namely, in those instances where true aspirations for serious theological thought are exchanged for theological slogans and religious loquacity. We can build upon the above-mentioned foundations with constructive and creative zeal, but not by imitating and copying. The crucial question, then, is not whether modern, neopatristic theology can adopt certain cultural-philosophical concepts, but whether its hermeneutical and epistemological attempts, based on biblical-patristic tradition, represent the only certain way to establish a creative dialogue with postmodern culture, and whether such attitude does justify various modern cultural and philosophical expressions of the modern humanity. With the right interpretation of dogmas in the light of today's and tomorrow's basic existential concerns, Orthodox culture, finding itself at the end of a historical culture shaped by the Enlightenment, should presented itself as an alternative to the culture of pluralism and, as such, should be proclaimed by all who share her treasures.

Chalcedon's Christology
Theological, Historical and Cultural Significance

Who do people say I AM? True God and True Man:
Chalcedon's Christology in a Postmodern World

Preface

Chalcedonian Christology is a quintessential ingredient of the continuing liturgical-dogmatic-ethical life of the Church. The Church has constantly re-received and transmitted this Christological truth—"one and the same Christ, Son, Lord, only begotten, to be acknowledged in two natures, unconfused, unchangeable, indivisibly, inseparably; the distinction of natures being by no means taken away by the union, but rather the property of each nature being preserved, and concurring in one Person and one Subsistence, not parted or divided into two persons, but one and the same Son, and only begotten, God the Word, the Lord Jesus Christ." In fact one can go even further and make the point that the Chalcedonian definition of Christ entailed not only a vertical perspective (consubstantial [co-essential] with the Father according to the Godhead), but also a horizontal perspective of the people of Israel to which Jesus belonged as Man ("consubstantial with us according to Manhood"). Without any doubt, Chalcedon brought about a helpful integration of "theology" and "economy," of transcendence and immanence. Being God, and belonging to a certain historical era and generation, Christ accepted what was the de facto human context as his own context. Thus Christology inevitably implies ecclesiology and even sociology.

For these reasons I propose to deal with my subject in the following way: First, I will try to point out Chalcedon's major theological issues in the historical life of the Church. Second, we will look at the present day situation and see what opportunities these issues provide for the Churches and society. Finally, we will also try to identify ways in which the Chalcedonian Christology can operate today with its theological, historical and cultural dimensions. Without going into the subtle, nuanced formulations of Chalcedon's Definition—for this is the most stunning dogmatic and doctrinal text of all Ecumenical Councils—we will attempt to present the significance of Chalcedon in a way that is accessible to a wider audience.

I. A Quick look at history

It is not possible for this presentation to offer a detailed historical analysis of the Concilium universale Chalcedonense (=Fourth Ecumenical Council), which, given its importance, deserves a separate monograph. That Council, held in the city of Chalcedon, near Constantinople, in 451, is one of the seven ecumenical councils accepted by the Eastern Orthodox, Catholic, and many Protestant Christian churches. However, it is the first Council not recognized by any of the Oriental Orthodox churches, in spite of the fact that it was designed to heal the growing Christological division. The Chalcedonian creed was written amid controversy between the western, eastern and oriental churches over the meaning of the Incarnation. We must, however, know a few historical facts.

The Council of Chalcedon was a courageous and quick response to the Synod of 449, and was aimed at overturning its decisions. That gathering, dubbed the "Robber Synod" by Pope Leo of Rome, had articulated an extreme Alexandrian Christology. The bishops at Chalcedon disclaimed the council of 449 and deposed Patriarch Dioscorus of Alexandria for his role in that gathering. It is commonly held that the Council of Chalcedon was more or less a "Cyrillian" Council; it followed his theology and thus continues the Third Ecumenical Council.

The Chalcedonian Definition includes the main expressions from the Formula of concordance in 433. It also uses Flavianus' Homologia, and the Tomos of Pope Leo. So it is a synthesis of Alexandrine, Antiochean and western Christological elements in the Definition, but this synthesis was produced completely within the framework of Cyril's Christology. However, we must not forget that Chalcedon's principal aim was to condemn monophysitism and to exclude the possibility of an asymmetrical monophysite interpretation of Cyrillian Christology. The

Fathers of the Council could have chosen either the formula "out of two natures" (ἐκ δύο φύσεων) or the formula "in two natures" (ἐν δύο φύσεσιν), and they chose the latter. The reason for this was that the Cyrillian formula ἐκ δύο φύσεων did not clearly indicate the existence of a full humanity after the union. In addition, Dioscorus had used this formula at the Council of 449, which had rehabilitated the monophysite Eutyches. Thus, when the Fathers of Chalcedon had to choose between "Dioscorus, who denied the two natures in Christ, [and] Leo, who argued that there are two natures," they unanimously chose the latter, and this led them to adopt the expression ἐν δύο φύσεσιν.

But the latter developments have also made the entire matter even more complicated for the following reason: The distinction between φύσις and ὑπόστασις, affirmed at the Council, was too new and revolutionary in the theology of Incarnation to not provoke different interpretations and misunderstandings. The Council's definition thus gave rise to a couple of persistent questions that have bedeviled theologians up to the present day. One of the problems lay in the fact that Eastern Mesopotamia did not posses Greek conceptual tools. They could not understand what the Council's distinction was between nature and person, or hypostasis. Those who rejected Chalcedon—namely, the anti-Chalcedonian "monophysites"—thought that the Christologies of Cyril and Chalcedon were incompatible. According to them, there was no distinction between nature and person, or hypostasis, at least on the level of economy, hence their dismay at the Council, which had ostensibly restored the heresy of Nestorius by attributing two natures to Christ.

We cannot now investigate their reasons for opposing the Council in detail. We know that when the Definition was to be signed, unfortunately the bishops from Alexandria—although they accepted the faith—did not offer their signatures. They simply stated "we don't have our patriarch." He should sign it first and then us. When we come back to Alexandria we will elect one and let him sign it first. There were those who were disingenuously hiding behind this in order to avoid signing the definitions of Chalcedon. When they got back to Alexandria, the schism occurred because the Orthodox elected their own bishop Proterius, and the other party elected another. That's how the schism took place, and how the monophysite Church emerged. It happened initially in Alexandria, then in Antioch, Jerusalem and Ethiopia. These are the four Churches: the Coptic in Egypt, the Ethiopian, the Syrian in Syria and India and the Armenian Church with its roots in Lebanon.

The creed became standard orthodox doctrine, while the Coptic church of Alexandria dissented, holding to Cyril's formula of the oneness of Christ's nature as the incarnation of God the Word (μία φύσις τοῦ Θεοῦ Λόγου σεσαρκωμένη). This church felt that this understanding required that the creed should have stated that Christ be acknowledged "from two natures" rather than "in two natures." This miaphysite position, often known as "Monophysitism," formed the basis for the distinction of what we call the Oriental Orthodox churches—the Coptic church of Egypt and Ethiopia and the "Jacobite" churches of Syria and Armenia. Over the last 30 years, however, the miaphysite position has been accepted as a mere restatement of orthodox belief by the Eastern Orthodox Church and by the Roman Catholic Church.

II. Theological significance

So to the question: what is the existential meaning of its Christology in relation to the problem of the overcoming of death?—we can give an answer by analyzing the four adverbs of the Definition: ἀσυγχύτως, ἀτρέπτως, ἀδιαιρέτως, ἀχωρίστως.

Fr. John Meyendorff holds that these "four negative adverbs, while they condemned the two contrary heresies of Nestorius and Eutyches, excluded any pretention to explain fully in human terms the very mystery of the incarnation." It is true that this Creed, being an extraordinary theological and philosophical achievement, does not exhaust the whole Truth; neither does it detract from the personal character of this revelation. These verbal confessions refer to the living Person of Christ, and the Church through them receives above all a Person and not ideas. However, beyond this apophatical aspect, they offer a solid basis for further theological meaning. Metropolitan John Zizioulas, in his lucid study, "'Created' and 'Uncreated': The Existential Significance of Chalcedonian Christology" elaborated the meaning of two of these words: ἀσυγχύτως (without confusion) and ἀδιαιρέτως (without division).

Let us try here to see the significance of ἀτρέπτως, unchangeably and ἀχωρίστως, inseparably. The first of these adverbs ἀτρέπτως means that, in Christ—theologically, anthropologically, cosmologically and ecclesiologically—there is no change between the two natures, per se. The essence of the natures (so to speak) did not change. Their otherness is completely respected and preserved. So, anthropologically, man remains completely man, and not god, and vice versa; cosmologically, the created nature remains created, and not uncreated, and vice versa. On the other hand, ἀδιαιρέτως refers to such a union, being perfect and absolute, where nothing can separate them because of the hypostatic union (as opposed to "union of natures"). By preserving the two natures after the Incarnation, Chalcedon safeguarded the precious concept of otherness. We shall see below how important this aspect is for us today. Speaking existentially in terms of person and nature, Chalcedon affirmed both unitatis and alteritas, communion and otherness. This is the accomplishment of these apophatic formulations.

With this approach, an emphasis is placed on the biblical dynamic of God's presence and activity through Revelation via Economy of salvation. As such, Christ is not only the One who truly *exists* but is also the One who *works truth* (ποιῶν τὴν ἀλήθειαν: John 3:21; cf. 1John 1:6), from creation, through the Incarnation, and until the eschatological deification in the Kingdom. This most certainly provides an answer to the basic question that intrigued the Apostles, and biblical man in general, to which the Gospels bear striking witness. In fact, the Biblical-Semitic preoccupation did not even concern whether or not God existed, but rather when Yahweh would come and judge the world and how they were to enter into eternal life with him.

Chalcedon provided the Church with a terminology capable of protecting the faith from both Nestorian and monophysite aberrations. By stating that the one person of Christ is one hypostasis, it demonstrated its determined opposition to Nestorianism.

On the other hand, by saying that this hypostasis is known in two natures, not only in a divine but also in a human nature, it showed that it is unacceptable to confuse Christ's natures, to jeopardize his consubstantiality with the Father and with us, or to undermine the fullness and integrity of his humanity after the union. The Theanthropic reality of Christ does not represent a mere episode of human history but the ontological basis of its salvation.

The Chalcedonian Oros [Definition] presents Christ as the Savior of the world, as a cosmic Christ. However, it is not because Jesus Christ brought a model of morality or a teaching for humanity; it is because He himself incarnates the overcoming of death, because, in his own Person, the created now lives eternally. This was a profoundly Eucharistic approach to the Chalcedonian Christology, since the reception of Christ by the people of God always takes place within the event of Communion. Eucharist was not of course the focus of Chalcedon, but it is widely admitted that the Eucharist occupies the central place in its Christology .

All this leads us to the crucial observation that the very godly "face" of Revelation, as the Initiator (Αὐτουργὸς) of all the aforementioned, is Christ. In that sense, when Christ is spoken of, what is really referenced is the entire Mystery of Christ, that is, Christ *as* the Church. The Apostle Paul explains to the Hebrews that Christ is *the same yesterday, today and forever* (see chapters 12 & 13). In this way, in Christ, the encompassing and transcendent side of God's being is born into the concrete historical context of the Church, into which Yahweh-Truth becomes a *present* reality that, paradoxically, is also yet to come. It is immensely important, then that the profound *mystery and power of the Gospel* come from the future, precisely because of Christ, who *is yet to come*. With this biblical framework, we can see the fullness of a *Pneumatological* dimension. In fact, with the power of the Holy Spirit, the mystery of Christ is not brought about by an "anamnesis" in a mere "psychological-empirical" sense. On the contrary, in every Eucharistic experience of the Resurrection as a judgment-truth of this world, the Church of the Holy Spirit douses the paradox of Christ's Gospel, which not a single epistemology can fathom, since those paradoxes are a *remembrance of the Coming One*.

III. Postmodern cultural and existential significance

So, we deal here with the existential meaning of Chalcedon: Who is Christ? What is Christ for me (per me)? It is critical for the theology to regain its existential meaning and purpose, and to cease from being alien to the agonizing questions of contemporary man.

The problem lies with the alien theological terms that we have adopted without much discernment, because of which contemporary man's answer to the Lord's question: "what do men say about who I am?," is either, a) that Christ is of no interest to him because He cannot help him out of his miseries, or, b) that Christ has placed upon him an unbearable burden that has completely weighed him down. Very few are those who recognize Christ today as "meek and of a humble heart," or as the good Samaritan—being "consubstantial with us according to Manhood"— who "pours oil and wine over man's wounds." Maybe Christ loved sinners "more" than others.

We live in an age of individualism. In our so-called civilization, everyone thinks only of himself; this attitude is not limited to the "secular" world, but is also present among Christians. Individualism has crept in and each one of us tries to be reconciled with God by himself, on his own. He forgets his brother or looks at him as an object of his criticism and blame and forgets that the meaning of the spiritual life, the fulfillment of our salvation, exists in this very act of receiving our brother. Our ecclesial communities should expand Christ's prayer at Gethsemane to the whole world, offering themselves to the world instead of imposing themselves on it.

But in spite of this general wisdom of Chalcedon's Christology— which we must always bear in mind—its theological content acquired, over the course of history, a very important sense. This sense is mainly associated with the life of the Church as manifested in culture, in arts (iconography, architecture), and in parish life (with a transformative power of this truth in social life); one can go even further and conclude that Chalcedonian (and of course Post-Chalcedonian) Christology influenced the whole process of the inculturation of the Gospel. One can speak about the "cultural" epistemology proposed by Chalcedon that has an indisputably "incarnational" basis.

So, what is the contextual manifestation of the eternal Christological dogmas of Chalcedon? History has offered various responses to it, and we note just a few: the Russian Christology of kenosis, so evident in iconography; the Theanthropic Christology of St. Justin of Chelie (Popovich), the "asymmetrical Christology" of George Florovsky, and the "Pneumatologically conditioned Christology" of John Zizioulas. On the basis of Chalcedon's Christology, for instance, St. Gregory Palamas develops authentic hesychast anthropology, wherein only Christ enables us to come to God without losing ourselves—our otherness. He enables self-realization without destroying the god in us and without abolishing the human. The Mystery of Christ is not only the central dogma of our Faith but it is also the supreme gift of God—the Way in which God, as the Land of the Living (Psalm 26:15), gives Himself to man and accepts man in Himself, without abolishing either.

All the above-mentioned Christological expressions are faithful to Chalcedon, because they are also grounded on the four adverbs (ἀσυγχύ-τως, ἀτρέπτως, ἀδιαιρέτως, ἀχωρίστως). Inculturation inevitably involves the Incarnation of Christ, be it in forms other than, and in addition to, the historical one. There is no race and no culture to which the Word of God can be unrelated. It is critical for the Logos (both the eternal Word and the theological word) to regain existential meaning and purpose.

Yet, what makes this "true God and True Man" an inclusive corporate personality, that is, Someone who takes part in all human agonies and weaknesses? It is another Divine Person (about which Chalcedon does not speak)—the Holy Spirit who works with Christ. Christ relates to people's culture by the Holy Spirit, because Logos is inseparably connected with Pneuma. For now, we can say that "the Spirit allows Christ to enter again and again in every culture and assume it by purifying it, that is, by placing it in the light (or one might say under the judgment) of what is ultimately meaningful as it is revealed in Christ." Theology must not simply speak about God, but invite people to His Body, for Christ is not an individual, conceivable in isolation: He is "the firstborn among many brethren" (Rom 8:29). The brethren, by communing with the personal being of God through Christ in the Spirit, constitute the primary service that the Church can render to every person and to all humanity in the modern world.

With the help of these theological principles, drawn from a study of Chalcedon's Christology, we can make the following points regarding the arts. We should emphasize that Orthodox iconography depicts Christ as a full man, as opposed to the monophysite depiction. This God-man realism was also applied in architecture, as Hagia Sophia in Constantinople testifies. Within this broader theological and existential context, Christian art went beyond the dilemma of anthropological maximalism or minimalism. Byzantine architecture surpassed classical notions of symmetry in its embodiment of Christology; the iconography of the most representative temples similarly expressed theological principles in an art that complimented, but surpassed, classical models (Hagia Sophia, Pantokrator, Chora ton zoonton, etc.).

So, a Byzantine icon of Jesus Christ always indicates Christ's eternity (as the Pantocrator, "the Same through all Ages"), but, at the same time, the expression in Christ's face (e.g. his gaze or eyes) reveals his participation in human agonies and weaknesses. Gazing at Him we might say that this is an "existential" Christ Who, having become man, lives through the antinomies of human existence, through time and difficulties, through passions and suffering (ὁμοούσιον ἡμῖν κατὰ τὴν ἀνθρωπότητα). This is a Christ Who does not wish to be separated from human beings; He is descending to their level, taking upon Himself all human troubles and conditions (the human condition)—"everything except sin" (κατὰ πάντα ὅμοιον ἡμῖν χωρὶς ἁμαρτίας). In the Orthodox iconographic depiction of Christ's face (eyes), we can see a complete sympathy for humanity, which culminates in the Cross and in the Resurrection.

Our postmodern time demands a respect for otherness, as expressed through the effort to assert personal distinctiveness and both assemble and advertise one's identity. However, this otherness remains in tragic isolation; nothing is as dreadful as the "other" without the inseparable union with somebody else. How can the Chalcedonian dogma help in this situation? Respect for otherness is "covered" with four Chalcedonian terms: ἀσυγχύτως, ἀδιαιρέτως, ἀτρέπτως (unchangeably) and ἀχωρίστως (inseparably). Being inseparably united with us, Christ of Chalcedon identifies Himself with all of us. Not only does He simply bear man's infirmities, but also He assumes responsibility for all these, possessing as He does the true sense of being human. He took this responsibility on the Cross precisely because He was the one who was paying for the sins of others. He did not simply bear the infirmities of others, He paid for them.

This leads us to the next important aspect of this unchangeable and inseparable unity: that which is valid for Christ is valid for us all. We, too, are invited to "receive one another." What does it mean to receive our brother? Simply to tolerate him? At this point we often stop, but this is not the meaning of "receiving." Receiving means I receive him within me and I become one with him—like receiving food. And as in receiving food one element of its nature becomes part of our body, assimilated by our body, transformed and becomes one body with us, so by participating in the Body of Christ, we also receive one another and each receives Christ, leaving each participant fundamentally altered within the very constitution of his being.

Chalcedon does not address the ecclesiological dimension of the Mystery of Christ. However, Christ is inseparably connected with the Church, which is the Body of Christ, the very presence of the Divine gift to the world in each place. In our particular situation today, our divided Churches are called to receive from one another and indeed to simply receive one another. This raises all sorts of fundamental ecclesiological questions, since the highest point of unity in this context is that of mutual ecclesial recognition and not simply agreement on doctrine.

It now seems to be a matter of when, rather than if, the restoration of full communion between our Churches, which has been sadly interrupted for centuries, will occur.

IV. Concluding remarks

In this presentation, we tried first to identify ways in which the Chalcedonian Christology could operate today. It is obvious that there are different Christological approaches among the churches concerning the application of this Chalcedonian model. Yet, there are positive developments offering hope that this model can be of use today. In concluding, let me specify a few of the many fields in which Chalcedonian Christology can be realized: as an antidote to the prevailing individualism in society, to overcome Hindu-inspired spiritualism, to curb the growing psychologism, to transform the culture, and to answer questions of bioethics and modern biotechnology.

Chalcedonian Christology is holistic and not totalitarian. Christ appeared with his *parousia* (presence, visitation), and not with his *ousia*, by springing from an event of communion. The consequences are really astonishing, which is as it should be because they testify to Triadic Grace in action: when we say Χριστός, we mean the "anointed one," anointed of the Father by the Holy Spirit.

Where can this Christology be helpful? Pluralism is a tremendous opportunity. Instead of having one uniform Christology (e.g. patristic), we should cultivate a vision of the Christological transformation of the world in a Neopatristic way; that is what Neochalcedonianism offers in order to fulfill and clarify the Fourth Ecumenical Council. The Chalcedonian view of Christ contains many elements that can be helpful for our situation, if we view them theologically and make proper use of them. These are the crucial points where this vision can help modern man.

This Christology overcomes the individualism and autarchy of humanity by offering personal communion where freedom to be other concurs with full communion and excludes any totalitarian ontology. Instead of spiritualism or psychologism, we have a theanthropic encounter with Christ, Who reveals himself as the Church, as "Χώρα τῶν ζώντων" (the Land of the Living) where we can see, hear, feel, touch, and know Him. There are aspects of Church life, such as hymnography, iconography, architecture, and culture (e.g. Hagia Sophia as a master work of Chalcedonian Christology), that are so deeply bound to this Christological Definition that they cannot operate without reference to the Chalcedonian vision. The central point of this Faith is Christ as the Land of the Living, as the Living Space, Whom God was well-pleased to give us in order that we may live eternally in Him, with Him, around Him, before Him, together with Him, and thereby, with one another. In our times, humanity faces many problems, including increasing ecological problems that threaten humanity's living space. Thus, Christ as the Land of the Living is very pertinent.

This Christology, however, implies ascetical self-denial (αὐταπάρνησις). Nobody is as personal, nor as unique as Paul who said: "it is no longer I who live, but Christ who lives in me" (Gal 2:20) At the same time, it is prophetic, since Christ's presence is always a judgment, "κρῖσις of this world" (Gospel of John). This leads us to a Church that addresses the word of love, the "kenosis" or "self-emptying" of the Cross, and of understanding acquired through self-depletion rather than self aggrandizement. It is a Christological message that—when formulated properly— should strike the existential chord of man, to which he can harmonize his own being and, thereby, overcome the tragic dead-ends of this life. Beyond biochemistry, Christ existentially strikes our inner chord, our genes, the logoi of beings, as St. Maximus, who developed an amazing Christology founded in Chalcedon, confirms so eloquently and perceptively. Modern man, our neighbor, is fiercely tried and gripped by anxiety in the face of an uncertain future. He needs an outstretched hand leading to the Risen Christ; he needs to be opened toward communion and community. This opening of man to God—the opening of history to the future of earth leading to Heaven—is the message of Chalcedon. It should also be our message and our faith.

For us in the 21st century, it is important to highlight that this experience-event of Christ is experienced by every epoch within its very *own* context. Therefore it is immensely important that new Christological approaches and studies become available, allowing different cultures and mentalities to newly envisage the eternal significance of the Ever-existing God.

Chalcedonian Christology, concerning the historical-eschatological reality of Christ, indicates the wondrous synthesis gifted to us by the Biblical and classical Greek understandings of Truth. In this synthesis, the epistemological boundaries are shifted, so that with our "understanding" of the object, through our "envisioning" of the truth and the "doing" of truth, we arrive at the salvific *praxis* of living the Truth of Christ in our own life, yesterday, today and, eschatologically, forever.

Ecumenical Councils
(fresco in Dečani Monastery, Kosovo and Metohia – Serbia, 1330-40)

Neopatristic Christology in Postmodern Culture

Presuppositions and Criteria for a Contextual Theology

The theological sensitivity of the organizers of this conference led me to consider the subject of Christology, as we have inherited it from the Fathers of the Church, in the light of the challenges of the modern era.[1] The Church cannot present society with an ethos other than that which springs from the life of Christ, nor can it preach a Christ who differs from the Christ preached to us by the Greek Fathers, in particular. The desideratum of Orthodoxy in the postmodern era will be a "Christ-centered ethos" (χριστοήθεια, St. Ignatios of Antioch), which is always realized as a paradoxical, *cross-centered*, and *self-emptying* experience. Imbued with this ethos of Christ and faithful to the patristic spirit, Orthodoxy must express the language of love, compassion, and immediacy, without suppressing our God-bestowed freedom to respond to the exigencies of the moment, thereby miring the Church in a sterile longing for the past.

Introductory remarks

In order to develop the future of Orthodoxy at the beginning of the third millennium after Christ, we need to examine the current age of postmodern pluralism, since this is the cultural framework within which Orthodoxy is called to act, to which it is called to adapt, though not to align Itself. If I may, I would like to clarify the key concepts in

[1] This study is a humble tribute to my teachers, Bishop Athanasius (Yevtich), Metropolitan John (Zizioulas) and Fr. Stamatis Skliris, from whom I was able to learn the criteria with which patristic Christology freely and creatively is incarnated in space and time, transforming it, i.e. changing the *mode* [tropos] *of existence* and not the *reason* [logos] *of nature*.

this introduction: Christology, Patricity, Neopatricity, post-modernity, and culture.

Christology. From the beginning, the Church experienced the complete synthesis of the paschal (Christological) and pneumatological mystery of Pentecost within the Eucharistic experience, in which the "One" (the Messiah) and the "many" (Israel) coexisted in love and freedom. "Jesus Christ is the same yesterday and today and for ever" (Heb. 13:8), "the first—fruits, mediator, and perfection,"[2] and the "composite hypostasis" that recapitulates the whole of creation (Eph. 1:10), since He is the Savior of the world.[3] Thus, we have a soteriological Christology, just as our anthropology is soteriological. Christ assumes history but He does not assume all aspects of culture, just as the world does not accept Him (John 1:10–11; as we will see below).

By the term *Patricity*, I mean the patristic conception and philosophy of life, which has as its starting point the mystery of the incarnation of Christ, as the criterion of His reception and assumption of that which is, or is not, receivable. This issue, however, is not self-explanatory, since the Patristic era—with all due respect—although in many ways unsurpassed, should not be romantically conceived as an era that cannot be repeated, because "the Fathers are all gone and there will be no more." We are thus dealing with a problem of methodology when approaching theology patristically.

"Neopatristic" means measuring our lives with the Patristic spirit and intellect, so that we can give new answers to today's problems. This is precisely what we know as the "Neopatristic synthesis," where the "neo" means new images and terms, while "Patristic" means the spirit and thought of the Fathers (without, of course, preaching "another Gospel"). A *Neopatristic* approach helps liberate us from protology (a romantic conception of the past) through immanent eschatology as a proposal for life in the *present*.

Postmodernity, properly considered, while religiously neutral (the principle that characterizes our era is summed up in the phrase "believing

---

[2] "Christ is the beginning, the middle and the end; for He is in all, in the first, the middle and the last as He is in the first. Christ is all things and in all people" (Symeon the New Theologian, *Chapters* 3.1).

[3] "This world and these people—in whatever situation it or they may be—has salvation because there is a Savior" (Saint Justin Popovic).

without belonging"), can, nevertheless, be a Christian concept, if "post" means "beyond" and "modernity" refers to "the here and now." Christianity embraces the moment with one's neighbor, and calls all to a loving participation in "guarding the place"[4] and the sanctification of spacetime (*Raumzeit*) in a Christ-like way. The concept of "post-modernity" has contributed to our understanding that there are no self-evident things, truths, identities, or principles. At the same time, however, the thirst postmoderns exhibit for *originality* betrays their fear of death and as they strive to fashion an antidote to death.

Culture or civilization is human creativity that aspires towards transcendence through created symbols and means.[5] The Church is culture par excellence because the Liturgy is a cultural event that sanctifies every human creation and institution: painting, architecture, music, education, philosophy, poetry, social and political institutions and religious sentiment. If the Church wants to serve people today, it must address and serve their *transcendent* needs, expressed today primarily through culture. This does not mean that Orthodox must become "culture vultures" nor that they must "build their own culture, come what may,"[6] through a social ethic; but it does mean that they should experience the truth that the grace of the Holy Spirit exists in the 21st century and, consequently, that genuine creativity still exists.

We are faced, then, with an issue of great importance and a crucial question: How can the Mystery of Christ—as the Fathers of the Church saw and explained it—be incarnated afresh today, in accordance with the teachings of the Fathers, but at the same time in the new forms and experiences of postmodern people, within the framework of their own culture?

[4] See the Gerontikon or work of the iconographer Fr. Stamatis.
[5] In Wikipedia, we find the following definition: In the twentieth century, "culture" emerged as a concept central to anthropology, encompassing all human phenomena that are not purely results of human genetics. Specifically, the term "culture" in American anthropology had two meanings: (1) the evolved human capacity to classify and represent experiences with symbols, and to act imaginatively and creatively; and (2) the distinct ways that people living in different parts of the world classified and represented their experiences, and acted creatively (http://en.wikipedia.org/wiki/Culture).
[6] On the margins of C. Kern's book, *The Anthropology of St. Gregory Palamas*, St. Justin Popovich (of Chelie) wrote: "It is not man's purpose to create culture, as Kern wants, because cultures come and go." "For the form of this world is passing away" (1 Cor. 7:31), but not the world itself, adds Fr. G. Florovsky.

In this short paper, I will try to see what *bridges* can be constructed, on the basis of Christology, between the Orthodox Tradition and Western postmodern culture. It is a difficult task,[7] especially today, despite all the answers and solutions that have been given in the examples of the inculturation of the Gospel into the historical conditions of Christianity at various times in the past, most notably in the age of the Fathers in the 4th century. The solutions of the past do not automatically transfer to the present, and therefore what is needed first and foremost are *theological criteria*, and also hard spiritual struggle (*podvig*). Although every age has lived and experienced Christ in its own way, and articulated this experience through its own means (theoretically, intellectually, politically and so on), there have always been problems in the cultural expression of this experience. This relationship is always *dialectical* and *critical* ("now is the judgment [κρῖσις] of this world," John 12:31). One could go even further and claim that every age has a legitimate need and even a *right* to receive (in the sense in which the Apostle Paul used the word) in its own way Christ—Who is the same forever, but therein lurks the great temptation of secularization, utopianism, romanticism, sentimentalism, aestheticism and so on. In order for us to *judge* what is received by the Church from among cultural achievements, we must have *criteria*. In other words, if the Church transforms the world, *into what* is it transforming it? To this question, the Church's only response is Christological.

Christ assumed history but He did not assume all aspects of culture; the world did not receive Him[8] ("He came to his own home, and his own people did not receive him," John 1:11, as also in, indicatively, John 7:1–13). Interestingly, in the Gospel according to Luke, Jesus is presented as a "foreigner" and a "stranger" in this world (2:4, 39; 8:1; 13:22; 17:11; 4:29–30; 9:53, 58; 24:18), though this does not exclude His hypostatic connection with the world. It ought to be noted that Christ Himself rejected many of the cultural expressions of Israel, maintaining, for example,

---

[7] Even if it is difficult. See D. Magriplis, "Θρησκεία καὶ φιλελευθερισμὸς στὸ δρόμο γιὰ μιὰ πολυπολιτισμικὴ—πολυθρησκευτικὴ κοινωνία," *Σύναξη* 108, 2008, p. 41. See also the volume of collected works, *Ὀρθοδοξία καὶ νεωτερικότητα*, ΙΝΔΙΚΤΟΣ, 2007.

[8] Mt. 8:20: "Foxes have holes, and birds of the air have nests; but the Son of Man has nowhere to lay his head." For this aspect of Christology, see A. Denaux, "A Stranger in the City: A Contribution to the Study of the Narrative Christology in Luke's Gospel," *Louvain Studies* 30 (2005), pp. 255–275.

a clearly negative attitude toward the Pharisees (whom He saw as representatives of a social institution that hindered entrance into the Kingdom, Mt. 5:20 and chapt. 6), as well as towards the Sabbath (and related cultural traditions). He was also wary of being classified as part of an ethnic cultural heritage. When Christ entered a particular cultural milieu, He did not adopt it but corrected it and *introduced innovations* to it: "You have heard that it was said...but I say to you..." (Mt. 5:21–22, etc.), just as He does not abolish, but endows with meaning: "I have not come to abolish but to fulfill" (5:17), not, however, in a subsidiary role, but as He who acts to make all things new (Rev. 21:5).

It seems, then, that throughout its history, the Church has employed both approaches, i.e. both *positive* (pro-culture) and *negative* (anti-culture). It expresses the first through its *Eucharistic* tradition, and the second through its ascetic tradition and *monasticism*, which, by its very nature, was a *denial of culture*.[9]

I. Historical paradigms

In its dissemination of the Gospel, the Church operated in accordance with the principles of pluralism and respect for both cultural diversity, on the one hand, and the particular features of the peoples to whom it was imparting the message on the other. Therefore, *reception* or *assumption* requires the adaptation of the Gospel to its cultural environment (which later became known in the canon law of our Orthodox Church as "economy" or dispensation, οἰκονομία). The reverse, however, is also true,[10] and here we must be especially careful. In assuming a culture, the Church "*baptizes*" it. We must not forget, however, that Baptism is also a *death*, from which a new person emerges. In the case of baptizing a culture, aspects of that culture must die and a new culture emerges. Inculturation means not simply respecting the identity, traditions, and locus[11] of a particular people, but primarily (and simultaneously) *care* for the existential—not merely passing—needs of people

---

[9] See G. Florovsky, *Christianity and Culture*, Collected Works Vol. 2.

[10] If God adapts the way of salvation to us, not changing the goal, the Church has no choice but to do the same. See how St. Maximos the Confessor (PG 90, 812) interprets divine "contrition" (μεταμέλεια).

[11] The Sinaitic idea of a ladder that leads to Christ is simply a *spiritual* adaptation to the cultural-geographical environment of Egypt.

today. If, with the Incarnation of Christ, "natures were innovated,"[12] how can cultures not be innovated through their Baptism with His Gospel? This is particularly true when we know that different cultures mean different ways of approaching the faith and expressing it.[13] However, ought we not to look at the criteria used in this "baptism" of culture? What is assumed (Christ's positive attitude) and what is rejected (Christ's negative attitude)? A culture includes both the existential and the ephemeral, and culture is always "in earthen vessels" (2 Cor. 4:7). I think that Orthodoxy *today* has not yet clarified what its criteria are for inculturating a postmodern society. The Fathers, however, did, and because we Orthodox have no other models, we must look to the Fathers to consider what we can do today.

1. Some examples of Patristic Christology can show us the ways in which the mystery of Christ was embodied throughout history in a positive way. The *positive* attitude toward a cultural, Christological expression has as its starting point the following principle of St. Maximus: "For always and in all things, the Word of God, Who is also God, desires to activate the mystery of this incarnation."[14] Thus we begin with the Apostle Paul (e.g. at the Areius Pagus) and the post-apostolic period.[15] In translating the faith into culture, the Apostles did not follow always the same paradigms. For instance, they did not follow the Septuagint, in which the name, "Yahweh" appears together with the phrase "ὁ Ὤν" (=*The existing one, the one who is*), a word which is, in a certain sense, a philosophical-ontological translation. That term would undoubtedly become significant for the conversion of the Greeks in the Gospels. The Apostles, rather, translate this Tetragrammaton in a providential, historical-eschatological, i.e. in a specifically Christological, sense. Thus, John

---

[12] Gregory the Theologian, *Oration* 38, 2.

[13] See David Tracy, *The Analogical Imagination: Christian Theology and the Culture of Pluralism*, New York, Crossroad, 1982. See also T. Matulić, *Metamorfoze kulture*, *Glas koncila*, Zagreb, 2009.

[14] Maximos the Confessor, PG 91:1084 cd. See J. Zizioulas, "Truth and communion," *Being as Communion: Studies in Personhood and the Church* (London: Darton, Longman & Todd, 1985), pp. 67–122. A. Yevtich, "Vaseljenski Sabori i saborno predanje Crkve," *Bogoslovlje* 1–2, 1973, pp. 43–80. C. Yannaras, Ἀλήθεια καὶ ἑνότητα τῆς Ἐκκλησίας (Athens Grigoris: 1997). See also the classic work by H. Richard Neibuhr, *Christ and Culture* (New York: Harper and Row, 1951).

[15] See J. Zizioulas, Ἑλληνισμὸς καὶ χριστιανισμός, συνάντηση τῶν δύο κόσμων, Ἀποστολικὴ Διακονία, Ἀθήνα 2003.

carries the word "YHWH" over with "the One Who Is, Who was and Who is to Come" (*Rev.* 1:8 & 22:13), while for Paul "Jesus Christ is the Same Yesterday, Today and Forever" (*Heb.* 13:8). Nicene and post-Nicene Christology expressed the great Trinitarian truth with audacious, non-traditional terms (such as the First Ecumenical Council's "consubstantial" [ὁμοούσιον]). The Christology of the Cappadocian Fathers was inspired by Trinitarian theology, but articulated in a contemporary language that underwent so much change that the ancient philosophers would not have understood its new meaning.[16] The Fathers transcended (neo-)Platonism, assimilating and transforming (Christianizing) it *from within*. The criteria for the Chalcedonian conception of the union of the two natures of Christ were based on four negative adjectives and the insistence on a hypostatic union. The "subsistent" [ἐνυπόστατον] of the period after the Council of Chalcedon emphasized the need for hypostatic assumption, and this Christology influenced the architecture (and all the art) of the Byzantines. After the Christological synthesis of Maximus and Symeon the New Theologian, we come to St. Gregory Palamas, who had at his disposal Maximus' "logos-tropos" distinction, yet wanted—in accordance with philocalistic *tradition*, his *surroundings*, and the spiritual pursuits of the Holy Mountain—to express the mystery of existence through the distinction between essence and energies. Additionally, in the realm of Western Christology, St. Augustine is seen as an example of a theologian of "cultural transformation."[17] In the realm of Christology, our age can cite similar models, such as the asymmetric Christology rec-

---

[16] The transmission of the dogmas cannot be done without their interpretation, i.e., through explicating old concepts and terms by means of contemporary concepts, which is something beyond the mere translation of texts from one language to another. Meyendorff and Zizioulas have traced many answers that have been offered over the centuries, showing how the meaning of many theological terms has changed and expanded far beyond the original (Platonic or Aristotelian) conception. They illustrate this with certain terms and concepts that the Church borrowed from Greek culture for dogmatic purposes. Zizioulas takes, for example, the terms καθολικός, πρόσωπον and ὑπόστασις, while Meyendorff writes about ὑπόστασις and φύσις in connection with the Chalcedonian definition. Historically and culturally, they are Greek words but those who established them (e.g. Aristotle, Platon etc.) most probably would not understand their meaning had they been given the Nicene or Chalcedonian Creed to read. See our paper "An Existential Interpretation of Dogmatics" in this book.

[17] For us, it is debatable to what degree Augustine molded the culture of that era with his use of Neoplatonism, rhetoric and ethics, contrary to the claims of H. Richard Neibuhr (*Christ and Culture*, New York: Harper and Row, 1951, p. 209).

ognized by Florovsky, the "pneumatologically-conditioned Christology" of Metropolitan John Zizioulas (which was formulated in opposition to the "double economy" of Lossky and the Slavophiles), the "soborniy (catholic) Christ" in the theology of St. Justin (Popovich) of Chelie,[18] the Eucharistic Christ "for the life of the world" of Fr. Alexander Schmemann,[19] the Christology of the *Land of the Living* in the theology of Bishop Athanasius Yevtich[20] and so on.

2. In none of the above cases of reinterpretation of teaching is there any doubt about each generation's right to express in its own way—without introducing anything novel (other than personal renewal)—the mystery "of the faith which was *once and for all* delivered to the saints" (Jude 1:3). Historically, however, there was always a tendency to transfer the Chalcedonian principle of "unconfusedly and indivisibly" from Christology to sociology and culture. The question remained open, however, as to whether the union has to do exclusively with nature or with something more, which we might call culture.

We ought really to mention here models of the *positive* embodiment of Christology on the cultural level of the Byzantines[21] and other peoples in the course of history, but such a parenthesis, because of the wealth of relevant examples, would exhaust the remaining time for this chapter and would depart from the issue at hand. The references, therefore, to Hagia Sophia and other churches in Constantinople, and to Byzantine architecture and art in both its ecclesiastical and lay expressions, will, unfortunately, have to be omitted, but we can at least note the main feature of this tradition. Due to its contextual nature, the Orthodox Tradition is a *custom-dominated* (*cultural*) tradition rather than *reason-dominated* one, which means that it addresses the whole person (and not just their intel-

---

[18] See his *Dogmatics* (Belgrade 1934) as well as his book *Man and the God-Man*, (Sebastian Press: 2009).

[19] Schmemann was the one representative of the Neopatristic synthesis who spoke in a language that was relevant to contemporary people, by translating the functional-eucharistic tradition, like "new wine [...] in fresh wineskins" (Mt. 9.17). See *For the Life of the World* (St. Vladimir's Seminary Press 1988).

[20] See his "Christ—The Land of the Living," *Christ—the Alpha and Omega*, Sebastian Press: 2007, pp. 41–52.

[21] The example of the iconic representation of the ancient Greek philosophers in the narthex of Great Lavra expresses Tertullian's view that all "good" culture is Christian: "whatever is good in the world is from Christians." He also said: *Quid ergo Athenis et Hierosolymis*, of course.

lect) at the level of *morals and daily life*. There are other cultures, on the other hand, such as the Western, which require "intellectual" explanations, a continual "catechesis." How did the Orthodox peoples survive under the rule of the Romans, the Franks and the Turks without catechesis? As Christos Yannaras has observed, "even when the Greeks[and, I would add, the other peoples of the Balkans]were enslaved, uneducated and poor they did not cease to produce culture and active alterity, a proposal able to reach out to peoples. From the time they became nation-states, they have simply imitated."[22]

3. Allow me to mention one example of the inculturation of the Gospel from the local, Serbian ecclesiastical culture: what we call "Svetosavlje," which is a particular philosophy of life and application of Orthodox dogmas and the Orthodox ethos, in a positive and organic way, in the particular situation of an Orthodox people. For many of my fellow-countrymen, "Svetosavlje" is the quintessence of Serbian history, a spiritual category of life and practice, a *constanta* and *constituanta* of our people.[23] Yet, there are certain negative aspects and repercussions of the phenomenon of Svetosavlje that demonstrate exactly what happens *when culture is assumed without criteria* and slides into a "patriotic theology."[24]

An unsuccessful but noteworthy attempt at assuming culture was the "Orthodox Gallicanism" of Kovalevsky.[25] Many scholars believe that the theology offered by the Russian diaspora was a cultural event. The Russians who emigrated to Europe after the Soviet revolution entered into dialogue with Western culture. Among these, Vladimir Lossky delivered

[22] C. Yannaras, "Ἐθνεγερσία, σύγκρουση δύο ὁραμάτων," http://kratylos.blogspot. com/2007/04/blog—post_06.html.

[23] Bishop Irinej Bulović, "Pravoslavlje, svetosavlje, duhovnost...," *Vidoslov* 1, 2000. The same author is also quick to point out some negative aspects and repercussions of the Svetosavlje phenomenon.

[24] See D. Najdanovic's insistence on "ethnological ontology" ("Pravoslavlje i svetosavlje," *Srpski dogovor*, vol. 1, Westmont–USA 1973). On the other hand, a genuine patriotism of the Holy Fathers "was not geocentric (i.e. limited to one particular location) or autonomous, nor was it idolatrous, but rather it was ecclesiastical and 'hierocratic,' i.e. soteriological and universal, and because of this, it was incomparably deeper and more genuine than common patriotism" (Εἰρηναίου Μπούλοβιτς, *Τὸ μυστήριον τῆς ἐν Ἁγίᾳ Τριάδι διακρίσεως τῆς Θείας οὐσίας καὶ ἐνεργείας κατὰ τὸν Ἅγιον Μάρκον Ἐφέσου τὸν Εὐγενικὸν* [Irinej Bulovic, The Mystery of the Distinction between the Divine Essence and Energy in the Holy Trinity according to St. Mark the Evgenikos of Efesos], Πατριαρχικὸν Ἵδρυμα πατερικῶν μελετῶν, Θεσσαλονίκη 1983, p. 3).

[25] A. Yevtich, Report to the Holy Synod on the ECOF, April 2005.

a decisive blow to the traditional Western perspective. He influenced contemporary (Western and Orthodox) theology, and this influence is still evident today. Yet, some of Lossky's views contained certain weaknesses that have had serious repercussions, and these have been noted.[26] The immigrants' cultural agenda did not effect a change in French culture, however, but merely inspired an appreciation of Orthodoxy as an exotic brand that impresses with beautiful icons, music, etc. (which generate interest, as does any Near Eastern culture). This, of course, accords well with multicultural post-modernity, which is *competitive*: we all need to be in there, and we watch to see who will "sell" the most. Orthodoxy, too, has its shelf in the supermarket of culture. This issue needs careful study and is meaningless unless we clarify the Church's position on such matters.

4. The case of the *patristic* conception of culture demonstrates that theology is the most powerful weapon in the Church's hands, more so than any other (political, diplomatic or whatever). Yet, again, what are the criteria? The misrepresentation of dogma leads to life that is out of joint and *faith* without *works* is of no help. When theology (Christology, Triadology, Pneumatology, etc.) has no existential influence on the Church's cultural expressions, as is the case today,[27] then we have a capitulation of the Church to culture, which should cause concern. Theology disconnected from life is just as bad as life without theology. Yet, we must not be overwhelmed with a sense of irresolution and purblindness, which comes from a mistaken and indiscriminate respect for tradition. Ready-made answers taken from the past are not the tradition of the Fathers. Rather, with them as a basis, we must see what we can do today. It sometimes seems as if we have Tradition in our hands and do not know what to do with it.

Let us, therefore, look at the Christological criteria of *lex vivendi* and *lex credendi* in the relationship between Church and postmodern culture.

II. Theological criteria (the requisite)

1. The re-reception (or reception anew) of Christ on the part of each successive generation is directly related to the activity of the Holy Spirit.

---

[26] See A. Papanikolaou, *Being with God: Trinity, Apophaticism, and Divine-Human Communion* (Notre Dame, Indiana: University of Notre Dame Press, 2006).

[27] G. Florovsky, "A Criticism of the Lack of Concern for Doctrine among Russian Orthodox Believers," *SVTQ* 3 (1995); also in *The Collected Works of Georges Florovsky*, vol. 13, pp. 168–70.

Beginning with Pentecost (Acts 2), the New Testament testifies most clearly to the fact that Christ is revealed and known "in Spirit and truth," and that the epistemological, cultural, and even psychological-biological preconditions of this reception are created and transformed because of a special act of the Holy Spirit. Consequently, Pneumatology is and remains a *conditio sine qua non* of every new embodiment of Christ in any culture, whether it be Near Eastern, African, Asian, or whatever. It is the Holy Spirit Who makes all different ways of thinking acceptable to the Person of the God-Man.[28] Christ is immanent in the world, present, active and activated in history ("You Who are enthroned on high with the Father and are invisibly present here with us"), but due to the descent of the Holy Spirit, Whom the Church invokes at every Liturgy, the Church's stance is *invocational*, i.e. par excellence eschatological. The Church is not based only on institutions, but also on gifts (or, better yet, institutions = gifts), as works of the Spirit, Who comes and acts in the Church, in history, and in the world, removing the obstacles, so that people can enter the Kingdom of God. (As A. Yevtich emphasizes, an institution itself can sometimes be an obstacle, as was the Old Testament[29]).

2. Therefore, in the Orthodox patristic tradition, the Spirit *constitutes* and makes present not only the event of the Liturgy, but also Christ Himself. The end things also become present in each historical generation through the action of the Spirit—our own generation included. With a measure of self-criticism, we must admit our inability to authentically experience the Christological transformation of life through the perspective of Pentecost. In the main, we see tradition as an ideal located in the distant past, from which we borrow *ad hoc* solutions. A modern theologian, iconographer, or hymnographer can today copy an old hymnological text, or an icon, *choosing*—in a most postmodern way—whatever seems acceptable to him without any reference to *his own* culture and the existential questions of his neighbor. In this perspective, people today are unable to see what Christ offers them. This approach is sterile worship

[28] See Acts 10:47–48: "'Can any one forbid water for baptizing these people who have received the Holy Spirit just as we have?' And he commanded them to be baptized in the name of Jesus Christ." Note here that the visitation of the Holy Spirit preceded Baptism.

[29] A. Yevtich, "Η ἐσχατολογία στὴ συγχρονη Ὀρθόδοξη θεολογία" (talk to "Goulandris–Horn," Athens), *Zagrljaj svetova*, Srbinje 2006. But see especially his talk, "The Eschata in Our Daily Life," in *Living Orthodoxy in the Modern World*, London 1996, pp. 37–49.

of the past and is prone to romanticization of our living Faith. We are Orthodox inasmuch as we respect the past, but we do so because the great events of Church history and Divine Economy, as a gift of God, took place then. However, we must understand that these gifts refer to both the past, the future—the Second Coming—and the present. The most representative icon of this synaxis of time is the Divine Liturgy, in which the operation and actions of Christ, past, present, and future, occur without distinction as a sacred Mystery. Moreover, our faith in this gift should be rendered in an atmosphere of hope and optimism.

3. And yet, the Neopatristic theological synthesis in our postmodern pluralistic culture will have the difficult task of demonstrating how Christ is shown, through the Spirit, to be the "communion of the many," the Church, i.e. a free multiplicity of persons united in one spirit[30] as an antidote to individualism. Since Christ is incarnated *as* the Church (and does not remain simply *in* the Church), the ecclesiology of the 21st century will remain the only locus for meeting Him. The Church's relationship with the world must be understood not only anthropologically, but also cosmologically, and always with the help of the concept of "communion." The Church exists not for itself, nor only for humanity, but for the whole of creation. The Church, therefore, is not essentially different from the Kingdom, inasmuch as its *raison d'être* and its purpose is to serve as an icon of the Kingdom and to become identical with it (and not with this world).[31]

4. Reprioritizing the *eschatological* perspective on life and ontology is necessary for our postmodern era. Every effort must be made in this direction, because when people do not have before them the eschatological view of the Kingdom that sanctifies and gives meaning to time, then they see only darkness and the unknown. By losing this eschatological sense, the postmodern age and culture turns to the past in the belief that it can find the meaning of its existence in old traditions. Consequently, Neopatristic Christology in postmodern culture must have two basic characteristics: a) firm adherence to the patristic spirit and pulse preserved in Church tradition, and 2) an authentic originality transcend-

---

[30] Adoption occurs through the Spirit which is called the "Spirit of adoption" (Cf. Gal. 3:27 and 4:6; Rom. 8:15). See A. Yevtich, [in Greek]. Ἐκκλησιολογία τοῦ Ἀποστόλου Παύλου,[2] Athens, 1967.

[31] Just recently, Hollywood produced a movie called *Knowing* that featured a dechristianized eschatology.

ing the mundane through the Resurrection and the gift of Pentecost, a gift bestowed as a blessing of the Church. As S. Skliris somewhere notes: "We must be careful not to symbolize rather than theologize in the context of the correct meaning and content."

5. The postmodern era is the "litmus test" for postmodern people. If we want to see what hurts and wounds them, and what interests them, we must look at their works of art (painting, architecture and so on). Then we shall see how heartsick they are with the "coordination," "principles," and "traditions," which hinder human creativity. And Orthodox anthropology is entirely in accord with this, since it does not view any one era as the ideal,[32] and this is because in *every* phase of history people are still created, mortal beings, and only Christ can free them from their passions. Salvation can come only from the end times. A rejuvenated Orthodox art will be in a position to show and offer postmodern people a Christ Who suffers with those who are suffering, who are disparaged through a variety of political and other manipulative practices, or who are wounded and alienated by life. A modern Orthodox icon of Christ[33] will speak directly to the hearts of people who have failed and are exhausted, rather than from a textbook on dogmatic theology. The point, however, is not to discard one or the other, but to find ways for them to bear fruit. The Christ who pours "wine and oil" on people's wounds is the Christ of postmodern culture.

6. This Christology, however, should be "catholic" in the real sense of the word, which means: holistic and transcending divisions (whether they be social, racial, or any other). But how can this "holistic" Christology avoid becoming overweening, since, if it does, it will not touch postmodern culture, which, by definition, seeks to transcend all totality? The answer rests with our Christ Who does not manifest Himself totally with His essence, but with His presence, a personal presence that embraces us only if we want it, respecting our alterity but changing the manner (the "hardware" stays the same but He changes our "software"). History, human nature, and culture thus become a "flaming but unburnt bush.." In every facet of His life, and how much more so in His Resurrection, Christ acts discreetly and powerfully, uniting, in a paradoxical way, His "divine weakness" with His omnipotence, just as we see in the icon of Resurrection: in the intensity of the surrounding imagery, He draws our ancestors,

---

[32]   As the Greek say: "God has children but not grandchildren."
[33]   Such as those by Stamatis Skliris, *In the Mirror*, Los Angeles, 2007.

Adam and Eve, from the darkness of death into the light of life. This is how Orthodox peoples traditionally experienced Christology: "The reason that such an experience of the Trinity, of the Father and of the Son and of the Holy Spirit, was possible in Orthodoxy was because Christ was seen and experienced at its centre."[34]

7. The postmodern era is anti-traditional and anti-totalitarian. As a result, we live in a very difficult age, in which people today rebel and revolt, with good reason, against a culture imposed on us and experienced as a system of rules without rules. While modernity was a deliberate revolt against traditional rules (in art, for example, the rules of the Renaissance), a violent rupture in the natural evolution of culture towards the deciphering of the laws of art, postmodernity is—after the split with modernity—a movement in the opposite direction, towards ancient cultures. Postmoderns re-examine everything, and are tired of the monotony, the repetition of created time. So in an entirely arbitrary manner, they use the same words, ideas, and concepts but give them different content, depending on the interests of the various groups. People today believe that they will exist only if they find something new, something that leads them out of the greyness of the mundane and stereotypical.[35] In essence, postmodern thought is thought that does not believe in itself. Yet, in spite of this, we cannot be allowed to lose faith in the possibilities of a "postmodern Christology" (which will have at its center the Christ of the Gospel, of the Seven Ecumenical Councils, the Christ of the Church presented *nove, sed non nova*). This faith illumines and gives hope to the kenotic victory. Just as the icon is a cultural representation (as we can see in architecture, psychology, biology and nature) of light free from the natural laws of creation, so also today Christian culture must liberate whatever it assumes, in an act that is at once ascetic and Eucharistic.

6. We have already said that in the 21st century we cannot present an ethos that differs from that which springs from the life of Christ, and that this ethos must be consistent with the spirit of the Fathers. What ethos springs from the life of Christ? First of all, the God-Man took on all aspects of human life—from the physiology and psychology of the

---

[34] A. Yevtich, "Πατερικὴ Τριαδολογία καὶ οἱ κίνδυνοι αἱρέσεων στὴ σύγχρονη τριαδολογία," *Χριστὸς Ἀρχὴ καὶ Τέλος*, ΙΝΔΥΚΤΟΣ 2007, p. 271.

[35] For this reason, it comes as no surprise that (as of 2009) only 13% of Roman Catholics in France believe in the Resurrection, while 60% believe in reincarnation.

human person, via customs and social relations, to culture—and so He embraces, not an abstract humanity, but becomes an identity of relationships as a "corporate personality" or a "universal man." Preaching the Resurrection must remain the kernel of the transmission of Christology. At the same time, however, this Christ is the antidote to sin[36] and to every false approach to life (Pharisaism, Utopianism, Romanticism or Nationalism). There is no direct route to salvation except through the Cross to the Resurrection, as Orthodoxy has lived it throughout the centuries: "Saul [the Greek, the Serb, anyone] must die in order for Paul [the Christian] to be born," as Bishop Athanasius emphasizes. Therefore we, too, must be catholic beings, persons in relationship with others, *ready to repent and be sacrificed for others*, as generously as Christ. When we seriously consider the accomplishments of modern culture—positive or negative—we show love toward man and acquire relationships that are fecund for life, and we are also able to construct culture. Otherwise, we will be confined to the margins of cultural-social life, as if we were a sect and not a living faith that gives meaning to and transforms people's lives.[37]

We are all postmodern because we do not concern ourselves with something foreign to us that we can cure from on high. We are at the side of contemporary people, like the patient in the next bed (as Haralambos Stathakis, a physician, said). Therefore, we are studying our own sickness, and it is difficult to find the medication.

III. Critical remarks (what must *not* happen?)

Christos Yannaras has already lamented that the Orthodox have ceased to create their culture. They have accepted the Western culture of the 20th century. Whether we like it or not, we Orthodox have also become multi-cultural. In the postmodern era and culture, Orthodox theology must recognize the elements of secularization and ideology, identify them, and avoid them, while it must highlight the authentic Christological elements and, bringing them into a relationship with eschatology, must place them in the light of the Eschaton.

---

[36] "Sin no more, that nothing worse befall you" (Jn. 5:14; 8:11), as well as "No one who abides in him sins; no one who sins has either seen him or known him" (1 Jn. 3:16). See also the Definition of Chalcedon.

[37] See H. Richard Neibuhr, *Christ and Culture* (New York: Harper and Row, 1951).

1. In this perspective—as the One, Holy, Catholic, and Apostolic Church—we ought to attempt, in a new, dynamic, and creative way, to repeat the Fathers' achievement—with other key concepts, "updating (innovating) the terms"—and to remain faithful to the Fathers' selection and legacy. This, however, will be achieved only if we try to belong to their world of light, truth, and love, the world of eternal values that inspires a human ethos to acquire a Godlike existence, and a culture that champions a beauty that does not depart. The criterion of this compassion and love toward postmodern man will be a Living Church which, first and foremost imparts the message arising from the Resurrection: hope of attaining the Heavenly Kingdom. This, however, involves a Eucharistic community that experiences a foretaste of the Truth. Preaching the Resurrection is not incompatible with culture.

2. We must rid ourselves of prejudices conflicting with the dogma of the Incarnation. If we, too, today believe in women's ritual impurity (it being a prejudice of a bygone culture), then not only do we undervalue women, we also undervalue the Incarnation of our Lord and its repercussions for our salvation.[38] Yet, how can a Christological faith be applied to contemporary cultural problems, such as we find, for example, in African culture? Polygamy is such a basic feature of African culture that an African cannot be African without also being a polygamist! Is there room, then, for the assumption of this cultural aspect—one that is contrary to the Gospel? And with what criteria will the Church accept or reject a given cultural feature? And why does it reject it? Today, there are a host of challenges (co-habitation, homosexuality, abortion and so on) and how are we to take them on board? Can we be flexible or not? Can we receive in Church a woman who has had an abortion? Or, in relation to art, how can we today make an icon that is not an imitation or repetition of a Byzantine icon? (Because the Byzantine icon is, as we suggested, a shelf in an aisle in the supermarket of religions that, with its beauty, can

---

[38] Cf. Φύλο καί θρησκεία — ἡ θέση τῆς γυναίκας στὴν Ἐκκλησία (συλλογικὸ), ΙΝΔΙ-ΚΤΟΣ 2004. Also, V. Larin, "What is 'ritual impurity' and why?," *SVTQ* 52:3–4 (2008) p. 292. See more generally Christ's position vis-à-vis women, which, like many of his positions, was especially "scandalous" for his time. When his disciples came across him speaking with the Samaritan woman, they were astonished that he was speaking with a woman. The Jews condemned him for eating with prostitutes and tax-collectors. It is also well known that his broader circle of disciples included women, who were the first to carry the joyful message of the Resurrection.

attract even someone who does not believe). Do we want the Church today to appear beautiful or do we want a Church that expresses people as they are today? How can this happen in a multi-cultural world? With what symbols?

3. By saying that our faith should be resurrectional and eschatological, we do not deny the foolishness of Christianity and our Cross-centered experience. As in apostolic times, so also today, we preach the "foolishness of the Cross" ("we preach Christ crucified, a stumbling block to Jews and folly to Gentiles," 1 Cor. 1:23) in a non-Christian cultural context. In the transmission of the Gospel, the Church and our ecclesiastical education will not rely on some guarantee of success, because our theology is *referential* and *kenotic*: Christ always was and always will be "a sign that is spoken against" (Lk. 2:34). Through kenotic (in a Christ-like way[39]) *self-criticism*, we will recognize our failure to speak the language of love, of Cross-centered self-emptying, and of understanding, for which people thirst today, hedged in as they feel. The truth and love that Orthodoxy invocationally "possesses" must not be understood activistically, but as a taste of the existence according to which whatever we have accomplished in history is experienced through eschatological transcendence.[40] It is precisely in the Eucharist that the communion of the Church is experienced and expressed as *a gift from above* and never as an achievement of the historical existence of the Church itself. Thus in the cultural activity of the Church, the basic rule must be the awareness that the Kingdom can judge any action of ours (of us who are Orthodox), not only as inappropriate, but as mistaken.[41]

4. If our Christological experience ends in the production of books as—irony of ironies—a substitute for inspired witness (to invoke St. John Chrysostom[42]), then we will remain anonymous, on the sidelines, and

[39] Phil. 2: 5–8: "Christ Jesus, who, though He was in the form of God, did not count equality with God a thing to be grasped, but emptied Himself, taking the form of a servant, being born in the likeness of men. And being found in human form He humbled Himself and became obedient unto death, even death on a cross."

[40] Cf. J. Zizioulas, "Comment on Communal Spirit and Conciliarity," *The One and the Many*, Sebastian Press 2010, p. 220.

[41] Elder Aimilianos of Simonos Petras also said this.

[42] "It were indeed meet for us not at all to require the aid of the written word, but to exhibit a life so pure, that the grace of the Spirit should be instead of books to our souls, and that as these are inscribed with ink, even so should our hearts be with the

will fail in our mission. First of all, the supposedly self-evident things in dogmatic theology must be challenged and reexamined and their contemporary significance made clear to us. This can happen if we are well-acquainted with Patristic dogmatic theology. Fr. Florovsky criticized Orthodox Christians' indifference to dogmatics and the prevailing trend in contemporary Orthodoxy of disparaging our own day.

5. Our failures and disappointments, however, should give rise to repentance and self-criticism. The main problem is that we Orthodox—in spite of the astonishing "Christological hope" we have been given—are still not ready to grapple with new challenges.

6. A kenotic, postmodern Christology will *help us avoid the automation* that is the primary characteristic of our age. Everything happens now at the push of a button or the tap of a computer key (the 20th century was already known as "the push button century"). Postmoderns have difficulty understanding the process involved and the effort required for each thing to happen, and the time that is needed for it to happen. People in an agrarian society knew that a certain amount of time, care, and effort were required to get from seed to harvest. "See how the farmer waits for the land to yield its valuable crop, patiently waiting for the autumn and spring rains. You too, be patient and stand firm, because the Lord's coming is near" (James 5: 7–8). Theology ought to inspire us to take responsibility for the effort required for the process, dispelling the illusion that someone who presses a button is omnipotent. It is a theology of patience, humility and so on.

IV. Suggestions/bridges for a postmodern—Orthodox cultural synthesis

What remains for us today is to find the *points of contact* with postmodern culture, while attending to the content and method of our Christological theology. We should not delude ourselves into thinking that method does not influence content.[43] If, however, we follow the example

Spirit. But, since we have utterly put away from us this grace, come, let us at any rate embrace the second best course. For that the former was better, God has made manifest, both by His words, and by His doings. In other words, it would be much better to learn the word of God directly from the Holy Spirit" (John Chrysostom in his first homily on the Gospel of Mark).

[43] Let us remember the establishment of non-critical Orthodox theological schools in the 19th and 20th centuries, which were modeled on Protestant and Roman Catholic

set by the Apostle Paul at the Areopagus ("I also found an altar with this inscription, 'To an unknown god,'" Acts 17:23), the Cappadocians (the common way of expression with the Hellenistic in Neoplatonic terminology), early Christian iconography (which borrowed the Greco-Roman vocabulary so that the people could understand), and other examples, then we would embrace postmodern elements (art, film, philosophy and so on) in order to speak to the people of our age. In this way, we would emphasize today also that life is Christ-centered.[44]

It is our duty to do this for the following reasons:

1. Every attempt at inculturation, since apostolic times, has aimed to translate and interpret the Gospel and its *resurrectional* message using the tools and features of the local culture. Perhaps this is what makes it necessary for acceptance and reception to take place, first of all, through the local Church.[45]

2. Patristic Christology involves cosmic, universal, environmental, social, cultural, and every other anthropological concern and care. Without our consent and initiative, others will not draw near us or understand. If we do not find the points of contact with people today, if we do not discover what their interests and concerns are, and if we do not "analyze" our *Truth* in a way they can understand, our voice will not be heard, and patristic Christology, which aims to treat their infirmities, will remain unknown.

3. The Church, however much it assumes culture, is an eschatological reality, which, within history, *can never be in harmony with it*. Today, when we talk about assuming culture, we run the danger of removing the element of persecution and conflict from the life of the Church. But on what issues am I prepared to be in conflict with and under persecution by culture? In a "fundamentalist" version of Christianity, I could be in conflict over the issue of abortion but not, say, over the war in Iraq, as is the case today among some Christians in America. For them, contempo-

---

universities, with near-tragic consequences for ecclesiastical education. More on this topic Cf. C. Yannaras, "Theology in Present-Day Greece," St. Vladimir's Seminary Theological Quarterly 16:4 (1972): pp. 195–207.

[44] "A true Christology must always be found in Trinitarian theology, i.e. inseparable from it, and therefore inseparable also from Pneumatology (A. Yevtich, op. cit, p. 271).

[45] See J. Zizioulas, "The Theological Problem of Reception," *The One and the Many*, Sebastian Press: 2010, pp. 118–125. It is true that every nation accepts the Gospel and Christ in different ways.

rary culture is unacceptable with regard to abortion, but they saw no problem with the bombing of innocent victims in Serbia, Iraq and elsewhere. We are in such confusion that the Church must deal with this issue on a very profound level and not superficially.

4. What stance should we take toward the phenomenon of a *lack of stable identity*? In postmodern culture, an electronic image can be constructed and deconstructed, and we can make a copy of anything (photocopies, etc.) that was previously impossible to duplicate. For example, in earlier times people only ever had one suit of clothes. Christianity and postmodernism differ here. Postmoderns have difficulty seeing others within a relationship in which they are unique and inimitable. It is difficult for the Church to inculcate this awareness in our time. Again, I believe that only the Christology of the Resurrection can offer the solution. 1) We must find human experiences (such as, for example, when a loved one dies and we find it difficult to continue with life) that will help us understand the existential need for the uniqueness of the person. 2) In an age dominated by a utilitarian mindset, theology ought to counter with *the theology of the person* (a unique and non-utilitarian relationship) and the difference between this and a relationship with things (a non-unique and utilitarian relationship). The theology of Metropolitan John Zizioulas is perhaps the most advanced in terms of addressing postmodernism.

5. Remaining faithful to its Christ-centered ethos, the Church needs to cultivate monasticism as a *critical* and prophetic stance. Monasticism in the patristic era was the expression of the *denial* of culture, e.g. a monk who lived on top of a column. Or when a monk rejects basic social issues such as *justice*, believing that the essence of the ascetic ethos is voluntarily to assume the sins of others, thus subverting culture, because this is considered "*unjust*" within the framework of a culture of justice (this is particularly interesting in the context of human rights). The monk subverts culture, but he does not denounce or condemn it. When a monk visits a bishop who puts meat on the table, he will eat it—although he would never normally do so—as if he were saying: "I have a way of life that I do not want to impose on you; I simply want to bear witness to another way of life." So the Church will not be all of a piece; it will have both those who adapt and those who refuse to adapt, but not in an attempt to impose change through coercion. The Church

has never imposed anything on monasticism except Eucharistic discipline, designating the day of the Eucharist as a non-fast day. It is forbidden to fast on the day of the Resurrection! The fact that the Church has made this the exception demonstrates that there are *criteria* for deciding whether something constitutes a denial of culture or an assumption of culture.

6. We must exhibit the treasures of our art through which people can come to understand the existential content that this art expresses.[46] Of course, there must be room for free expression and a variety of cultural forms in the process of reception. The criterion, however, must be "The truth is not in our words, but in our actions" (as Gregory the Theologian and other fathers of the Church put it). Theology should not, by necessity, be an intellectual exercise but rather a "cry" of praise, an iconic/hymnographic expression: "This is the faith of the Apostles, of the Fathers."[47] In all these things, the Church should beware of the danger of aestheticism, since its art is of an ontological character, which means it speaks about the Truth, which is beyond any aesthetic.[48]

7. It is not necessary for us always to be explicit (Hitchcock said of his films: "People do not fear what they see, but what they do *not* see"), but rather to cultivate the Orthodox apophatic approach,[49] es-

[46] In order to articulate a clear Orthodox *cultural* proposal, we need aesthetic studies, because these are being read today. Thus we ought to start from aesthetics in order to formulate a theological and spiritual content for art—in the way the Fathers did. As S. Skliris emphasizes, it would be *desirable* for studies to be undertaken that would demonstrate the nihilistic and demonic tendency and content in modern art.

[47] As is well known, in the Orthodox Church the commemoration of the Seventh Ecumenical Council, which dealt with the issue of the *Icons*, is proclaimed to be the Sunday of *Orthodoxy*. When the Fathers of the Council declared, "This is the faith of the Fathers; this is the faith which has sustained the oecumene," they pointed to a form of "theology," the Icon, which was a form of liturgical experience of the community and did not require any subscription to conceptual statements" (Cf. J. Zizioulas, *The One and the Many*, Sebastian Press 2010, p. 354).

[48] In modern Orthodox theology, there is an emphasis on the "empirical," on the "vision of God," as something essential, but this approach needs other elements in order to be in accord with patristic theology. These elements are: the Eucharistic, the repositioning of eschatology, the transcendence of "aestheticism," apophaticism, and epistemology.

[49] See Athanasius Yevtich, "O apofatičnom i katafatičnom bogoslovlju" [Apophatic and Cataphatic Theology], *Znak preporečni*, Srbinje 1994, pp. 203–208; see also, John Zizioulas, "On Being Other—Towards an Ontology of Personhood," in *Persons: Divine and Human*, (ed. Gunton, London 1996) where the author first proposed his "ethical apophaticism" as an Orthodox cultural proposal.

pecially when it comes to questions of ethics. But, with the proper criteria; we will not relativize sin and falsehood. The question is: by what criteria will we say, for example, that murder is *not* a matter of indifference, while adultery—especially today[50]—*is* a matter of indifference? How many things has the Church accepted from among things that once it did not?

8. Our Christology is not something separate from worship, which, in the 21st century, must become the source and means of cultural proposals. We have only ourselves to blame if we let other proposals be heard while we are silent. This is unforgivable passivity.

9. We live in the culture of images (digital and otherwise), in which an image is worth a thousand words. People today are no longer familiar with the language of philosophy (which gave birth to the theological sermon), but legitimately communicate in other ways, digitally or with artistic images, i.e. they speak in the language of culture (otherwise we cannot speak to a Frenchman). This does not mean that we must become "culture vultures": contemporary culture has not stopped seeking ontological truth, so patristic ontology continues to be relevant.

10. Through this approach of more recent theology, empirical epistemology has been strongly emphasized. It may be that we will achieve something by shifting our knowledge- and reason-centered education away from the dominance of the intellect and reason to the sphere of the experience of personal relationships.

11. Orthodox artists must achieve an expression (both abstract and other) that is simultaneously postmodern and Christian. The ideal solution would be to express the Resurrectional/Eucharistic experience at the same time as adopting elements of contemporary culture.

12. The local Churches (metropoles, dioceses with institutions in the diaspora) must take the initiative to organize exhibitions and events with *authentic* artistic products that present Orthodox culture dynamically to the major cities of the world, which is where large-scale movements emerge. It will be of no assistance if we wish merely to transfer, for example, Mount Athos to America, thereby imposing cultural uniformity. The incarnate aspect of Christology leads to an ecclesiology that respects cultural and historical multiformity and diversity. Our Lord accepted

---

[50] Many of the ancient inadmissible practices (abortion, adultery, etc.) today are so widespread that the Church has ceased to react.

not just human nature, but also a specific historical people, with its cultural characteristics.[51]

13. Although our culture springs from and derives from the East, its future depends—as never before—on the West. And even though the West wounds us, provoking uncertainty, we should not reject it, out of prejudice or a superiority complex. Rather, we should accept it with genuine, brotherly love.

14. Finally, postmodernism can be seen in the following way. All the old cultures are projected onto one and the same screen, which expunges time differences, and people can take whatever features they want from any culture and combine them with elements from other cultures. It therefore eliminates prejudices such as "we're good and they're bad." We Christians have always had this example in Christ, who highlighted the Samaritans, even though the Jews hated them (the Good Samaritan, Lk. 10:30–37; the grateful Samaritan from the ten lepers, Lk. 17:16; the Samaritan woman at the well, Jn. 4:9). Here, Christianity and postmodernism are in accord.

❖ ❖ ❖

The Church is not producing culture, as Yannaras rightly points out, and this symptom is very worrisome. There will be no resolution merely with deliberations and conferences. We are simply deliberating because deliberation and awareness are the necessary prerequisites for finding a solution; unless we are aware of this, no solution will ever be found. The solution, however, if it comes, will come naturally and not ready-made from our deliberations. Just as the great philosophical and artistic movements were not prefabricated, but arose both spontaneously and through collaboration. To this end, what is needed is awareness, but especially an authentic experience of the mystery of the Resurrected Christ within the Church. And, finally, our Lord must make us worthy to provide personalities who will live authentically and will provide solutions. Let us admit it: Orthodoxy today is feeding an inability to relate, an aphasia, through Byzantine romanticism, avoiding reflection, and missing rather than finding solutions. The Church should therefore be more aware of the messages it is receiving.

Having said all that, we need to take people today seriously, their existential needs, and their postmodern understanding of life. Only in this

[51] See my remarks above. See also J. Jeremias, *Jerusalem in the Time of Jesus*, Augsburg Fortress Publishers, 1975.

way will Orthodoxy shape culture as it is happening. In everything we do, we should proceed with the knowledge that the "perpetrator of *new* mysteries"[52] is Christ, Who, as a Church and a true Eucharistic *community* and *synaxis*, heals and saves the world, through the Cross and the Resurrection, offering to it love as the mode of personal existence and eternal life.

[52] Maximus the Confessor, *On the Lord's Prayer*, PG 90, 876.

Lord Jesus Christ as Pantocrator
(icon in Chilandar Monastery, Mount Athos, 13th century)

The Old and New Wine of Liturgical Theology

The Task of Liturgical Theology Today

It is a privilege to attend such a conference that marks the twenty-fifth anniversary of the blessed repose of one of the greatest liturgists of our time, Fr. Alexander Schmemann (1921–1983).

One of the many gifts evident during Fr. Alexander Schmemann's long service to the Church and which has impressed most of us very much, was his ability to unite his liturgical interests to a remarkably theological mind. For him theology and liturgy were inseparable twins and for this reason, when two days are devoted to his heritage involving the east-west ecumenical engagement, Saint Vladimir's Seminary wants to affirm the intermarriage between *lex orandi* and *lex credendi*, the law of prayer and the law of belief. This occasion motivates this school to acknowledge all those scholars who recently have shown great interest in Eastern liturgical themes.[1]

For a bishop, it is an inspiring opportunity to speak about the *raison d'être* of his own ministry, which is: presiding over the Divine Liturgy and *unifying* all charismata and rites, being "in the image and place of Christ" and thus reconciling the people of God with the kiss of peace... and thanksgiving, through the *Mystery* of the transformation and "ἀνακεφα-λαίωσις" (the summing up) of the entire reality of the salvation of the world, in the Eucharistic *movement* (kinisis) and *synaxis*. It is there that we understand the Eucharist as "not merely linked with the Kingdom which is to come, [but] it draws from it its being and its truth"[2] and *manifests* it in the material context of the Synaxis, with the communal and "catholic" character of the Eucharist as a "gathering in one place," which

---

[1] See for example a recent study of one of the invited speakers, Michael Aune, "Liturgy and Theology: Rethinking the Relationship," *Worship* 81, 2007.

[2] J. Zizioulas, "Eucharist and the Kingdom of God," *Sourozh*, nos. 58/1995, p. 7.

ends with our participation in the Supper of the Kingdom, our union and communion with the life of God in the Trinity.[3] So at the end of this Resurrectional and festive Economy and the *common work* (leitourgia), the presiding bishop can—precisely because of this manifestation, prefiguring and foretaste of that Kingdom—say doxologically:

> "*Completed and perfected, so far as is in our power, O Christ our God, is all the mystery of thy dispensation, for we have had the memorial of thy death, we have seen the type of thy Resurrection, we have been filled with thine unending life, we have enjoyed thine inexhaustible bounty, which also in the age to come be pleased to vouchsafe us all, through the grace of thy Father... and of thy Holy Spirit.*" (Prayer of St. Basil said on Consuming the Holy Things).

One of the reasons why we are here is a belief that what will result from this conference and all of its conclusions, will and must concern our local Churches. Therefore, here are a few brief, yet important, thoughts concerning the role of such liturgical symposia in the life of the Church and for the unity of the Church.

❖ ❖ ❖

The last century was an amazing period of liturgical rediscovery and revitalization of the Orthodox worldview concerning patristic iconic ontology, anthropology, and cosmology. The many facets of this renewal, which was no mere "religionization" of the Church, expose the ontological reality of the Eucharistic Liturgy through the empirical revelation of the mystery of salvation. Recognizing these achievements, liturgical symposia are important for many reasons:

1. First, Orthodox Christians, especially those involved in spreading the Gospel, desire to interpret our liturgical practice existentially within the context of modern pluralism, all the time fully aware that our pluralistic society must be reinterpreted in light of the Church's Liturgy. From this experience, I see two items of import emerge.

As the *cult* par excellence, Liturgy is a highly *cultural* event which should be brought more into the discussion of the new cultural problems. In order to show the broader cultural and ecological significance—or more accurately, the anthropological and cosmological consequences—

---

[3] Ibid. Cf. N. Μιλόσεβιτς, *Ἡ θεία εὐχαριστία ὡς κέντρον τῆς θείας λατρείας* [N. Miloshevich, *The Divine Eucharist as the Centre of Divine Worship*], Pournaras Press: Thessaloniki 2005. In the ancient Church the entire liturgical or sacramental life of the Church was united with the Divine Eucharist and constituted extensions of the Eucharist.

of the eschatological character of the Eucharist, we must first pay attention to the *way* we celebrate the Eucharist and worship. Fr. Schmemann insightfully taught that behind the liturgical typicon and rite is hidden a profound theological and existential significance. Other theologians (Staniloae, Zizioulas, Yevtich, Yannaras etc.) of our time stress that we must celebrate the liturgy properly if we are to offer anything to the world of existential significance. So, the liturgical texts of the Holy Eucharist inspire us to express a deep social and cosmic concern.[4]

This immediately leads to a conviction that we must interpret our liturgy in existential terms. In other words, we need a liturgical dogmatics which entails a *liturgical* understanding and expression of dogmatics. Then, we must put that theology into action, evaluating the current state of liturgical theology, evocatively described as a pluralism of particularities. Our current period shows a tendency of imposing cultural uniformity on every tradition, unlike the practice in the early and Byzantine Church. Since different mentalities mean different ways of approaching the faith and expressing it, our liturgical customs must also be different.

2. In a period when some of our contemporaries sadly and untraditionally introduce two liturgies in the same temple on the same day (and some other uncanonical innovations), it is quintessential to stress the communal and "catholic" character of the Eucharist as a "gathering in one place" of the whole of the local Church with all *leitourgemata*. It is not simply because this is the image that we have inherited from history, but mostly because the Kingdom of God is a gathering that is structured in a particular way, with Christ as its center and head, surrounded by the Apostles.[5] Today, even in Orthodoxy, we see a tendency of promoting the individualistic pietism of a "charismatic sociology"—which reduces dogmatics into ethics and ecclesiology into sociology—rather than advocating the ecclesiastical consciousness of the liturgical-canonical existence of the Church.

---

[4] Ion Bria's expression "liturgy after liturgy" means an extension beyond the Divine Eucharist, into the life of the faithful in his relations with others, in his relations with the material world.

[5] See for instance the Book of Revelation. "This structure, imaged in the Eucharist and transferred to the structure of the Church itself as a unity of the people of God around the bishop, is rooted in the eucharistic imaging of the Kingdom and for this reason contains an ultimate truth which may not be overlooked for the sake of a supposedly 'spiritual' understanding of the Church" J. Zizioulas, "Eucharist and the Kingdom of God," *Sourozh* 60/1995, p. 45.

3. Perhaps such Symposia will give us some hints about how to overcome the emergence of the dichotomy between *academic ecclesiology* and *ordinary liturgical Church life*, a dichotomy that is still responsible for some of the problems of contemporary Orthodoxy. Today we expect to see historians of liturgy with profound theological and ecclesiological awareness and not merely a historical and archeological disposition. Consequently, this conference also might help us to understand that:

"The Church is defined (σημαίνεται, is revealed) by the Sacraments."[6] The Eucharist is a *gathering* and a *Liturgy*. Holy Fathers (such as Chrysostom, Basil, Maximus etc.), reflected on the Eucharist as the expression of Truth and a place of theosis, and examined it in *an organic unity with all the basic liturgical actions*. Only together do they constitute the summing up of the divine Economy and the imaging of the Kingdom. St. Justin of Chelie used to emphasize that mainly in the Eucharist does the Church behold and experience the truth as both historical and metahistorical; as communal and trans-societal; as deeply human but also theanthropic, i.e., experienced as *theosis*, sharing the trinitarian life of God.

There is a common misconception of the Eucharist as existing apart from the Liturgy; this is reflected in academic theology that continually speaks of the Eucharist without reference to the Liturgy. "The theologian concerned with the doctrine of the Eucharist should be a *liturgiologist*, or at least well informed in the questions of liturgics" (J. Zizioulas) in order to treat, for instance, the theme of the transformation of the Gifts and the "real presence" of Christ not separated off and examined in isolation from the entire liturgical context.

4. These Symposia are useful both internally and externally. As Orthodox, we need not only self-reflection, but also, and probably even more, an outsider's view: the insider is not anointed with truth just because of existential intimacy with the object of study. There are deeper reasons for this, which I will touch on in my next few points.

Externally, these conferences increase Orthodoxy's visibility within the American environment, which is a kind of witness to the contributions Orthodox theology has made. On the pan-Christian and ecumenical level, many scholars know Orthodoxy for its contribution to liturgics; it is what makes it "famous." So it is important to stimulate the intellectual side of Orthodoxy by meeting with other Christian

---

[6] Nicholas Cabasilas, *Interpretation on the Divine Liturgy*, chapter 38:6.

confessions (Catholic, Protestant). We are grateful to many such people for the revival, starting at the beginning of the twentieth century, of biblical, patristic and liturgical studies, which have drastically changed our own focus. "This revival has recovered the ancient link between Church and Eucharist that was obscured, if not lost, in the Middle Ages. Thanks to the work of scholars such as G. Dix, O. Casel and W. Elert and others in the West, Orthodox theologians themselves have been reminded of the Patristic concept of the Eucharist as leitourgia, a work of the people and a gathering *epi to auto* to realize the ecclesial event par excellence."[7]

Now, *internally*. Historians of liturgy with their archeological expertise provide useful information about early liturgical practice. Indeed they are digging for the truth and a symposium is an opportunity to see the relevance of such textual and archeological findings. As their work shows, most things (in today's Liturgy) are part of a heritage that goes back to the very earliest centuries.[8] Fr. Schmemann's "Byzantine synthesis" is a prime example of such an endeavor.[9] However, Orthodox theology has not, I am afraid, worked out a satisfactory answer to the question of how this synthesis is applicable to ordinary liturgical life on the local level. Very few of the findings from academic liturgical theology ever seem to make any impact on the actual liturgical practice at the level of parishes and monasteries.

5. Strangely, our theology in recent years until Fr. Alexander does not seem to have given appropriate weight to the importance of the inseparability of the *lex credendi* (dogmatics) from the *lex orandi* (liturgics). Its principle focus appears to be on one or the other rather than the intertwining of both. It is not enough to have only "Liturgy" or solely "Orthodoxy," but—as Bishop Athanasius (Yevtich) emphasizes—"a Catholic fullness and balance between πίστις and ἱερουργία, between faith and life. We both realize the Economy of salvation and enter into the theological life of the Trinity through participation in the Divine Liturgy. However,

---

[7] J. Zizioulas, "Ecclesiological Presuppositions of the Holy Eucharist," *The One and the Many*, p. 66.

[8] Cf. Gregory Dix, *The Shape of the Liturgy* (London: Dacre Press, 1945); R. Taft, *The Great Entrance: A history of the transfer of gifts and other pre-anaphoral rites* (Rome: Pontificium Institutum Studiorum Orientalium, 1978).

[9] Schmemann personally tried to make such a historical review in his well-known "Introduction to Liturgical Theology."

within that Economy, Christ is Archpriest, the Incarnate Word, not only the Son of the Father. The core of the Triadic Mystery of the Church is revealed through Baptism-Chrism-Eucharist.

It is precisely because the Liturgy of St. Basil the Great contains the full and complete Triadology, Christology and Pneumatology that it is acceptable and fully Orthodox, whereas the Church does not so recognize the Liturgy of the Apostolic Constitutions.[10] And we see that in this eucharistic and iconic approach where the entire notion of "sacrament" is not based on assurances deriving from history—e.g. the words of institution in the Eucharist—but rather that it is conditioned pneumatologically: this means that whatever has been given by Christ in history cannot be a sufficient basis for the ultimate eschatological reality without the *new* action of the Holy Spirit. Through the *epicletic* character of the Eucharist (to which Orthodoxy attaches particular importance) the local ecclesial community ultimately escapes "the laws of sociology."[11]

For the Orthodox it is of vital importance to insist that Baptism, Chrismation and the Divine Eucharist form a unified and inseparable liturgical unity, whereas in the West (for both Roman Catholics and Protestants), these three Sacraments have been liturgically separated, and there is an intervening time between the Baptism, Chrismation and the Divine Eucharist, on various experiential pretexts, in the personal sense of experience (i.e., the child has to grow up so that it can fully comprehend matters, and then proceed to the Sacrament). These criteria are not considered in the Orthodox liturgical tradition.

6. Similar observations apply to the symbolism and order of service. Examining the words of the Apostle Paul in his epistle to the Romans: "to be a minister of Christ Jesus...in the priestly service of the gospel (ἱερουργοῦντα τὸ εὐαγγέλιον) of God," we discover that ἱερουργεῖν τὸ εὐαγγέλιον means *"ministering"* or *"acting as a priest,"* which is not only preaching. Saint Paul tells us that he did this "so that my offering of the Gentiles may become acceptable, sanctified by the Holy Spirit" (Rom 15:16).[12] There are deeper reasons for this interconnection between πί-

---

[10] For more on this, see, A. Yevtich, *Hristos Nova Pasha, Bozhanstvena Liturgija* I-II (Vrnjacka Banja, 2007).

[11] Cf. J. Zizioulas, "Comment on Communal Spirit and Conciliarity," *The One and the Many*, Sebastian Press 2010, pp. 219-221.

[12] "εἰς τὸ εἶναί με λειτουργὸν Χριστοῦ Ἰησοῦ εἰς τὰ ἔθνη, ἱερουργοῦντα τὸ εὐαγγέλιον τοῦ θεοῦ, ἵνα γένηται ἡ προσφορὰ τῶν ἐθνῶν εὐπρόσδεκτος, ἡγιασμένη ἐν πνεύματι ἁγίῳ."

στις and ἱερουργία, which I will discuss in a moment. Orthodoxy today seems to have difficulty relating the rich and extremely important symbolism of the Liturgy to the theological hypostasis of the Eucharist *in an organic way*. In reading many liturgical studies, one misses a discussion of the significance of the existing Eucharistic symbolism for understanding dogmatics, an endeavor that certainly requires a solid ecclesiological foundation.[13]

Liturgiologists, who are too often historians of liturgy with no theological or ecclesiological interest, frequently fail to distinguish between the indispensable and the inessential in the theological content of the rites they study. However, we need them to help us "rescue the past from the tyranny of stereotypes"[14] preserving faithfully the liturgical tradition of the ancient Church. And sometimes there is considerable confusion in the liturgical manuscripts and liturgical material.

It is reasonable to expect liturgiologists to help us understand that the basic liturgical rubrics and actions are not ornamental trappings of the mystery but something more crucial: the very basis of the mystery.

In the same perspective, liturgiologists can also help many of us to stop thinking of the liturgical typikon as something secondary and unimportant, without deeper ecclesiological significance. The point here is not to justify a whole slew of secondary symbolisms and aesthetic decorations. Rather, the point, as we noted above, is that every rite in the Liturgy is related to its essence.

According to our tradition, these events in the order of the service have the deepest liturgical and theological meaning. The *Synaxis* (Entrance —"ἐπὶ τὸ αὐτὸ")—The *Readings* (The liturgy of the Word and the Sermon of the leitourgos/celebrant)—*Bringing* (Offerings—Proskomidi—Prothesis)—*Giving of Peace* (Kiss of peace, mutual Love and Credo)— *Thanksgiving* (Eucharist, "He gave thanks"—Anaphora & Anamnesis)— *Blessing* (sanctification, epiclesis of the Holy Spirit)—*Intercession* (Dyptichs—commemoratio sanctorum)—*Our Father* (Breaking of the

---

[13] There is a widespread and deeply seated assumption in the Orthodox world that history of worship—or liturgics, if you prefer the technical, theological term—is basically a matter of archeology. The liturgical science is assumed to be the sum of the different layers (strata), while the liturgical typika and the basic liturgical actions that make up the "conglomerate" are conveniently divided into different areas.

[14] A. Brown, *The Catholic Historical Review* 83 (1997) p. 754.

Bread)—*Communion* (Distribution).[15] Each of the above events has its exact place and cannot be shifted or removed for any reason.[16]

We need now to focus on the "theological" side of the development of leadership in our eucharistic communities in the twenty-first century. As early as the New Testament era, the leadership structure of the Christian community was seen as an integral part of the community's expression as the "people of God"—and this occurs first and foremost in the Eucharist and around the Bishop, which includes of course each ordo.[17] Only through a study of the early Eucharistic community and the way in which structure and communion are interrelated within it can we arrive at the proper understanding of the significance of liturgical order and typicon.

7. Since the nature of the Eucharist is *eschatological*, it would be important to see how historians of the Divine Liturgy explain this relationship between the image and the Truth (the Kingdom of God), and the way this has evolved. Is the Eucharist related more to Golgotha (past events) than to the Eschata (the last times)? If the former is the case then it is not permissible for either academic theology or liturgical practice to play down or in various ways obscure the eschatological character of the Eucharist. This character is to be found throughout Holy Scripture and Patristic thinking, and indeed in our liturgical typikon—often despised by dogmatic theologians—despite the alterations that this has undergone at various times (as a result of the indifference or ignorance of our clergy). It proves that what we have in the Eucharist is not a religious asylum from history, an escape or deliverance from choro-chronos, but the *locus* of the transfiguration of space and time as seen in the biblical perspective.

An additional upsetting moment that deserves particular consideration is the evidence that the Orthodox hierarchy has neglected the his-

---

[15] See, A. Yevtich, Ibid.

[16] For example, on the exact place of the sermon within the Liturgy, Metropolitan Zizioulas (op. cit.) comments: "The argument put forward to justify the inept and novel practice (introduced just last century) of shifting the sermon from its natural position after the reading of the Gospel to the time of the Communion Hymn, by which time the Anaphora has been accomplished and our communion with God's eternal life is imminent, is revealing. The argument that more people have gathered by that time shows that the missionary or pastoral criterion has prevailed over that of structure and imagery: it does not even cross our minds that by making this shift we are altering the image of the Kingdom and turning back to front the whole movement and progress from history towards the Kingdom, and it is like putting the first act of a play after the final act!"

[17] See the συνέδριον ἐπισκόπου, in St. Ignatius of Antioch.

torical development and milieu of the liturgical actions and put an accent on symbolism and formalism that leads to museum fossilization (a mere traditionalism and liturgical conservatism). A good portion of the blame, therefore, for our Church's inability to offer much of a cultural witness, based on the eschatological dimension of our Liturgy, is to be placed on Orthodox bishops and priests.

8. An equally significant contribution liturgiologists could make would be to help rid our people of conceptions and "experiences" of the Eucharist influenced by Western pietism—a pietism which has deteriorated our worship more than we could have ever imagined and that "tends to deprive our Liturgy of its resurrectional and festive character or to turn it into a medium for individual piety and psychological compunction and an instrument of mission or pastoral work."[18]

In its liturgical interests, Orthodoxy today, sadly, seems to follow the instinctual human "religious" (contrary to Schmemann's assertion that Christianity in not a religion) necessity to treat the liturgical space (both its architectural formation and interior organization) as scenery for an individual's search for metaphysical security. In order to reawaken within the Orthodox a true sense of the Eucharistic *offering* as something authentic, genuine and truthful—a chaste fruit of a community experiencing Resurrection—liturgical "dramaturgy" must again become an iconic representation of the Kingdom. In order to achieve this iconic ideal, the members of the Church must be heedful of the correct understanding of the liturgical "dramaturgy" and aesthetic expressions embellishing our worship: melody—an echoing of the paradisial doxology beyond every sentimental euphoria; iconography—an imaging of the unified landscape of Jerusalem that is above; hymnographic versification—a freedom from rationalistic submission in experiencing Parousia; lighting—an absence of artificial light-effects; reading and chanting—freedom from didactic expediency and enthusiastic exhilaration; sermon—logos deprived of rhetorical excursus into non-ecclesial thematics, etc. Our liturgical typicon does not aim to captivate the individual with psychological appeals or to emotionally subordinate it, but rather our typicon aims to include man into a liberated choro-chronos where he or she will acquire freedom from all individualistic priorities and become acquainted with the incarnate Logos through communion with the Spirit and in personal freedom and love.

[18] J. Zizioulas, *Eucharist and the Kingdom of God*, *Sourozh* 59/1995, p. 28.

All these hidden *dangers* of romanticism, sentimentalism, paganism and rationalism cannot be healed without a healthy ecclesiology. All this has resulted in a critical situation for liturgical science. A return to the Fathers without recovering the meaning of liturgical symbolism will not get us anywhere; for in the Orthodox Church, the *lex credendi* has no meaning without the *lex orandi*. Fr. Schmemann's achievement here is enormous. He was well aware that the rediscovery of liturgical symbolism (i.e., iconic ontology) safeguards Orthodoxy from both magical rites in a paganist manner and rationalism.

Such symposia might also help us to understand the significance of *the dimension of movement and progression in the typikon of the Liturgy*. It is a pity to give the impression that everything in the Liturgy is performed in a *static* manner (the abolition of the entrances is just a symptom).

This Liturgical Symposium offers an opportunity for discussion of a number of issues both of a theoretical and a practical nature. How can we arrive at an authentic and genuine synthesis of these two approaches? The first step is to realize that the two attitudes need one another and must try to understand each other better. The greatest enemy of liturgical science/theology is the self-sufficiency that *lex credendi* (dogmatics) and *lex orandi* (liturgics) have both felt, particularly since the end of the patristic era. The well-balanced approach sees them reconciled.

I am afraid, however, that Orthodox theology has not yet found a creative synthesis of these two aspects: the anthropological and cosmological consequences of the eschatological character of the Eucharist are often forgotten under the influence of the same individualistic tendencies that have invaded other areas of our Church.

Fr. Schmemann's achievements cannot be the end. Our liturgical theology must not be limited to a mere repetition of any authority of the past. Rather, it must be inspired by visions such as that of Fr. Alexander in continuing to bear witness, to confess, and to proclaim the Mystery of Christ, the transformation of the entire reality of the salvation of the world, with the communal and "catholic" character of the Eucharist as an eschatological "gathering in one place," which ends with our participation in the Supper of the Kingdom.

Unitatis et alteritas
Unity and Otherness in the Ecclesiology of Conciliarity

Introductory remarks

The Orthodox and Roman Catholic concepts of conciliarity[1] differ somewhat from each other even though they stem from the same synodal tradition. Their creative and more profound encounter is, nonetheless, beneficial and even necessary if we endeavor to fulfill sincerely the petition of the Lord's Prayer at Gethsemane. Although the differences that exist in both general and historical interpretations of the one and same conciliar tradition are not insurmountable, overcoming them presents a daunting task unless expressly pursued through theological dialogue. The attention currently devoted to the question of relations between the "one" and the "many" in the realm of ecclesiology indicates that dialogues and gatherings such as this are necessary as well as practical. Primacy (or *primus*) represents the *conditio sine qua non* of synodality, but the converse is true as well. The Church, as the icon of God, is the only place where the *freedom of being the "other"* represents sanctity in itself, for through her structure and salvific mission she has to express the freedom of otherness (*alteritas*).[2] If this holds true in disciplines such as

---

[1] The term conciliarity or synodality comes from the word "council" (*synodos* in Greek, *concilium* in Latin), which primarily denotes a gathering of bishops exercising a particular responsibility. The themes of "primacy" (*primus*) and conciliarity have recently garnered greater attention on the agendas of mixed ecumenical committees (e.g., Rome 2003, Belgrade 2006, etc.). Cf. *Ut Unum Sint* (*May they be one*) which emphasizes the gravity of this question (Pope John Paul II, Encyclical Letter, May 25, 1995, TN).

[2] Cf. *The Mistagogy* of St. Maximus the Confessor (PG 91, 657–717).

Triadology and Christology, it must also hold true for ecclesiology where the same ontological principles are applicable. This is the reason we speak of the synodality of the Orthodox, Catholic Church[3] primarily from a theological standpoint.

Despite its relevance, this brief study will not focus on the evolution of conciliarity in the life of the Church. A close study of the Church's historical development already reveals the message or idea essential to any genuine *theology* of synodality. Our primary interest is in the *ecclesiological* elements that played a role in the formation of this institution. Such an approach makes it easier to grasp the manner in which the fundamental ecclesiological content of the institution of the synod has remained unchanged despite the adoption of new expressions of Church unity. Finally, in the light of these theological, historical and ecclesiological considerations, I will address the question concerning which guidelines, related to the institution of the synod, should inform the Canons of the Orthodox Church in order to ensure that fundamental concepts such as community, otherness and freedom remain essential pillars of the life of the Church.

I. A theology of conciliarity

1. Conciliarity is a defining feature of ecclesiology.[4] It may be said that patristic ecclesiology gave ontological meaning[5] to the term "synod" (σύ-

---

[3] The term "Orthodox," denoting one of the attributes of the Church, has a historical rather than a theological meaning since "orthodox" is one of many terms applied to the Church (although not mentioned in the Nicene-Constantinopolitan Creed). This is why Orthodox Christians accept the term "Orthodox Church" conditionally because they are aware they belong to One, Holy, Catholic and Apostolic Church.

[4] As noted by John Zizioulas, "the institution of the synod (council), at least from the point of view of Orthodox theology, is at the foundation of the rule and canonical structure of the Church. Each autocephalous Church has its synod and it is inconceivable that any law-giver, be it ecclesiastical or secular, should supplant the synod with some other ruling body, either collective or individual." See his study "The Institution of the Synod," *Sabornost* 1–2/2000, pp. 27–55, and "The Development of Conciliar Structures to the Time of the First Ecumenical Council," *The One and the Many*, pp. 190–213. Also, A. Schmemann *The Idea of Primacy in Orthodox Ecclesiology, The Primacy of Peter*, London, 1963, as well as his essay *Towards a Theology of Councils, St. Vladimir's Seminary Quarterly*, 4, 1962 pp. 170–184.

[5] For more information on the usage of the term by the Church Fathers see G.W.H. Lampe: *The Greek Patristic Lexicon*. The Slavic word "*sobornost*" semantically connotes both synodality and catholicity.

νοδος). The theological *raison d'être* of synodality, or the institution of a synod, has its rationale in the idea that *community* (a feature common to both Triadology and Pneumatology) is also an ontological category of ecclesiology; it is impossible to apply those concepts to ecclesiology without making reference to Trinitarian theology. The historical emergence of the first councils can never be considered independently from the *early* conciliarity or synodality that was their predecessor and integrally linked to the eucharistic community (local community). Therefore, a) the basis for the institution of the synod can be found within the very *practice* of the Church, b) the oldest sources for this can be found in the writings that constitute the New Testament, such as the epistles of St. Paul, and c) we find it attested to in the structure of the first eucharistic communities.

2. The history of synodality indicates that the goal of the Church councils was none other than the confirmation of *eucharistic communion* (κοινωνία), be it as reconciliation between the *Other* (the Only Holy—Christ) and an *"other"* (a Christlike person), or between *"others"* (eucharistic communities). The main theme of the canons is therefore the restoration to full communion of those excommunicated (τῶν ἀκοινωνήτων) (Canon 5 of the First Ecumenical Council is but one of countless examples). Issues regarding the correct relationship and salvific activities within the Church community are given special attention ("let an inquiry be made"), which would lead to establishing the regular convening of the councils ("it seems good that synods be held twice every year in each province," the same canon). Questions of *otherness* (*alteritas*) and the essence of the Church have thus been posed from its very beginnings.[6]

"Otherness" (*alteritas*) is a dominant theme in the modern humanities (Buber, Levinas, socio-ethical conception of otherness, etc.) In our case, the "otherness" of the local Church denotes not only her particularity (distinctiveness), "catholicity" and "sovereignty," but also her uniqueness that should under no circumstances be jeopardized. This is why "oth-

---

[6] See, for instance, Canon 8 of The Third Ecumenical Council, where the attempt to establish authority over another local Church is described as "an attack on the liberty of all". Cf. also Archbishop Peter L'Huillier, *The Church of the Ancient Councils: The Disciplinary Work of the First Four Ecumenical Councils* (St. Vladimir Seminary Press, 1996), pp. 163–169. This Canon does not speak about "independence" or "autocephaly" but states that it has seemed good and proper that "the rights acquired from the beginning and established according to ancient usage from the immemorial be safeguarded intact and inviolate in each province".

erness" is a term suitable to express the fullness and wholeness of the local episcopal Church in relation to One Church.

The Church is *per definitionem* the space where one can freely live one's *otherness* and *uniqueness*. It is along those lines that the relationship between the local and the universal Church, seen in the light of synodality,[7] must be such that it precludes the ontological priority of the universal over the local Church. This is one of many efforts that the Church Fathers made in order to refute the argument that the "one" precedes the "many," and that essence has precedence over existence. The problem of the "one" and the "many," posed in the spirit of Greek philosophy, can be formulated like this: is unity (oneness) that which gives being to many churches? Are we true to the spirit of theological substantialism if we claim that one Church precedes and "subsists" in every local Church? The answers to these difficult questions should be sought in what modern theology calls a *"pneumatologically constituted Christology,"* alluding to the Body of Christ ("the one") formed (animated, brought to life, preserved) by the Holy Spirit (κοινωνία of "the many"). The following is thereby achieved: a) the being of the Church cannot be understood as given *a priori*, as an indispensable fact (datum); b) the "one" (Christ) cannot precede the "many" (He coexists with the community), and the otherness cannot occupy a secondary position in this unity; c) the "many" must have a constitutive rather than a derivative role in the being of the Church; d) finally, the local and the universal have to coincide in a particular way.

3. By the very fact that the Eucharist is the Mystery that best evidences the paradox of the *"One"* (Christ) and the *"Many"* (the church community), it is also the *locus* where their mutual interaction and relationship is manifested. Just as the many individuals of the local Church must be united in and through the ministry of the One (the bishop, representing Christ), in the same way the many local Churches must be united into one for their Eucharist to be proper ecclesiologically. Metropolitan John Zizioulas points out that ecclesial unity on a universal level is essential for the Eucharist.[8] Every local Church gathered around her

---

[7] K. Rahner and J. Ratzinger co-authored a book in which they discuss the relationship between the local and universal Church (*Episcopat und Primat*, Freiburg 1962).

[8] See his study "Eucharist and Catholicity," *Being as Communion: Studies in Personhood and the Church* (London: Darton, Longman & Todd, 1985), pp. 143–170.

bishop to celebrate the Eucharist is a *catholic* Church in totality (this is an ancient understanding of the Church in the East, and the Second Vatican Council is in agreement with this at most points). The unity of those Churches and one Church is *adequately* realized through the *synodal* system. According to this system, regardless of how many difficulties have been encountered historically, a single local Church cannot act without the consent of other local Churches when it comes to questions that affect them all. Moreover, the local Church or the council of local Churches cannot interfere with the affairs of a particular local Church (unless the exercising diocesan Bishop gives his permission[9]). Namely, neither the *primus* nor the synod can have jurisdiction over the otherness and fullness of the local Church. Both the *primus* and the synod belong to the *esse* (being) of the Church, though this will be discussed later.

4. This catholicity characterizing the Eucharist introduces a number of practical implications, particularly the emergence of the synodal system in the early Church. As Zizioulas has remarked, synodality is closely related to the Eucharistic community—in theory as well as in practice—and all its prerogatives. If two or more Churches are in schism, the eucharistic life (and perhaps also "validity"?) of all local Churches is upset. Conciliarity, as an expression of the unity of the local Churches in one Church, constitutes a fundamental condition for the Eucharist. Taking this a step further, the synodal tradition of the Church implies that all members of the Episcopate—not merely as successors to the Apostles, but as the heads of Eucharistic communities that contain "the whole Christ"—*collegially hold equal authority*. Therefore there can be no global or universal Church

[9] The practical operation of local (autocephalous) Orthodox Churches makes clear that they depend on the "strength" of the first—that is, on his initiative, influence, stamina, organizational abilities. It is not uncommon that a "stronger" primate (the first) can exert influence on the life of one "independent" diocese. While the concrete power of the foremost bishop of the Moscow Patriarchate, the Patriarch, seems to reduce other bishops to the rank of vicars, the weakness of the primus of the Pec Patriarchate in turn contributed to the insecurity of synodality more recently. One hardly needs to point out that in such cases the "otherness" of the local Church is in danger. Having too powerful a primus may stimulate inertia in the entire ecclesial body. This is why in theological circles we hear of the "hypertrophy of the first" (the Roman bishop) and the "atrophy of the first" (heads of the Orthodox Churches). It seems that in this case the middle way is best. Protestant ecclesiology, being mostly congregationalist in nature, prioritizes the local community without giving due regard to the one Church, at least not in any formal way.

that exists as an underlying *structure* in the Orthodox Church, for it would threaten, perhaps even contravene, the paramount importance of the local Church's *catholicity* (its otherness, wholeness, and fullness). The reason for this is that every discussion about synodality and episcopacy is built on a *Christological* foundation (cf. St. Ignatius, St. Hippolytus, etc.), and only then introduces elements and aspects of apostolicity. Thus the emphasis on the Church as an "icon" of the Kingdom of God—of critical importance for both the Eucharist and eschatology—does not, in turn, lead to seeking a "*vicarus Christi*" outside or beyond the apostolic (and episcopal) community. However, episcopal sacramental grace is inconceivable without automatically involving jurisdictional power. Within the local Church where this jurisdictional power operates, however, the peculiar otherness of the Bishop cannot exist without direct reference to other people to whom the Bishop is linked and from whom the identity[10] of his office is established: "Grant, Father who knows the heart, to Your servant whom You chose for the episcopate, that he will feed Your holy flock, that he will wear Your high priesthood without reproach, serving night and day, incessantly making Your Face favorable, and offering the gifts of Your Holy Church."[11]

5. We are forced, therefore, to reject the notion that speaking of the Church "synodal" and the Church "local" necessarily gives rise to an antinomy. This has already been resolved when we established that synodal-

---

[10] The Orthodox Church, contrary to Roman Catholic practice, refuses to ordain a bishop *in absoluto*—that is, without reference to the name of a specific diocese (Canon 6 of the Third Ecumenical Council). Roman Catholic theology teaches that through ordination a bishop is united to the "body of bishops and apostles" in general, even before he is appointed to a concrete diocese. In the West, the right to rule over a diocese is not conferred upon ordination, but subsequent to the Pope's decree issued only later. Canon 6 of the Third Ecumenical Council, for example, forbids ordination without reference to a concrete place. This indicates that this personal otherness in the Church does not exist without the others with whom the particular bishop is linked and from whom he draws his identity. The newer practice of ordaining titular bishops, even in the Serbian Church, or moving bishops from one diocese to another, speaks volumes about the corrupted understanding of the connection between the otherness (and person) of the bishop with the otherness of his diocese, which represents his bride. The likely cause is the strong influence of a universalist ecclesiology on the Orthodox. This is not merely a juridical question, but fundamentally one of theology. One local Church (diocese) with its members is the only bride and it represents the icon of the Bridegroom Christ.

[11] St. Hippolytus of Rome, *On the Apostolic Tradition* (prayer at the consecration of a bishop).

ity is a necessary aspect of the local Church and the defining feature of its ecclesiastic nature. What about universality, a contrasting concept that, at first glance, negates the concept of locality? Concerning the apparent negation of locality by the Church's claims to universality,

J. Zizioulas observes:

The emergence of councils represents the official negation of the division between the "local" and the "universal," a negation which must be taken with all its implications. The eucharistic mentality which led to this solution would not allow for any structure which would deny the fact that each eucharistic community revealed in a certain place *the whole Christ* and the ultimate eschatological unity of all in Him.[12]

He continues:

But the same mentality would not allow any provincialism that would fail to see the same reality in the other eucharistic communities. The whole Christ, the catholic Church, was present and incarnate in each eucharistic community. Each eucharistic community was, therefore, in full unity with the rest by virtue *not of an external superimposed structure* but of the whole Christ represented in each of them. The bishops as heads of these communities, coming together in synods only expressed what St. Ignatius, in spite of—or perhaps because of—his eucharistic ecclesiology wrote once: "The bishops who are at the extremes of the earth are in the mind of Christ" (*Eph.* 3:2). Thanks to a eucharistic vision of the "catholic Church" the problem of the relationship between the "one catholic Church in the world" and the "catholic Churches" in the various local places was resolved apart from any consideration of the local Church as being incomplete or any scheme of priority of the one over the other, and in the sence of a *unity in identity*.[13]

6. Historically, synods (councils) were composed of bishops, and the theological reasoning behind this has already been addressed. Since bishops are the heads of their communities—inside these communities they stand "in the place of Christ" as "the image and likeness of Him," according to St. Ignatius of Antioch—they were the representatives of their entire communities at the Councils as much as all other bishops were the representatives of theirs.[14] The importance of the bishop in his local com-

[12] "Eucharist and Catholicity," p. 157.
[13] *Ibid.*
[14] The principle of equality of all bishops and local Churches comes precisely from the eschatological perspective of the apostolic community as an indivisible

munity goes even further. Because he is the head of the eucharistic community, the early Church considered him the one through whose hands the whole local community would have to pass in its being offered up to God in Christ.[15] There are two main lines of argument offered by Zizioulas for this conclusion.

Because of the character of the eucharistic community as the expression and manifestation of the whole Christ and the whole (therefore "catholic") Church, through the bishop, as the one who offers the Holy Eucharist, the Church transcends every concept of "locality" and is united with other local Churches in One, Holy, Catholic and Apostolic Church. In practical terms this means that if one is a member of a particular eucharistic community (or local Church), one is thereby also a member of all the eucharistic communities of the world: one can commune in any one of these communities. It was precisely this nature of the Eucharist and its practical implications that led to the emergence of the synodal system in the early Church. Conciliarity is closely connected with eucharistic communion—both in its theory and its practice—and with its presuppositions.[16]

7. From this we may discern several fundamental ecclesiological (dogmatic) rules of the ancient Catholic Orthodox Church:

a) Only *diocesan* bishops (not retired or vicar bishops, except by invitation) who are heads of defined communities can participate in a council—they cannot delegate their powers to another bishop or send a representative body of priests in their stead.[17] The unifying equality of episcopal communities forms the foundation of conciliar infallibility. A council is not authoritative in and of itself, but only as it is *received*. A

---

structure reflected through every bishop. The importance of this principle can be seen in the early Church (e.g. Cyprian) and Orthodox Canon Law (compare with Zizioulas' study).

[15] Apostolic Canon 39: "Let not the presbyters or deacons do (ἐπιτελείτωσαν) anything without the sanction (γνώμης) of the bishop; for he it is who is entrusted with the people of the Lord, and of whom will be required the account (τὸν λόγον) of their souls."

[16] Cf. J. Zizioulas, "Eucharist and Catholicity," pp. 156–157.

[17] The exceptions to this are the delegates of the Roman Pope who attended the Councils in the East. The reasons for this are to be found mainly in the hardship of travel to such distant destinations and also in the system of representation by proxy that could be verified upon their return by comparing signatures. A Council needed Papal approval (and—awkwardly—his *absence*, as Fr. John Behr has asserted) in order to be deemed Ecumenical.

council is the supreme authority in faith, not because it has juridical power, but because it has charismatic authority that has withstood the test of reception over time. Councils do not have automatic infallibility—it is the Church that affirms the council, not the Council that affirms the Church.

b) There is little to support the notion of a bishop belonging to the college of bishops as a whole rather than a particular local Church.

c) Local churches are not superseded by "independent" or "autocephalous" Churches as they are not "parts" of the catholic Church and are far from being dependent or subordinate to any other entity; rather, each diocese (or episcopal Church) exists as the whole, catholic Church because it realizes in itself the concrete presence of the whole Christ (*totus Christi*).[18]

d) This, in turn, does not imply that the local Church exists as a collection of isolated, "independent" or "detached" entities, but is, rather, in constant communion, in shared liturgical unity, in Eucharistic communion with other Churches.[19] Had these local Eucharistic communities allowed themselves to become self-contained—either completely, by severing all connection with other communities, or partially, by refusing to commune faithful from other communities or allowing those who have been excommunicated by their own communities to partake of the Holy Eucharist—they would simultaneously abandon the true Eucharistic nature of their catholicity as well as the catholic character of the Eucharist.[20] The emergence of the council, therefore, was an inevitable response to this dilemma, and its institution should be understood in the light of this situation.

Based on the above observations it should be clear that each episcopal Church is not subordinate to any other, while *at the same time* is de-

---

[18] See the *Epistles* of St. Ignatius of Antioch and the *Martyrium Polycarpi* (bishop of Smyrna).

[19] Only from this standpoint can we understand the "intervening" of Clement of Rome in the affairs of the Church in Corinth. It was normal at the time to show pastoral care and responsibility for other catholic Churches throughout the world, and this pastoral and ethical care of other centers (Metropolia) was not the exclusive privilege of Rome. In fact, Rome was for quite some time regarded as the final arbiter of questions linked to the preservation of faith and the unity of Churches. Such are by no means isolated cases in the history of the Church.

[20] J. Zizioulas, "Eucharist and Catholicity," p. 157.

pendent on all other episcopocentric Churches. This is why the authority of any one of the ancient Patriarchates (a Pentarchy that also included the Church of Rome) was not understood in a monarchic sense—their authority was bestowed by virtue of remaining true to the Orthodox faith rather than through any sort of institutional prerogative.[21]

8. Clearly, the authority of the Church does not come from the structure of the institution itself but rather from a *communal event* inspired by the Holy Spirit. The Holy Spirit, as has already been established, unites all Christians in the body of Christ simultaneously on both a local and universal level.[22] Catholics and Orthodox Christians alike have traditionally accepted that the highest authority in the Church is the ecumenical council. No ecumenical council, however, embodies authority in and of itself—it is not an institution, but becomes an event in the interactive gathering that takes place. The authority of the council is derived from its relational nature. In order for it to be authoritative, its decisions must be accepted and received by the local Churches. Not all councils met the criteria necessary for them to be considered ecumenical (e.g. the controversial proceedings and questionable teachings at the Council of Ephesus in 449, or the Council of Florence in 1442, etc.) and were never accepted by the Church. It is generally held that without an institution that holds teaching and decision-making authority, there can be no unity in the Church; but, in the end, even the decisions of such an institution must be put to the test of being accepted and received by the community before they come to be considered as possessing full and undisputed authority.[23] As is the case with every other ecclesiological aspect of the community, this au-

---

[21] Y. Congar gives as an example the Sixth Ecumenical Council (680–81) and Pope Agatho, whose decrees were acknowledged not because of his authority but because the other Churches recognized in them the authentic faith.

[22] Each meeting of the Synod is opened with the *epiclesis*, a prayer of the invocation of the Holy Spirit.

[23] "The government of the Churches is carried out by those to whom the chief offices in them have been entrusted, but their hands are strengthened by the laity." (St. Basil the Great, *Letter* 230, *To the magistrates of Nicopolis*). Compare Bishop Athanasius' *An Ecclesiological Reminder of the American Schism*, in: *Zagrljaj Svetova*, (in Serbian), Srbinje 1996, p. 166. According to J. Zizioulas, even reception has to be on a universal rather than only a local level. He argues that it is necessary to have reception on a universal level because it is inherent to all forms of conciliarity and that it should be exercised through local bishops (cf. his book *The One and the Many*, pp. 262–273).

thority is *relational*—that is, it must never lose sight of the "otherness" of the people (*laos*), the fullness of the church community.[24]

9. In this same theological vein of Orthodox ecclesiology, *primacy* is understood as the *conditio sine qua non* of synodality. The reverse is also true, as set forth in Apostolic Canon 34. Recent studies have drawn particular attention to this canon and several authors consider it to be a very old precept, if not the oldest canon of the First Ecumenical Council. It sets forth the following principles:

a) the bishops of every *nation* (ἐκάστου ἔθνους) must acknowledge him who is *the first* amongst them and account him as their *head*;

b) they should do nothing of consequence (περιττὸν) without his consent, and each is to operate only on things regarding his own area (τῇ ἐκείνου παροικίᾳ) and the territories that depend on it;

c) but neither shall he (who is head) do anything without the consent of all.

The jurisdiction and power of the *first* is set forth in a manner deserving of attention. His relationship with other bishops is one of mutual dependency: *the first* can do nothing without the consent of others as much as the others cannot, naturally, do anything without *the first* concerning issues that involve more than one local Church. Set forth here is a notion of the true community of Churches modeled on the life of the Holy Trinity (invoked even in the Trinitarian doxology concluding the Canon). The spirit of this Canon[25] grants that the institution of the synod does not represent a pyramidal hierarchical structure of the Church,

[24] In the practice of the Roman Catholic Church, the councils, regional and general, are subordinate to the "primus." The Bishop of Rome may or may not, if he does not agree or so wishes, ratify the decisions brought by the entire college of bishops gathered from all over the world. Compare *Lumen Gentium*, 22:

> But the college or body of bishops has no authority unless it is understood together with the Roman Pontiff...The Pope's power of primacy over all, both pastors and faithful, remains whole and intact. The order of bishops, which succeeds to the college of apostles and gives this apostolic body continued existence, is also the subject of supreme and full power over the universal Church, provided we understand this body together with its head, the Roman Pontiff, and never without this head.

[25] This canon does not directly deal with the question of councils but it is evident that it is linked with what represents the beginning of the canonical foundation of the local and regional councils. Although it was originally connected with the issue of the metropolitan system, many theologians consider it applicable to all forms of primacy.

but, rather, the community of Churches represented by their bishops. *Primus inter pares* in Orthodoxy plays a far more important function than that of honorary presidency, preserving the balance between the local Church and the institution of the council, where the local and the universal must coincide.[26] This canon overcomes, *in practice*, the dichotomy between "democracy" (the rule of many in some loose confederation that rejects primacy) and "monarchy" (the rule of "one" over many).[27] But, in theory, on the theological-philosophical level, it establishes that the "one" cannot precede the "many" and *vice versa*, and that otherness (*alteritas*) cannot come second to unity (*unitatis*). The Church also addresses the holiness of the *protos* (the first one) and the holiness of "*many*" (local Church). Conciliarity that invalidates the otherness (catholicity and integrity) of the local Church only leads to ecclesial universalism,[28] whereas on a philosophical level it denotes theological substantialism.

In summary, in any given ecclesiastical community (κοινωνία), each local (regional) Church is the Church in the full meaning of the term

[26] There are many different approaches to the application of this rule on the universal level offered today in Orthodox theology. While some consider this canon relevant at the local and regional levels, others think it germane to all three levels (that is, including the universal). The position of the Moscow Patriarchate is that justification for primacy on the universal level cannot be found in tradition, but it wholeheartedly applies it within its own autocephalous structure. The Ecumenical Patriarchate of Constantinople and other ancient Patriarchates in the East have always supported the idea of primacy on the universal level. The question of central authority in the Church is a question of faith as well as order. It is their opinion that the Church, if it cannot speak with one voice, cannot truly be an image of the Body of Christ. In order for it to function, the Orthodox system of autocephaly requires some form of primacy that, in fact, already exists. Their argument is this: theology that justifies or even asks for the service of bishops on the level of the local Churches implies that the same is required on the regional and even universal level.

[27] It appears that the synthesis of the two precluded the possibility of the primacy of the universal Church over the local. Namely, the relationship between the "local" and the "universal" catholic Church must be seen as a *unity in identity* and not a *unity in collectivity* (J. Zizioulas, "Eucharist and Catholicity," p. 158). It is an interesting simile: in the first case, the various local Churches form *parts* added to one another to make up a whole, whereas in the latter, the local Churches are *full circles* which cannot be added to one another, but coincide with one another and finally with the Body of Christ and the original apostolic Church.

[28] The statement made by the Congregation for the Doctrine of the Faith about the Church as community reads that the universal Church is "a reality ontologically and temporally prior to every individual Church," *Vatican Bulletin*, 1992.

catholicity because of the Eucharist that is celebrated according to the model established by Christ and "transmitted" to the Apostles and their successors. All bishops are equal, presiding over the Church in the fullest sense possible, regardless of the size or the number of faithful of the local Church.. For this reason, neither the Synod, nor the Council, nor the *protos*, nor any other institution should act in a way that might question or invalidate the otherness and fullness of a local Church. The system of autocephalous Churches and synodal practices (currently in something of a crisis) also reinforces what has been said about the "many" needing the "one" in order for their potential to be fully realized. The mystery of the "many" and the "one" is deeply rooted in the Church's *biblical* theology, especially in her Christological (the "one") and Pneumatological (the "many") natures. From an institutional perspective, this mainly concerns the question of primacy inherent to all forms of synodality—absent, however, is a convincing ecclesiology of community. This is why Zizioulas gives the imperative: We must find the golden rule, the proper balance between the "one" and the "many," and that cannot be achieved without a deeper insight into Trinitarian theology. The God we believe in is the "one" because He is the "many" (Trinity), and is the "many" (Trinity) because He is the "one."[29]

II. A look at the history of conciliarity

There are discernable consequences that the above understanding of conciliarity created in the life and organization of the Church,[30] and it makes sense to examine these directly rather than attempting a comprehensive historical survey on the subject.

[29] J. Zizioulas, *The One and the Many*, p. 368.

[30] The exact place that the synod occupied in the context of the Church's catholicity is one of the more difficult problems of Church history. This historical retrospective owes a lot to the efforts of J. Zizioulas (works mentioned in this paper) and A. Yevtich (e.g. *Zagrljaj Svetova*, Srbinje 1996, pp. 153–168; also *Svešteni Kanoni Crkve*, Beograd, 2006). The basic idea that permeates these works is that in order to understand the content of an institution we must go back not only to its theological but also to its historical roots. Many institutions have been subject to change over time. This caused their original purpose to become somewhat obscured. The Orthodox Church does not deny the changes that took place over time, but tries, rather, to preserve unchanged the basic relation between those institutions and the essence and nature of the Church.

1. The Church's early experience and understanding of synodality gave rise to one of the fundamental and unalterable canons of the ancient Church, later formulated by the First Ecumenical Council in Canon 8: *"...there may not be two bishops in the city,"* that is, there can be only one bishop per city.[31] The bishop in a given city (usually including the surrounding area, and perhaps also involving *chorepiscopoi* in outlying districts), as Bishop Athanasius says, was the bishop of all the faithful in that city regardless of their race or ethnicity; therefore the bishop was originally the bishop of the citizens and not the city itself, e.g. "the bishop of the Antiochians." Only later was his title gradually changed to the "bishop of Antioch" or "the Antiochian bishop."[32]

2. The logic inherent in such an attitude elicited a basic rule in the ancient Church both in practice and theory: a bishop is to be selected and ordained by the bishops of a particular region or province.[33] Later, after the emergence of the metropolitan and patriarchal systems of organization, an elevation to the episcopate could not take place without the prior consent of the metropolitan (or patriarch) of that region, as noted in Canon 4 of the First Ecumenical Council. The ancient rights of patriarchs and metropolitans are defined in Canon 4, but these never invalidated the spirit of Canon 8—if any Patriarchate be dissolved, as happened to the Serbian Patriarchate of Pec at one time, the rule of local, regional bishops becomes effective immediately.

3. Larger organizational structures such as Metropolitanates, Patriarchates and autocephalous Churches, could not have damaged or diminished the *wholeness* and fullness (catholicity) of each episcopal, local Church; the local Church being the only one that existed in a

---

[31] See Apostolic Canon 35 and Canon 16 of the First–Second Council. Comp. J. Meyendorff, *One Bishop in One City* (Canon 3, First Ecumenical Council) in St. Vladimir's Seminary Quarterly, 1961, pp. 1–2, 54–62.

[32] Bishop Athanasius Yevtich, *An Ecclesiological Reminder about the American Schism*, p. 157.

[33] On the meaning of the ordination of a bishop by many bishops, see A. Schmemann's essay "The Idea of Primacy in Orthodox Ecclesiology" in "The Primacy of Peter," London, 1963; also G. Florovsky, "The Sacrament of Pentecost" (A Russian view on Apostolic Succession) in *Sobornos*t, March 1934, pp. 29–35: "Under normal conditions of Church life, Apostolic succession should never become reduced to an abstract enumeration of successive ordainers. In ancient times, Apostolic succession implied first of all a succession to a definite *cathedra*, again, in a particular local *sobornost*. Apostolic succession does not represent a self-sufficient chain, or order of bishops."

particular region. Two or more episcopal Churches existing simultaneously in one city or in the same region would be ecclesiologically nonsensical, as it undermines the basic principle that the Church of God is One.[34] At the same time it negates the "otherness" of the local Church in its city.

4. The cohesion of all episcopocentral Churches is based upon unity in one Christ, one Spirit, one faith and grace, one uninterrupted eucharistic communion that embraces all other unities[35] while at the same time preserves the wholeness and fullness of each local episcopal Church. This is why the episcopocentric structure of the Church was and remains inviolable and unaltered through the history of the Orthodox Church. All *systems of organization* that served to keep the episcopal Churches united (metropolitanates, patriarchates, autocephalous Churches) have seen changes to both their structure and content over time: "The episcopocentric structure of the Orthodox Church is eucharistic, dogmatic and unalterable; all other organizational structures emerged over the course of history and are subject to change."[36]

5. It is in this spirit that Cyprian of Carthage formulated the idea of apostolic succession, which made a crucial impact on subsequent generations. The fundamental principle of his ecclesiology is based upon the notion that *each bishop occupies the seat of the Apostle Peter*—not only are

[34] A. Yevtich, *ibid*, p. 158. The current state in the American Orthodox "diaspora" presents a problem; it is not only about failing to keep the spirit of genuine ecclesiology alive, but also about adopting secular criteria entirely foreign to the life of the Church. It is true that the Church cannot remain unaffected by various political or nationalistic factors (it exists in this world, though is not of the world), but it is also true that these should not be determining factors that dictate the structure and operations of the Church.

[35] According to an ancient Church tradition, every newly consecrated bishop sends a letter (εἰρηνικὸν) to all other Bishops informing them about his consecration in the spirit of brotherly love and unity. In the Roman tradition, a new Catholic primate enters into the fullness of the episcopal office once he is bestowed the pallium (a vestment similar to the omophor) by the Pope. This is particularly evident with the primates of the Eastern Catholic Churches (so-called Uniate Churches), whose ecclesiastical status is not recognized by the Orthodox. Not even the Uniate Patriarchs, according to the Code of Canons of the Eastern (Catholic) Churches (CCEO), can consecrate new bishops in their own Churches or summon synods unless they receive a letter of approval from the Pope. In Orthodox ecclesiology, the Pope himself is a bishop and all other bishops are sacramentally equal to him, as they have received the same grace.

[36] A. Yevtich, *ibid*, p. 158.

all bishops equal but they are also equal successors to the entire congregation of the Apostles presided over by the Apostle Peter. Although *cathedra Petri* is one of the most important elements used by Cyprian, it is incorrect to conclude that Cyprian is a proponent of some sort of universalistic ecclesiology. He does not understand *cathedra Petri* in relation to the universal Church, but, rather, it is applicable to each local Church with a bishop at her head.[37] Cyprian's perspective of the Church is encapsulated in the letter sent to Pope Celestine from the Fathers of the Council of Carthage in 424:

> The Holy Fathers [of Nicea]... did not think that the grace of the Holy Spirit would be wanting in any Province, for the bishops of Christ wisely to discern, and firmly to maintain the right...unless it be imagined that God can inspire a single individual with justice, and refuse it to an innumerable multitude of bishops assembled in council.

It should be clear that the notion of preserving the "otherness" of the local Church was incorporated in the foundations of the ancient Apostolic-synodal Church's general ecclesiology, which, despite all the upheavals it has witnessed, has been preserved in the East.[38] The following examples should help illustrate this.

6. With the development of the metropolitan system and subsequently that of Patriarchates in the ancient Church, the center of local

[37] The attitude of the Eastern Fathers toward Western ecclesiology can be formulated as follows: according to Tradition and the established order of the ancient Church, the bishop of Rome is the first bishop in all the Church. He is the head of the local Church of Rome—the basis of his primacy on his succession to Peter is problematic and does not confer universal jurisdiction, which would empower the Pope to interfere in the affairs of another local Church. When the Orthodox speak of primacy, they speak of the *primacy of the Church of Rome* of which the Pope is the executive.

[38] It is interesting to note in the context of this discussion that in the East the Archbishop of Constantinople enjoyed some kind of primacy, albeit in quite a different way than the Bishop of Rome. Until the second half of the 20th century, the bishop of Constantinople represented a certain "reference point" to the historically "younger" autocephalous Churches. A letter of the Metropolitan Mojsije of Belgrade (Ἐπισκόπων Σερβίας, Αἴτησις τῷ Οἰκουμενικῷ Πατριάρχῃ ὅπως ἐπιτραπῇ τῷ Μητροπολίτῃ αὐτῶν Μωϋσεῖ μὴ νηστεύειν, pp. 686–688,) signed by three other bishops in 1723, may serve as an illustration of this: he asks the Patriarch of Constantinople to be exempted from fasting because of illness. See Καλλινίκου Δελικάνη, *Πατριαρχικῶ ἐγγράφων* [K. Delikanis, *Formal Documents from Patriarchal Archives*], τόμος τρίτος, ἐν Κωνσταντινουπόλει, 1905, vol. 3. See also V. Phidas, "Le Primat et la conciliarité de l'Eglise dans la tradition orthodoxe," *Episkepsis*, 671 (2007) pp. 36-42.

unity shifted from the diocese to larger geographical areas, encompassing the eparchies of provinces under the rule of the bishop of the Metropolis (the Metropolitan). The emergence of the Metropolis, a term which is purely nominal in the Orthodox Church today (some bishops are called "Metropolitans," but the Metropolis as an entity no longer exists—it disappeared together with the notion of ancient Roman/Byzantine provinces), did not significantly change the understanding of the local Church as being equal to the diocesan Church.

a) The development of Metropolitanates was closely related to the conciliar practices of the primitive Church because it represented a "temporary" or "accidental" kind of Church "locality"—it coincided with centres where council sessions were held. Since the principle that essentially *all bishops are equal* became the basic underpinning of Canon Law in the Orthodox Church, neither Metropolitans nor Patriarchs ever assumed the position of the prelate of a certain Church with a ranking higher than that of a diocesan Church.

b) There are permanent synods in the Orthodox Churches today, but they are never regarded as separate church "bodies" that can be called "local Churches." The observed theory and practice of the Pentarchy in Byzantium was in accordance with the ancient division of the *oikoumene* (the inhabited world) into five parts, and represents a historical attempt to provide structured communication between Churches and guarantee their unity.[39]

c) It is difficult to label Patriarchates as "local Churches" since the principle of equality of all bishops, with regard to their ecclesial status,

---

[39] As noted by Bishop Irinej of Bachka (*The conception and significance of autocephaly*, a paper submitted at the symposium on Problems of Contemporary Canon Law, Belgrade, 2003), we do not see a decrease in the number of autocephalous Churches today. Historically, from the 4th century onwards, Metropolitanates tended to be enfolded into Patriarchates and thus the number of autocephalous Churches was reduced from hundreds to only a few. Today we have a different process altogether and the number of independent entities is increasing—as if we are returning to the state where practically every Metropolis will have become autocephalous. I think that it is unrealistic to expect the wheel of history to start turning backwards, especially in our world where all structures, even on the state level, are being globalized. It seems difficult, with such trends, for the old system of small autocephalous Churches to survive. Although this is theoretically possible, we should not hold our expectations high or direct our efforts toward it, but we should take upon ourselves the task of sieving through all these novel 19th and 20th century theories and practices related to autocephaly.

makes it impossible to create a distinct ecclesial entity *outside* the Patriarchate. A genuine argument for the development of autocephaly is that a certain geographic region which comprises several eparchies has the right to elect its "primate," and must be formally recognized by all of the other local Churches. This area, however, *must not* coincide with national borders.

d) In addition, the ecclesial status of any given unit in the Orthodox Church (apart from the diocese) is not derived from that unit itself, but from the diocese or dioceses comprised by that unit. This pertains not only to units smaller than an eparchy (e.g. a parish), but to larger ones as well.

e) *A Metropolis, Archdiocese or Patriarchate cannot be considered a Church per se* except in a broad sense because it is comprised of one or more dioceses of local Churches. Namely, it is only those—because of the bishop who celebrates the Eucharist—that can rightfully be called the Church. This means that each Orthodox Metropolitan, Patriarch, etc., does not owe his ecclesial status to the fact that he is the "primus" in a broad geographic area, but to the fact that he is *the head of a concrete local Church.*[40]

7. Therefore, by addressing the place that a "synod" or "council" occupies in the context of catholicity (conciliarity) in the primitive Church, this entire historical-theological retrospective shows that there was no concerted effort made to create a structure of "universal catholicity" transcending the local Churches and invalidating their otherness. J. Zizioulas summarizes thus:

a) With regard to the question of authority, St. Cyprian, one of the people most involved in this aspect of synodal activity, considered the authority of a council in a *moral* context. Each bishop was directly responsible to God for his own community or diocese.[41]

---

[40] In the final analysis, local Churches in the Balkans are Metropolitanates, without exception. Although there are bishops who carry the titles of Metropolitans in those Churches (Serbian, Russian, Greek, Romanian, etc.), they are still—by virtue of not having a Council of Metropolitans—only titular Metropolitans (without canonical justification). The only true Metropolitans are the primates of those local Churches who actually carry the titles of Patriarchs or Archbishops.

[41] J. Zizioulas, "Eucharist and Catholicity," pp. 155–156. But the very fact of the gradual acceptance of the "council" as a norm in the life of the Church proves that its roots must have been very deep (*Ibid.*).

b) Respect for the "otherness" of the local Church won the battle over precedence by some superimposed entity. The various local Churches had to wrestle—perhaps unconsciously—with the problem of the relationship between the "catholic Church" in the episcopal community and the catholic Church in the world. The moment they admitted a *supra-local structure over the local eucharistic community*, be it a synod or another office, the eucharistic community would cease to be in and of itself (by virtue of its Eucharistic nature) a "catholic Church."[42]

It is in this context that the only acceptable consideration of universal primacy in the Orthodox Church must be one that does not work against the fullness of the local Church. In the interest of unity (in faith and order), the Orthodox would not object to yielding such primacy to the bishop of Rome, based on the model from the first millennium.

9. In Orthodox ecclesiology, as already stated, the Christological dimension of episcopal ministry (the bishop as the "icon of Christ") takes precedence over apostolicity (the bishop as the successor to the Apostles). It is apparent, nonetheless, that Church practice recognizes a special apostolic character in those Churches that have historical connections with one or more of the great Apostles. We need not be confused by the profound and fundamental concept of apostolic continuity, which permeates the very nature and structure of every Church and is relevant not only to its *historical* but also to its *eschatological* aspect as well. Those sees have traditionally been held in highest regard and enjoyed special primacy (as Patriarchates or their equivalent), but they have never been treated differently than other episcopal sees because of the apostolic continuity in which the historical and eschatological dimensions come together. Such an approach may serve to illustrate further how deeply this synthesis is rooted in the ethos of the Orthodox Church. It is, however, difficult to say whether the honor bestowed on the "first" bishop by a college of bishops is merely an honorary recognition: first of all participants, one who presides over the synod has (by his canonical authority, not in essence) a greater prominence and role since he is the "first": he has the right to convene the sessions, guide the discussions; he has two votes and can change the agenda of the meeting, etc.[43]

---

[42] J. Zizioulas, "Eucharist and Catholicity," p. 157.

[43] The list of the examples of the exclusive "interventions" of the *primus* in the Orthodox Church is not as short as it might seem. It is not unusual in the practice of some

III. Some closing remarks

The central notion of the "first" (one, *primus*) in relation to the "many" in the field of ecclesiology, as well as the fact that the *primus* represents *conditio sine qua non* of synodality (and vice versa), requires a careful consideration of "otherness" (*alteritas*) in the Church. As the icon of God, the Church is the only place where the freedom of being "other" is held to be sacred, where it has been enthroned within her own structure and salvific mission. The first part of this treatise discussed the relationship originally established between the local and universal Church—due to the emergence of *conciliarity*, this relationship developed from the outset with an understanding that precluded ontological priority of the universal over the local Church. The synodal tradition of the Church implies that all members of the episcopate share the same authority, not only because they are the successors of the Apostles, but also because they are the heads of the Eucharistic communities where the "whole Christ" dwells. This is why in the Orthodox Church there is no global or universal Church—not as a structure—for it would threaten (perhaps even negate) the primary catholicity of the local Church.[44]

As Bishop Athanasius[45] holds, in the *First Letter of Clement to the Corinthians* we find no mention of Roman legal theory or jurisdiction, let alone the primacy of Rome or the Roman Bishop over others. By reading into this ecclesial Epistle some "proof" that Rome enjoyed primacy at that early stage, it seems that Roman Catholic theologians misinterpreted this early Christian text of brotherly love and Christian solidarity, general ecclesial care and self-awareness. The fact that the Epistle was sent from Rome to Corinth, that is, from "the church of God which sojourns (παροικοῦσα) at Rome, to the church of God sojourning at Corinth" (1:1), does not designate any power but the "bond of the love of God in Christ" (49:1–6), such as the Holy Apostles and

local autocephalous Churches that the *first* obstructs the work of the synod if he so decides; also, the other bishops cannot make decisions in his absence. The bylaws stipulate that in the absence of the Patriarch, or if there is no Patriarch currently occupying the throne, new bishops are not elected and no amendments to canonical acts can be made. Is this not a clear example of *primacy* that goes beyond mere honor?

[44] When it comes to the question of the ecclesial status of a parish and its otherness, it should be noted that it is a part of the diocese whose head is the bishop. A parish does not have the fullness and otherness of an episcopal Church.

[45] A. Yevtich, *Dela Apostolskih Učenika*, Vrnjci-Trebinje 1999, pp. 37–38.

their disciples and successors manifested in their "care of all the Churches" (2 Cor 12:28). Clement, the humble Bishop of Rome, wrote one *Letter to the Corinthians*, but not even a full century later (latter half of the 2nd century), Dionysius, the humble bishop of Corinth, wrote seven encyclical letters to the Churches in Laconia, Athens, Nicomedia, Gortyna, Amastris, Knossus and Rome, to show his love for the brothers, teaching Orthodoxy, and enjoining peace, union and order in the Church of Christ. This is confirmed by yet another example: shortly before the convening of the First Ecumenical Council at the beginning of the 4th century, the anti-Arian bishop St. Eustathius of Antioch interfered in the disputes of some neighboring Churches. He was criticized for this, and his disciple, the rhetorician St. John Chrysostom, responded some time later (in his *Homily on Saint Eustathius*): "Truly he was well trained by the Spirit's grace that a church's leader should not just be concerned for the church entrusted to him by the Spirit, but also for the entire Church situated throughout the world. Indeed, he learnt this from his holy prayers. 'For if one is obliged to offer prayers,' he said, 'for the universal Church from one end of the world to the other, one should show far more forethought, too, for it all, and, similarly be concerned for them all and care for all of them.'"[46]

Ultimately, one must address the question of whether unity in the Church can exist without primacy at all three levels: local, regional and universal. This is particularly relevant to the contemporary Orthodox experience, at least on an ecclesiological level. It is only through one "head," one "primus"—be it Christians as individuals or as members of the local Church—that the Church can speak with one voice. But the primus must be a constitutive part of the community and in genuine relationship with it. This is the only way we can realize "otherness" on both an ecclesiological and synodal level. To be "other" (and "others") and be free are fundamental aspects of Triadology (the perfect union of three Persons in their otherness), Christology (union of two different natures in One Person) and cosmology (respect for the otherness of the world by its Creator). The concept of conciliarity in the East has contributed to creating such a concept in the field of ecclesiology.

---

[46] *On Saint Eusthathius,* in: St. John Chrysostom, *The Cult of the Saints* (Crestwood, NY: SVS Press, 2006), p. 57. Cf. A. Yevtich, *Dela Apostolskih Učenika,* pp. 37–38.

Christ the Great Archpriest
(fresco by Stamatis Skliris in Los Angeles)

The Icon and the Kingdom of God
Theological, Cultural and Artistic Implications

We live in times awash with man-made images, in a postmodern epoch where each person struggles to produce the most convincing image of himself and his idea, where people try to attract the most people they can through their self image in order to impress and to impose their "icon" or, better yet, their "idol," on others (as St. Andrew says : "αὐτείδω-λον ἐγενόμην," "I have become an idol to myself"; Canon of St. Andrew of Crete, Ode IV). It is an era that offers falsehood, delusion, and fantasy without transcending the antinomies and limitations of history.

We live in such times; yet, this moment in time—The Sunday of Orthodoxy, the feast of the icon—proposes an alternative image: one Divinely-revealed rather than human-made, one that is convicting rather than convincing, one that is iconic rather than idolatrous—the icon of God.

This icon represents humanity having received the opportunity to circumscribe and depict the Transcendent God, which only became possible once God became man, expressing his Divinity in human form, bringing the Kingdom of God into the Divine Liturgy, and demonstrating the reality of the Resurrection by asking one of His disciples to verify what he saw by touching Christ's hands, feet, and side (Jn 20:26). Similarly, the language of the Fathers about icons, especially that of the Seventh Ecumenical Council, has to do with both seeing and beholding the vision of God. But this language introduces significant questions: What is the real image of God? What is the real image of man? What is the real image of this world? Does the icon depict a Platonic ideal? Or does it represent Greco-Roman art? Or does the iconic image capture the corrupted world of Pieter Brueghel or Salvador Dali? Maybe, we Christians present an image that itself can obscure the image of the Kingdom? Do we not, instead of iconizing the transfigured world of Paradise, most often represent the mere fallen world? This problem faces us in our present-day Church and it is necessary to ask ourselves: does our image of the world and the Church overshadow the true image of the Kingdom?

What is the difference between the icon and the image, between the Divine Image and the image of this world? The two are altogether different.

The first, and significant, difference is that the icon is not naturalistic; it does not represent something ephemeral, but rather it represents both a Person and a personal relationship. "But if anyone dare to make an image of the immaterial and incorporeal and invisible and formless and colorless divinity, we reject them as false" (St. John Damascene, *Three Treatises on the Divine Images*, II, 10). It is not only that in Christ "all the fullness of Deity dwells in bodily form" (Col. 2:9) but also "the Son is a living, natural and undeviating *image* of the Father, *bearing in himself the whole Father*" (I, 9). "I am not speaking of the flesh of the incarnate Son of God; for that is called God immutably by hypostatic union and participation in the divine nature, not anointed by the energy of God as with each of the prophets, but by *the presence of the whole* of the one who anoints." (I, 19)

Contrary to conventional wisdom—although quantum physics to a degree anticipates this truth—Christ shows in himself the Father and replies to Philip: "anyone who has seen *me* has seen *the Father*" (John 14:9). The icon of Christ is not presented as an *individuum* or individually, but is revealed as the Mystery of the Church, as the One who co-exists with the many and where the many are gathered in Him as Saints (in the Pauline sense). So, the icon is an unusual image that presents the landscape of this world, not corruptible as it is now, but incorruptible, as God the Father will look upon it in the Eschata or end of time, when the Son of God will introduce the resurrected people and all creation to the Father, saying: *Behold, I and the children that You have given to me*! (Isaiah 8:18) In this way, the icon depicts the restoration of fragmented, corrupted space and time.

❖ ❖ ❖

One of the most significant points to emerge from the Seventh Ecumenical Council is that one Divine Person—the Son of God—became man, demonstrating that we cannot speak about God or imagine God without the Person who revealed God to us. An image that does not refer to the Person of Christ is an image that refers to the corrupted world and thus leads to death. The icon is not of this world; it is eschatological both in origin and in content. Not being drawn from history, we can call the icon meta-historical.

Nevertheless, the Kingdom can only be depicted by using created means. The icon is distinct from the Truth, not because it is false, delusional, or fantastic, but because it borrows its means of expression from still-corruptible nature (Cf. St. John Damascene, *Three Treatises on the Divine Images*, I, 16).

Although its means of expression derive from fallen nature, the icon refers to inexpressible Truth by encouraging our personal relations with Truth; a proper icon creates true personal relationships. That is why an icon is indivisibly linked with Love: we cannot speak about Truth without Love, and we cannot speak about an icon that does not lead us to Love. "The fifth kind [of veneration] is that whereby we venerate one another as having a portion of God (προσκυνοῦμεν ἀλλήλοις ὡς μοῖραν Θεοῦ ἔχουσι) and having come to be in the image of God, humbling ourselves before one another and fulfilling the law of love (νόμον πληροῦντες ἀγάπης)" (St. John Damascene, *Three Treatises on the Divine Images*, III, 37).

For Orthodox Christians, this means that the icon leads us to the Church. There we will meet the other in his or her true state. As St. Justin (Popovich) of Chelie used to say, "in the Church we are taught to see (iconically) in every man our future brother/sister [as he or she is in] Paradise." There, in the Eucharistic synaxis, we will see and meet God through our communion with others. So, the icon gathers (*synaxis*) the community we call the Church. The icon, then, is not only an object that we kiss and venerate, but an eternal synaxis that exists in moments, movements, and actions during the Divine Liturgy. Outside the Church, there is not the Kingdom of God; inside the Church, all is iconic.

Here we understand the next characteristic of the icon: it refers to another, not to itself, leading us, thereby, out of solipsism. It encourages us to go out and meet the other. The icon is person-oriented! When we venerate an icon of Christ or a Saint, we demonstrate our victory over individualism and show that we are not self-reliant. When the icon traces this relationship between persons (God and man) and gathers the Church, then the Church becomes a real depiction of the Kingdom of

God, leading us to the Divine Eucharist, which St. Maximus the Confessor described as the image or icon of the Kingdom (σημαίνουσα καὶ προτυποῦσα δι᾽ ἑαυτῆς τὴν ἀλήθειαν, ἧς εἰκὼν ὑπάρχει καὶ τύπος: St. Maximus, *Mystagogy*, PG 91, 688). In the primitive phase of the ancient Church, the icon was closely linked with the mystery of the Eucharist. The Eucharist is the celebration that makes the earthly Church what it is, namely, an *Icon* of the Kingdom.

⁘ ⁘ ⁘

From the very beginning of Christianity, the theme of *icons* has been a fundamental component of theology, and most especially of Christology. On the occasion of the Sunday of Orthodoxy, as we celebrate this day in history, we know that icons have been central to the life of Christians since the 8th and 9th centuries, culminating in the thought and work of theologians such as John of Damascus and Theodore the Studite, who made them key subjects of their theological discourses. However, we also know that the theology of the icon is as old as Christianity itself, as is evident from the place it occupied in the Pauline writings.

Here it is also worth mentioning that St. John of Damascus began his great theological work, *An Exact Exposition of the Orthodox Faith*, with the words of St. John the Evangelist: "No man has seen God at any time; the only begotten Son, who is in the bosom of the Father, He has *explained* (ἐξηγήσατο, made known) Him" (Jn 1:18). "Who first made images? God himself [the Father] first begat his Only-begotten Son and Word, his living and natural image, the exact imprint of his eternity [ἀπαράλλακτον χαρακτῆρα τῆς αὐτοῦ ἀϊδιότητος]; he then made humankind in accordance with the same image [of His Son] and likeness." (St. John Damascene, *Three Treatises on the Divine Images*, III, 26)

The evangelical truth expressed in these words concerning the mystery of God and his Incarnation reveals to us the solution to the two-fold question that has historically surrounded icons and especially the icon par excellence, the icon of Christ: on the one hand, the complexity of describing God, Who by nature is indescribable (ἀπερίγραπτος), and, on the other hand, the theological attempt to describe the indescribable (τὸν ἀπερίγραπτον) God, who, by the nature of His Being, is limitless and infinite.

Through the reality of the Incarnation of the Invisible God, we have been given the possibility of Christian iconography, iconology and icon-veneration, knowing very well that on the one hand, it is impossible to make any adequate picture or description of God, for He is Invisible and incomprehensible, and because no one has ever seen God. But on the other hand, we have come to know that it is the only-begotten Son who is the image of the invisible God (Col. 1,15), who, in His Incarnation revealed the invisible God with a human face, as Saint John of Damascus paraphrased from the words of the forefather Jacob: *I have seen the human form (face) of God, and my soul has been saved!* (Gen 32:31, *On the Divine Images*, I,22).

When we speak about the relationship between God and the icons, we should always bear in mind the Incarnation of the Word, the Son of God by Whom God in Christ became visible. That is the reason why the Person of the God-Man, Christ, One Hypostasis in two natures, is the basis for iconography. The Seventh Ecumenical Council (787) expressed this relationship in its dogmatic *oros* which states that *honor rendered to the image ascends to its prototype* (St. Basil the Great, *On the Holy Spirit* 18,45, PG 32, 149c.) and he who venerates an icon adores the person of the one portrayed. It was the decision of this Council therefore, that affirmed, once and for all, that the rejection of the holy images was the rejection of salvation by God in Christ and the Holy Spirit.

"For if you make an image of Christ, but in no wise of the saints, it is clear that you do not prohibit the image, but rather the honor due to the saints.... For to make an image of Christ as glorified and yet spurn the image of the saints as without glory is to endeavor to show that the truth is false. 'For I live,' says the Lord, 'and I shall glorify those who glorify me,' and the divine apostle, 'So you are no longer a slave, but a son, and if a son, an heir of God through Christ,' and 'if we suffer together [with him], so that we are glorified together.' You are not waging a war against images, but against the saints." (St. John Damascene, *Three Treatises on the Divine Images*, I, 19)

Holy icons and the ultimate state of being

But, there is yet one more difference between the icon and the image. The image "fixes" reality, as opposed to the icon which does not fix it but liberates it from natural laws. We celebrate the Fathers of the Seventh Ecumenical synod who gathered to testify that the Church could not exist without icons, without iconizing the Person of God. When an image becomes an icon, it no longer refers to itself anymore—to its ephemeral existence; rather, it refers beyond itself: to something beyond this corrupted world. When an image becomes an icon, it redeems a person or landscape depicted in it and situates that person or landscape in relationship to the Kingdom ("the law and everything done in accordance with it was a kind of shadow of the image to come[σκιαγραφία τις ἦν τῆς μελλούσης εἰκόνος], that is, of our worship, and that our worship is an image of the good things to come [ἡ δὲ καθ' ἡμᾶς λατρεία εἰκὼν τῶν μελλόντων], the realities themselves, that is Jerusalem above": St. John Damascene, *Three Treatises on the Divine Images*, II, 23). In the historical life of the Church, everything is an image of the future. The icons which depict the Saints are not photographs of their historical faces, but the images of the future they portray. "John the theologian, who leant on Christ's breast, therefore says, that *'we shall be like him.'* For just as iron plunged in fire does not become fire by nature, but by union and burning and participation, so the deified man does not become God by nature, but *by participation....* Because by deification *the saints are gods*, it is said that *'God stands in the company of gods, in the midst he discriminates between the gods,'* when God stands in the midst of gods, distinguishing their several worth, as Gregory the Theologian interprets it" (St. John Damascene, *Three Treatises on the Divine Images*, I, 19).

Therefore, in the iconic ontology of the Greek Fathers, an *eikon* is normally an image of things to come, the future gathering in the Kingdom. So, there cannot be an icon of the Kingdom without the community.

This reality of the icon's relationship with the Kingdom of Heaven is why the Fathers of this Synod repeated what St. Basil the Great said in the fourth century: "the honor paid to the icon passes on to the prototype" (ἡ γὰρ τῆς εἰκόνος τιμὴ ἐπὶ τὸ πρωτότυπον διαβαίνει). Therefore, when we venerate an icon, that relationship goes beyond the icon and reaches the Original source of the image, which is a Person. That is why in the Church, the *word* is an *icon* and an *icon* is the *word*. And this is something that our Church has experiences throughout the ages. In our Churches, the Kingdom of God is depicted and represented through icons, through chanting, through harmonious architecture, through all manner of aesthetic endeavors that are part of our Liturgical expression. How did the Orthodox survive under the Ottoman rule without catechism or schools? Only through this iconic approach to embodying Truth. The pious people spoke with God through icons (iconographic depictions) and hymns and not through

216

human words or rational formulations; God, in turn, revealed Himself to His people through icons and hymns.

This, in the final analysis, means that the Divine worship in its liturgical-iconical context has saved the Orthodox Church and not the verbal descriptions and rhetoric of the homilists.

There will be those who assert that an iconic image conveys the Platonic idea of a shadow empty of reality. But such a position makes it difficult to speak of the Church as an icon without falling into the realm of the imaginative or unreal. The *iconic* nature of the Orthodox Church does not imply a lack of reality, although it does imply a lack of objectified and autonomous reality. As Metropolitan John of Pergamon states, "by being iconic in her existence the Church is two things: (a) she is an image of something else that transcends her—hence, again, a *relational* entity; and (b) she is in her institutions and structure so *transparent* as to allow the eschatological realities to be reflected in them all the time. This can hardly be achieved outside the context of worship, for it is there that transcendence and transparency are experienced par excellence." (*The One and the Many*, Sebastian Press 2010, p. 144)

In a society permeated with the *illusions of multimedia*, where image-pollution of all sorts has blurred our vision, we are invited to promote the true icon of the Kingdom, we are invited to liberate our everyday life from slavery to the natural world through this iconical ethos that our Tradition bequeaths to us; an *iconological* ethos that leads to an affirmation of the other, which leads very often to "silence" and to deference before the other, whom we prefer over ourselves ("honor one another above yourselves"—Rom. 12:10).

Unfortunately, Orthodoxy in our times tends to become an ideology, wherein slogans and accusations of betraying the faith and tradition—understood ideologically—are hurled at one another. But, significantly enough, our Orthodox Church has chosen the commemoration of the Seventh Ecumenical Council to be *the* Sunday of Orthodoxy. As is well known, this Council dealt with the issue of Icons and did not put forth any propositional definition of the faith. In declaring, "*This is the faith of the Fathers; this is the faith which has sustained the oecumene,*" the Council pointed to a form of "theology," the *icon*, which was the liturgical experience of the community and required no subscription to conceptual or ideological statements.

This declaration of the Seventh Council ended the Christological debate of words by testifying to the *reality of the Mystery* in the icon of the Crucified and Risen Lord. This icon removes our forgetfulness of the eschatological Coming of the Risen One, the eschatological *newness* of the Living One (Apoc. 21, 5; 1, 17). Now "we call Christ's image 'Christ'... The Icon of Christ is nothing other than Christ, *apart, of course, from the difference in essence*" (St. Theodore the Studite, *Antirrheticus*, 3.3 [14], PG 99:425).

In our own time there is vast agreement that Byzantine iconography has a particularly unique value. But, the difficulty arises around the question: wherein lies that value? One perspective is that Byzantine iconography is essentially a *spiritual* painting, contrary to the secular, which underlines the merely bodily dimension. Still others consider that Byzantine iconography expresses the heavenly reality and secular painting the earthly one. We insist that the difference lies in the fact that Byzantine iconography expresses the ultimate reality of this world. It depicts the world as it will be transformed in the Kingdom of God.

Secular art usually expresses the mere passing, the temporal world that does not succeed in transcending its limitations: space, time, corruption and death. One such example of a master actually anticipating the corruption of this world is evident in Picasso's response to a critic who noted that his portrait of Gertrude Stein did not look like her: "She will," he said. So, iconography depicts just the opposite: a world free of aging and decay. But, at the same time, it continues along the same line of thinking, but goes even deeper than Picasso's chronological anticipation of Stein's ideal image: for iconography depicts a saint as he or she will appear and become known in the Kingdom of God. Instead of the decay and corruption of modern portraits, the icon depicts the image of sanctity bathed in the uncreated light of Paradise that expunges the features of corruption possessed during a saint's earthly life. So, we might say, with Fr. Stamatis Skliris, that an icon is a *portrait of transfigured life in the future kingdom*.

From the artistic point of view, we can summarize the theology of the icon with these four simple points:

First, the icon is not a naturalistic portrait, but a *light-portrait* (photo-portrait). Icons express ontological participation in the Uncreated Light.

Secondly, this Light transcends the laws of optics. It expresses the freedom of the Uncreated.

Third, icons of Christ are not presented as an *individual* or individually, but are revealed as the Mystery of the Church, where the many are gathered as saints. Each saint depicted in the icon bears all the properties of the Light of Christ, which implies that he is a *christ by grace*.

And fourth, as every icon is depicted transcendentally, the lighting *equalizes* every saint with Christ, "the most handsome of the sons of men" (Ps 45:2) and other saints within the ontological community of persons, that is, the Church.

"It is not said of them [the angels] in Scripture that they will be seated together with, or be partakers of, the divine glory...nor that they will reign together, nor that they will be glorified together, nor that they will sit at the Father's table, but the saints are sons of God, sons of the kingdom and heirs of God and fellow-heirs with Christ. Therefore, I honor the saints and I glorify them together with Christ as his slaves and friends and fellow-heirs: slaves by nature, friends by choice, and sons and heirs by divine grace, as the lord said to the Father." (St. John Damascene, *Three Treatises on the Divine Images*, III, 26)

The icon reveals an existential attitude and disposition. When we stand before an icon, we do not kiss a mere photograph, but rather, the eschatological (ultimate) person of a Saint depicted. And in the same manner, it is especially important for us to know and remember that when we stand with our fellow man we should also see in him primarily his future restored, transformed and resurrected face, free of passions, overlooking his weaknesses and iniquities.

This explains why, historically, Orthodox people did *not* differentiate between ecclesial and secular painting. Their eyes were transformed by the eschatological vision of the world. Thus they looked not only at the saints, but also to the ordinary men and women, and our landscape and environment as well all as transfigured from the temporal to the eternal, the mortal to the immortal, the corruptible to incorruptible. "But now, since the divinity has been united to our nature [ἡ θεότης τῇ ἡμετέρα φύσει συνεκράθη], as a kind of lifegiving and saving medicine, our nature has been glorified and its very elements changed into incorruption [πρὸς ἀφθαρσίαν μετεστοιχειώθη]" (St. John Damascene, *Three Treatises on the Divine Images*, II, 10).

To more fully understand this, let us now briefly consider what distinguishes Byzantine art from secular aesthetics. Byzantine art is not carried away by the phenomena caused by the laws of optics. It does not empirically observe and represent the appearance of what exists; rather these are appreciated on account of their partaking in *another light*, which is not determined entirely by the laws of optics. Everything in the icon is painted in such a way, with such conventional, flexible shading, that it lends *permanence* to its characteristics.

The fullness of Byzantine aesthetics is also expressed in the iconographers freedom to depict not only what is visible, but more so, what is invisible. Byzantine art thus gives a *complete view of the subject, not given to fragmentation*. While western art is *often* restricted by natural laws of the linear transmission of light so that everything that is behind or inside something else is not seen; in contrast, *Byzantine art has absolute freedom to depict everything*. One such example among many, in the many icons of saints and feast days which we venerate, as well as those which are part of the exhibition here at the museum, we can see depicted such things as the roof of a house, even though we are looking at it from below; however according to the laws of western perspective that would not be possible.

❖ ❖ ❖

In the restoration of icons, we celebrate this perspective and vision of life, transformed and transfigured by the person of Jesus Christ. We celebrate in them the possibility of what remains ahead for those who believe and have lived faithful to Christ. It is precisely this vision of life that Byzantine iconography communicates to us and the culture in which we live.

So, icons are our spiritual treasures because they ultimately reveal our relationship with God; that we belong, not to our self, or to our work, or to ambition in this world, but that we belong to God. They are our treasures because they reveal that we are not alone, not isolated, but part of a communion of saints, loved by God with a love that this world with all of its adversities and all of its trials and tribulations cannot take away. The Lenten season certainly calls us to joyfully rediscover this vision of life and our relationships with the world and one another. It is, in a very real way, the foundation and purpose of our fasting, prayer and almsgiving. Through our ascetic efforts, we are led to this essential understanding of our relationship to God, to the world, and to one another as citizens of His Kingdom to come.

Fully aware of our rich treasure of faith in the holy icons, we honor the memory of those who have handed down this precious heritage to us, and by so doing, we solemnly rediscover this vision of life, and once more, rededicate ourselves to our faith in Christ, our service to Him and to one another as we await the ultimate transformation of the world that has already begun within and through the Church. This is central to our spiritual growth and this celebration, as summarized in the historic Synodikon.

The identification of the selfsameness of Christ with His image leads to my final point: Orthodoxy *is* the Church and *not* an ideology! It is a gathering of the people and, particularly, a Eucharistic gathering of living icons. This is what we must emphasize today. Not an Internet—online—virtual *illusion* of communication, but the Icon as the visible and true communication of the Kingdom; such *must* be the future of Orthodoxy because such is the future Christ promises His Church. In the Eucharist, we are taught not only to venerate and greet icons, but also the other members of the synaxis, not passing the living icons—people—by, but greeting and embracing them. So, the Icon is indeed the right method of looking at the world. Only this iconic approach will save Orthodoxy from becoming a secular organization conforming to *the image of the world*.

The contribution of Stamatis Skliris to modern Orthodox iconography

Stamatis Skliris' contribution to modern art (both Church art, and art in general) through his painting and iconography is already a generally established fact. With this review we would like to sketch the historical context behind the appearance of Skliris the *zographos*,[47] and, by making a theological-aesthetical analysis of his iconographic opus, to emphasize clearly and objectively some of the particular qualities of his art in relation to the iconography of the second half of the twentieth century.

---

[47] Zographos: one who paints from life or from nature using fresh, natural colors.

1. *The iconography of the first half of the twentieth century.* During the first half of the twentieth century, Greek iconography was briefly dominated by lay tendencies. There existed an authentic lay tradition, e.g., Theophilos. After Theophilos, the lay tradition ended once and for all because the artist became a learned man, a *logios*. Already from the first half of the twentieth century, Photios Kontoglou initiated an attempt to merge lay tradition and the "learned" art of painting. He went to Paris in 1921, where he got into the general tendencies of the Romantics and their investigation of local traditions. He returned to Greece in this spirit and became inspired first by the monasteries of Meteora, and then by Cretan iconographies and lay painters (see the collection of articles on Kontoglou entitled Ἄνθρωπος ἐν εἰκόνι διαπαρεύεται, published by Akritas, as well as the text on Kontoglou by Nikos Zias).

The first half of the twentieth century was marked by the *anasynthesis* of Modern Greek society, which after the liberation from the Turks was again subjected to many Western influences due to Bavarian rule; and these influences ran parallel to Byzantine tradition. This *anasynthesis* occurred mainly due to Kontoglou, and later to Pelekasi. Kontoglou linked lay and post-Byzantine traditions, while Pelekasi established links with the traditional art of Eptanisa (the Seven Islands of Greece), which belonged to the Greek traditional mainstream but also contained a multitude of Baroque and Renaissance elements. Accordingly, the roles of Asia Minor and Kontoglou were very significant (Photios Kontoglou was from Kydonai in Asia Minor). However, the geographical and cultural environment within which Kontoglou was active was *Athens*. This proved to be the geographical and cultural setting from which arose the seminal activities and tendencies that characterize present-day Church iconography. Kontoglou did not bring along with him any concrete tradition from Asia Minor, but he brought a spirit of preserving tradition and of protecting dogmas by means of the icon. Greece had a very concrete and very well-developed lay and Church iconography. Kontoglou had the traditional spirit, and Greece presented him with the icons of Meteora, the Holy Athos, Panagiotes Zographos, and Theophilos, the last surviving lay painter of Kontoglou's time.

The first generation of Kontoglou's students turned to an *older* phase in the development of Byzantine painting as compared to the one which influenced Kontoglou. Spyros Papanikolaou was inspired by the twelfth-century Monastery of Chora, and Yannis Karusos by the Monastery of Sopochani in Serbia (1260–1265). Later on, the second generation, and especially Dimitrios Tsiantas, was inspired by Michael Astrapa, Euthychios and Panselinos (end of the thirteenth and beginning of the fourteenth centuries). Kontoglou was not partial toward these periods of Byzantine art, being under the impression that they were worldly, but he was greatly attracted to late Byzantine and lay art. It was his students who turned toward integral Byzantine forms. Kontoglou himself offered the wrong criteria for the evaluation of Byzantine art. He emphasized the element of tenderness (κατάνυξις) and dark colors, while Byzantium had light colors and emphasized doxological and eschatological elements. (The Brothers Lepur, for example, desired to be Kontoglou's students by their own free will, but they expressed a more lay articulation.)

Since Kontoglou's death, there has existed yet another generation of his students, who have gone beyond the problems relating to post-Byzantine and Byzantine art, between "doxologizing" and "tenderness." The exaggerated influence of the great teacher was abrogated, but they retained from him one other element which their predecessors did not utilize, and this was the fact that Kontoglou *painted worldly themes employing Byzantine style and techniques*. Thus they managed to open themselves to a new comprehension which connected worldly art with Church art, which did not differentiate between a saint and a worldly man. This used to be an unyielding rule of Byzantine art. It was Kontoglou who reintroduced this spirit into more recent times, especially when painting Greek history on the walls of the great assembly room of the Parliament in Athens. Thessalonica's John Vranos continued in this spirit (with comic elements), as did George Kordis (with elements of Cretan iconography), Spyros Kardamakis (Cretan and lay elements), Manolis Grigoreas (with his simple, childlike drawings), and Fr. Stamatis Skliris (with elements of a more Palaeologan art of painting).

In our day and age, when a renaissance of Church art is to be seen in all Orthodox countries and nations, Athens still manages to retain a uniqueness throughout the world, which history will know as the *School of Athens*. The majority of iconographers in Serbia copy Astrapa. This is the form that this renaissance of Church art is taking in Serbia. In Russia it takes the form of a return to more ancient sources such as that of Sinai (sixth to twelfth centuries): Hieromonk Xeno. Thessalonica is deeply immersed in research into Palaeologan and Cretan icons, which have been preserved on Holy Athos. Copies of Theophanes the Cretan (sixteenth century) are made in almost all Greek monasteries and in a grand workshop in Athens as well as related artists (Karusos-Leondas, Tsiantas-Vlachoyanis, Yorgos Kopsidas, Sideris, Kardamakis, Kordis, Manolis Grigoreas, Stamatis Skliris). All this is still in a state of development, and it is still too early for any conclusions to be made.

2. *Special elements of Stamatis Skliris' iconography.* The special characteristics of Stamatis Skliris' painting are the following:

a) *He ascends from the very beginnings of iconography (catacombs, Dura Europos, Sinai, etc) and from classical Hellenic presumptions of iconography*, striving to revitalize the initial solutions and choices made by early Christian art. Rather than following the ready-made mannerisms that were formed throughout the centuries, he chooses to observe the very first choices (for example, his works[48]: *St. Catherine*, p. 49; *Annunciation*, p. 71; *Caryatid with a Seashell*, p. 97; *Kouros*, p. 99; *Alexander*, p. 99).

b) He adopts elements of *Persian, Hindu and Turkish miniatures*, and "*borrows in return*": Anatolians borrowed from Byzantium, and Stamatis borrows from the borrower (painting: *The Primitives*, pp. 292, 295).

c) *He articulates a dialogue with modern art* by evaluating the brush strokes of Van Gogh and Cezanne, Monet's colors, Matisse's forms, Picasso's Cubism, and Post-modernism (paintings: *Melchizedek, Resurrection of the Son of the Widow of Sarep*, pp. 498 and 270–71).

d) *He is authentically post-modern*, because he employs purely artistic criteria; he does not adopt ready-made solutions from the iconographic past; he researches everything anew; a strong experimental sense is at his disposal, and he combines strictly traditional elements with those that are modern; e.g., *The Mighty Protectress* (Theotokos) is strongly traditional, but Christ has the movement, the colors, and brush deposits of modern, expressionist art (title page and p. 39).

e) *Light plays the most significant role*; it is Byzantine, but Stamatis looks at it in a neo-impressionist manner, i.e., he captures Byzantine light with brush strokes that emphasize dominant points in an impressionist manner.

---

[48] The paintings are listed according to the page numbers in Stamatis Skliris' book: *In the Mirror and the Enigma*, Belgrade 2005.

f) He uses *strong and clear color*, avoiding mixtures of different colors (painting: *Apostle Paul*, p. 403).

g) His colors and drawings relate to us a *beauty and a joy of a modern type*, which theologically expresses eschatological tranquility rather than Kontoglou's tenderness or penitence (painting: *The Mansards*, p. 157).

h) He gives anew to the *elements of nature* some of their basic characteristics which were neglected by Cretan painting and presented only symbolically. For example, water has a freshness and dynamic wave agitation rather than nicely combed waves (frescos and icons: *Ascension of Prophet Elijah, Elder Zosima Gives Communion to Mary of Egypt*, p. 179).

i) Although he basically employs a dark Byzantine under-painting, adding to it light "accents" (illuminations), he still plays with colors in such an impressionist manner that his work gains a "*non-determinism of color*"; he leaves sections of his painting uncolored and then treats these sections in an unpredictable manner with an eagerness to play and not to make use of the calligraphy that is usual in iconography (painting: *Transfiguration*, pp. 149, 151).

j) In spite of the strong eschatological dimension of his work, he allows for a somewhat dispersed manifestation of *tragic and psychological elements*, which puts him in line with twentieth-century painters (painting: *Nightmare*, p. 245).

k) Most characteristic of all is the strong *portrait dimension* which marks his icons, as well as the fact that he introduces into church interiors a contemporary facial expression (paintings: *St. Thomas and St. Demetrios*, in the church of Prophet Elijah in Piraeus, pp. 501, 397).

l) The *look in the eyes* is not only transcendent, as is the case with old icons, but it also has some special features which are applicable to modern man: I) an intense look; II) a look which creates a relationship with the observer-pilgrim; III) a psychological look; IV) a look that thinks and examines (paintings: *The Tree-Woman, The Thinking Girl*, p. 98).

Upon observing Stamatis' artwork, we see that he manages to link the *graphic* and the *chromatic* elements both harmoniously and with rare originality, thus anticipating with his *drawing* and *coloring* a wondrous world, God's world of love and light. With regard to the *graphic* element, by the mobility and expressiveness of his images, with the open, childlike looks in their eyes—through his excellent knowledge of anatomy (being a medical doctor) and of psychology (being a priest and a spiritual father)—

Stamatis overcomes the immobility and inertia of fallen human nature through a movement of *reaching out*, which is the feat of loving and of an eager progress toward Christ. As far as *coloration* is concerned, by a combination of color (warm-cold, complementary), by a gradation of tones, and by a multitude of vibrating shades brought on by the brush—employing the best solutions from the history of the art of painting (Byzantine, impressionist, cubistic, abstract, surrealist, etc.)—and in doing all this, illuminating everything by *light*, Stamatis anticipates the coloration of Paradise, the coloration of "a new Heaven and a new Earth" (Rev. 21: 1). In addition to this, he also offers a *thematic* contribution: he does not overlook emphasizing the historic, *tragic element* (agony, suffering, wounds, and pain) in the images of saints and martyrs depicted in his works, and especially in his most recent creations, which are, nevertheless, illuminated by the *Light* that overcomes the world and history.

The Holy Resurrection
(fresco in Chora Monastery, Constantinople, 14th century)

List of Sources

"Holiness and Otherness: From Holiness as an Ethical Concept to Holiness as an Hypostatic Concept" was first published in *Bogoslovlje*, Belgrade, and then in *Theologia*, Athens. Translated from Serbian by nun Mihaila Vavich.

"Truth and History: Implications in Theology and Science," was first published in *Bogoslovlje*, Belgrade. Translated from Serbian by nun Mihaila Vavich.

"The Ethos of Holiness: Between Ontology and Gnosiology" was first published in *Vidoslov*, Trebinje. Translated from Serbian by nun Mihaila Vavich.

"Is There a Biochemistry of Freedom" was first published in *Bogoslovlje*, Belgrade. Translated from Serbian by nun Mihaila Vavich.

"An Existential Interpretation of Dogmatics: Theological Language and Dogma in the Face of the Culture of Pluralism." A paper presented at the Dean Installation and Symposium *The Challenges for Orthodox Theology and Orthodox Theological Education in the Twenty-First Century*, St. Vladimir's Theological Seminary, New York, September 14–15, 2007. Published at *St. Vladimir's Seminary Quarterly* 51 (2007), 395–422.

"Chalcedon's Christology and Its Theological, Historical and Cultural Significance" is a paper presented at Loyola Marymont University in Los Angeles, March 2009.

"Neopatristic Christology in Postmodern Culture: Presuppositions and Criteria for a Contextual Theology." Presented at the International Conference on "Church and Culture" in Volos, Greece, May 7–10, 2009. Translated from Greek by J. W. Lillie.

"The Old and New Wine of Liturgical Theology," presented at the St. Vladimir Orthodox Theological Seminary international liturgical symposium, "The Past and Future of Liturgical Theology: Celebrating the Legacy of Father Alexander Schmemann," New York, January 29–31, 2009.

"Unitatis et Alteritas (Unity and Otherness) in the Ecclesiology of Conciliarity." An address entitled "Conciliarity in the Orthodox Church" delivered at a colloquium held at the Vrhbosna Catholic Seminary in Sarajevo, November 19, 2005, Paul VI Hall. Translated from Serbian by Teodora Simic.

"The Icon and the Kingdom of God" is a homily delivered on The Sunday of Orthodoxy Vespers, St. Steven's Cathedarl, Los Angeles 2010 adapted here in view of the present edition. The paper includes other two texts: "Holy Icons and the Ultimate State of Being," a homily on The Sunday of Orthodoxy Vespers, The Getty Center, Los Angeles, 2007 and "The Contribution of Stamatis Skliris to Modern Orthodox Iconography," published in S. Skliris's "In the Mirror" (Sebastian Press 2007, pp. 205–209) and translated from Serbian by Petar Sherovich.

Index of Scriptural and Patristic References

Index of Names

Subject Index

234

Salvation xiii–xv, 10, 15, 20, 28, 29, 34, 38, 40, 46, 48, 49, 61, 79, 89, 100, 108, 109, 114, 117, 121, 125, 129, 131, 135, 136, 140, 147, 149, 156, 159, 167, 169, 170, 179, 180, 183, 188, 215

Sanctity xviii, xx, 1, 10, 12, 19, 46, 56–60, 86, 189, 218

Schism 141, 145, 193, 198, 202

Science xii, 3, 10, 11, 21, 42, 46, 49, 50, 68–70, 72–74, 76, 82, 90–93, 112–114, 120, 134, 185, 188, 227

Scientific 4, 32, 46, 48, 49, 53, 69, 70, 73, 77, 79, 89, 92, 101, 102, 112–114, 116, 134

Scripture 186

Sin 1, 20, 26, 68, 70, 76, 86, 90, 91, 94, 95, 97, 106, 151, 169, 176

Sobornost 121, 130, 190, 202

society 2, 13, 18, 112, 124, 125, 127, 130, 134, 137, 144, 152, 155, 160, 172, 180, 217, 222

Son 4, 5, 8, 15, 22, 24, 27–30, 34, 35, 38, 41, 45, 48, 55, 119, 124, 125, 143, 158, 168, 212, 214, 215, 224

Soteriology, soteriological 6, 89, 99, 115, 122, 132, 134, 138, 156, 163

Soul 17, 32, 43, 49, 53, 57, 74, 79–81, 85, 88, 93–97, 103, 104, 107, 108, 111, 113, 116, 117, 137, 215

Source 109, 119, 176, 216

Spirituality 13, 60, 65, 70, 71, 75, 79, 83, 84, 91, 97, 102, 111

Structure 20, 31, 39, 41, 42, 45, 47, 48, 60, 69, 77, 97, 101, 108, 131, 181, 186, 189, 190, 191, 194–196, 198–200, 203, 206–208, 217

Substance 18, 42, 47, 121

Succession 133, 202–204

Suffering 17, 34, 35, 42, 58, 59, 62, 100, 108, 151, 167, 226

Symbol 59

Symbolism 184, 185, 187, 188

Synaxis 21, 45, 121, 122, 166, 178, 179, 185, 213, 221

Synod, synodality 20, 121, 144, 163, 189–196, 198, 199, 201, 202, 206–208, 215, 216

Theology ix, xi, xii, xv, xix, 2, 7, 9, 18, 21, 22, 42, 46, 47, 49, 68–70, 74, 90, 102, 109, 116, 119, 121, 122, 124, 125, 127–129, 134–139, 141, 142, 148, 150, 156, 163, 164, 171, 172, 174, 175, 179, 181, 183, 194, 200, 214 – aca-demic 182, 183, 186 – apophatic 138 – asym-metry in 139 – as Icon 175, 217 – biblical 201 – branches of 111 –Christian ix, 74, 129, 132 – Christological 172 – contemporary Orthodox ix, xx, 42, 136, 175, 181, 192, 200 – contemporary x, 124, 138, 140, 164, 176 – contents of 119 – contextual 155 – dogmatic 125, 137, 167, 172 – Eucha-ristic-ascetic 78 – form of ix – foundation of 117 – holistic 136 – application of 137 – inculturation of 132 – language of 134 – liturgical 179, 181, 183, 188 – methodol-ogy of 122 – natural 47 – negative theol-ogy 57 – neo-patristic 132, 139, 141, 142 – neurotheology 72 – New Testament 16 – ascetic 42, 107 – of Bishop Athanasius Yevtich 162 – of conciliarity 190 – of In-carnation 145 – of medicine 77 – of Met-ropolitan John Zizioulas ix, 174 – of Or-thodox Tradition xvii, 76 – of patience 172 – of resurrection xiii, 29, 36 – of sinodality xviii – of holiness 11 – of St. Cyril of Alex-andria 144 – of St. Justin (Popovich) of Chelie 162 – of synodality 190 – of the Church xiv, 22, 91, 140, 201 – of the icon 214, 218 – of the person 174 – Orthodox xiii, xvii, 58, 115, 119, 120, 121, 123, 129, 134, 136, 137, 141, 169, 182, 183, 188, 190 – pa-triotic 163 – patristic ix, 127, 133, 139, 142, 172, 175 – Protestant ix – Roman Catholic ix, 194 – synthesis 133 – trinitarian ix, 140, 143, 161, 173, 191, 201 – way of 129, 139

Theologian(s) xvi, 8, 11, 18, 29, 46, 70, 102, 104, 130, 145, 161, 182, 199, 214 – Ortho-dox ix, 67, 75, 112, 134, 141, 183 – Roman Catholic 208 – Church's 135 – contempo-rary/modern 49, 85, 165 – conservative 56 – moral 134 – systematic 131 – dogmatic 186 – St. John the Theologian 12, 89, 216 – St. Gregory the Theologian 12, 25, 29, 45, 61, 74, 81, 98, 103, 130, 160, 175, 216 – St. Symeon the New Theologian 57, 66, 156, 161

Theological xvii, 69, 72, 89, 111, 143–144, 146, 152, 181, 186, 191, 199, 200, 201, 214, 225 – achievement 146 – analysis 221 – ap-proach 135 – awareness 120, 182 – circles 193 – claims xv – conclusions 115 – confu-sion 142 – consciousness 131 – consider-

*) Index of Scriptural and Patristic References, Index of Names, and Subject Index kindly produced by *Maja Jovanović, Andrej Jevtić, Snežana Denker* and *Marko Vilotić*